3/94

A TASTE OF ANCIENT
ROME

A TASTE
OF ANCIENT
ROME

ILARIA GOZZINI
GIACOSA

TRANSLATED BY ANNA HERKLOTZ

WITH A FOREWORD BY

MARY TAYLOR SIMETI

THE UNIVERSITY OF CHICAGO PRESS
CHICAGO AND LONDON

ILARIA GOZZINI GIACOSA
is a writer based in Zurich who combines a scholarly background in
archaeology with a passion for all things good to eat.

THE UNIVERSITY OF CHICAGO PRESS, CHICAGO 60637
THE UNIVERSITY OF CHICAGO PRESS, LTD., LONDON
© 1992 by The University of Chicago
Foreword © 1992 by Mary Taylor Simeti
All rights reserved. Published 1992
Printed in the United States of America
01 00 99 98 97 96 95 94 93 92   1 2 3 4 5 6

ISBN (cloth): 0-226-29030-1
Originally published as *A cena da Lucullo: Come cucinare oggi i piatti
dell'antica Roma*, © 1986 Edizioni Piemme S.p.A. Via del Carmine 5,
15033 Casale Monferrato (AL), Italy
Illustration credits can be found on page 217.

Library of Congress Cataloging-in-Publication Data

Gozzini Giacosa, Ilaria.

    [A cena da Lucullo. English]
    A taste of ancient Rome / Ilaria Gozzini Giacosa ; translated by Anna Herklotz ; with a foreword
by Mary Taylor Simeti.
        p.   cm.
    Recipes in English and Latin.
    Translation of: A cena da Lucullo.
Includes bibliographical references and indexes.
    1. Cookery, Roman.   I. Title.
TX725.A1G613   1992
641.5937—dc20   91-44601
                                                                                 CIP

⊛ This book is printed on acid-free paper.

CONTENTS

Color plates follow page 84.

FOREWORD

First impressions of history linger. My ideas of how the ancient Romans ate were formed in fifth grade, and were very far removed from anything I wanted to try myself: sows' paps and flamingos' tongues dancing across the screen in the decadent banquets at *Quo Vadis;* a handful of dried figs and some goat cheese served up with the virtuous but unappealing austerity of Cato or Cincinnatus.

Nor did later and more serious research into the history of food do much to correct these youthful impressions. Early European translations of the chief Latin treatise on cooking, the *De re coquinaria* of Apicius, are little more than repetitive and unrevealing lists of peculiar ingredients in unlikely combinations. The first English translation, published in 1936 by J. D. Vehling,[1] made greater sense, but although Vehling, a professional chef, claims to have tried many of the recipes and to have found them "practical, good, even delightful," he neither invites nor even tempts his readers to follow his example.

In *A Taste of Ancient Rome,* Ilaria Gozzini Giacosa has done just that. Far more than a mere translation of Apicius and of the other culinary writers of Roman civilization, her book gives context to the ancient recipes by explaining to us how and where the Romans bought, cooked, and ate their food, and makes the recipes themselves accessible to modern cooks, suggesting substitutes for unavailable ingredients and supplying the procedures and the quantities omitted in the originals.

This achievement is the fruit of an unusual combination of serious archeological study and of a culinary curiosity marked by great passion and, given the difficulties involved, even greater patience. But it is also a child of the enormous changes in our eating habits that have taken place in recent

1. Apicius, *Cooking and Dining in Imperial Rome,* edited and translated by Joseph Dommers Vehling (Chicago, 1936; New York 1977).

decades. Ms. Giacosa is writing for a public that has become acquainted with ethnic cuisines from all around the world, that can find a much wider variety of foods in the markets, and that can accept and appreciate a much greater range of "taste sensations." Exotic ingredients in unusual combinations, and sweet-and-sour or sweet-and-salty seasonings in particular, are much less startling to us today than they would have been fifty-odd years ago when Vehling's book was published.

If anything is startling in *A Taste of Ancient Rome,* it is the modernity of the behavior that Ms. Giacosa describes. Her portrait of the wealthy Roman could be transposed to a New Yorker of the 1980s with very few changes in detail: a sophisticated gourmet, he patronized a five-story shopping center and was willing to pay extravagent sums for novelties and imported luxuries, or for produce growth in the right area—what I have heard a contemporary Californian call "designer lettuce." He sent fancy food baskets to his friends during the Saturnalia celebrations, and appreciated good food writing: witness the survival of many of the epigrams which the poet Martial wrote to accompany his holiday gifts.

Breakfast at home was followed by a light mid-day snack at a tavern in the Forum, or a working lunch after a session at the gym or the baths. The main meal of the day came in the evening, either dinner at home with the family or one of those infamous banquets. But these too acquire a familiar note: the guests, chosen for reasons of cultural and charitable patronage as well as networking, each brought from home a special napkin to serve as a doggy-bag.

If such parallels in behavior are amusing, even alarming (Rome fell, after all), the occasional familiarity of the food itself raises some tantalizing questions for historians. Establishing continuity in anything as ephemeral as food is especially difficult in the Mediterranean Basin, a vast region of fairly homogeneous climate and soil whose peoples have been trading with and colonizing each other for many millennia. Pasta provides a good example of this: the Italian agricultural historian Emilio Sereni[2] claims that the *laganum* called for in the recipe for Apician *patina* is the ancestor of modern Italian *lasagna* but suggests a much more roundabout history for the kind of pasta we know as *vermicelli:* a product of Arab Sicily first introduced into northern Italy in the early Renaissance, it was called *tria,* a word that appears to have progressed from Greek through Arabic into modern Sicilian dialect, perhaps east on the heels of Alexander's army and then, with the expansion of Islam, west from Syria along the African shore and north again to Sicily.

Ms. Giacosa plays with the idea of continuity by occasionally offering

2. Emilio Sereni, *Terra nuova e buoi rossi* (Turin, 1981).

modern versions of the classical recipes which she has culled from regional cuisines in Italy and other parts of the Mediterranean. My own research can provide a surprising number of similar parallels of Sicilian cooking.[3] According to Jean-François Revel,[4] the principal difference between classical cooking and that of the Middle Ages lies in the methods: the roaring blaze in the open medieval hearth did not provide the slow heat necessary for stewing, braising, or simmering sauces. But in a southern climate like that of Sicily, large fireplaces are almost unknown, and the kitchen described by Ms. Giacosa, with its dirt floor, brick oven, and burners fired with charcoal, could be found in Sicilian houses well into the present century.

Whether the result of continuity or merely of coincidence, the tastes of ancient Rome are still the tastes of Sicily today: the use of pinenuts and raisins to season; of reduced grape must to sweeten; of honey and vinegar to make a sweet-and-sour sauce. Specific dishes such as *apotermum* or the vegetable soup known in Latin as *tisanum farricam* seem to survive in ritual dishes like the *cuccia* that Sicilians eat on St. Lucy's Day or the *maccu di San Giuseppe*. Even the way Sicilian cooks use anchovies melted in oil to add zest to vegetables resembles the Roman habit of sprinkling everything with *garum*, their ill-famed sauce of fermented fish.

With so many of the ingredients already in my Sicilian larder, I lost no time in experimenting with some of Ms. Giacosa's recipes and, like Vehling, I have found most of what I have tried "good, even delightful." These recipes have gained much in precision and clarity through Anna Herklotz's pleasing and painstaking translation, but ingredients such as *garum* inevitably remain problematic. (I found I did best by diluting anchovy paste with a few drops of Worcestershire sauce.) If readers find that they must occasionally call on their own experience and imagination when trying out the recipes, they should not feel guilty: historical accuracy will always be a moot point where flavor is concerned. Botanists cannot agree as to which plant of the celery family it was that the Greeks called *selinon*, and there is an enormous difference, for example, between the stringy, dark green celery of Sicily and the bleached and fleshy vegetable sold in American markets. Centuries of selective cultivation and breeding have no doubt altered the flavors of most of what we eat, but to what degree and in what fashion we can only guess.

Despite such difficulties, *A Taste of Ancient Rome* does much to dispel the myths surrounding Roman meals and to reveal Roman cuisine in its true substance and flavor. The considerable culinary and archeological experience which Ms. Giacosa brings to interpreting the rather hermetic

3. Mary Taylor Simeti, *Pomp and Sustenance* (New York, 1989).
4. Jean-François Revel, *3000 anni a tavola* (Milan, 1979).

Latin texts, and the wealth of historical detail she provides, enriched by Patricia Smith's drawings of scenes and utensils from the Roman kitchen, make the purchasing and preparation of classical food intelligible and even familiar. Thanks to her efforts we can participate both with mind *and* with palate the celebrated banquets of ancient Rome.

Mary Taylor Simeti

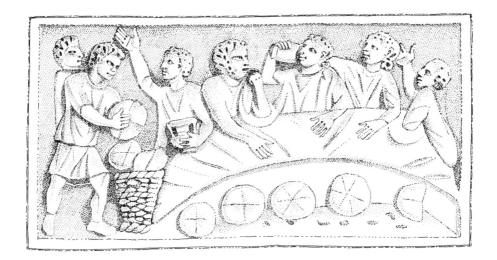

A TASTE OF ANCIENT ROME

TRANSLATOR'S PREFACE

Even a casual thumbing of Italian cookbooks past and present will encourage the observation that such a grand culinary tradition seems to owe little of its longevity to an exacting standard of transmission. Indeed, many of the very recipes under examination here could be considered the generative paradigm of this tradition, enticing riddles often consisting of little or nothing more than a formulaic inventory of ingredients. I therefore remind the reader that, notwithstanding Ilaria Gozzini Giacosa's considerable deductive detail, the successful realization of these ancient recipes still rests largely upon the individual cook's intuition, experience, and imagination. In other words, do not look to Giacosa for the prescription and employment of every drop and grain a given recipe might require. This, I believe, is as it should be, since it is quite in keeping with the spirit and example of the sources she celebrates.

Amounts given for all herbs and spices used in these recipes are for the dried forms unless otherwise indicated, a practical if reluctant concession to the often limited availability of fresh herbs in many areas of the United States. In any case, the cook always retains a fairly free hand to adjust for taste, and to omit or substitute when necessary. Giacosa has offered a few examples of such variations in the text; there are surely many other possibilities in keeping with her design and desire to provide the most closely representative sampling or substitution one can find.

Conversions from the metric to the American system of weight measurement have been rounded wherever possible and appropriate, in order to provide practical working units without destroying the proportions among the various ingredients in any one recipe. (Liquid and volume measures convert fairly closely between the two systems.) For simplicity, and in consideration of typical U.S. packaging and purchasing habits, 1 lb., 2 lb., and 3 lb. are used as the conversion for the ½ kg., 1 kg., and 1½ kg.

weights respectively. The following table provides both the close and rounded conversions for comparison:

Original measure	Close conversion	Rounded conversion
50 g.	1¾ oz.	2 oz.
100 g.	3½ oz.	3 oz.
150 g.	5¼ oz.	5 oz.
200 g.	7 oz.	7 oz.
250 g.	8¾ oz.	9 oz.
300 g.	10½ oz.	10 oz.
400 g.	14 oz.	14 oz.
500 g.	17½ oz.	16 oz. (1 lb.)
600 g.	21 oz.	20 oz. (1¼ lb.)
700 g.	24½ oz.	24 oz. (1½ lb.)
750 g.	26¼ oz.	26 oz.
800 g.	28 oz.	28 oz. (1¾ lb.)
1000 g.	35 oz.	32 oz. (2 lb.)
2000 g.	70 oz.	72 oz. (4½ lb.)

Brackets in the Apician texts and their translations indicate derivative or explanatory editorial insertions. The majority of these insertions—along with the numbering system used for the individual recipes—reflect the thorough investigative reading provided by Jacques André (see the Bibliography), whose critical apparatus and source description will be most useful to the reader seeking further detail regarding *De re coquinaria*.

INTRODUCTION

It seems these days, with magazines full of the latest dietary fads and bookstores bursting with beautiful cookbooks, that more people are beginning to consider cooking not as a chore but rather as a creative art. Healthful eating is also a prime concern. Thus it is both timely and intriguing to include among these culinary endeavors an exploration of the long-forgotten cuisine of the ancient Romans, perhaps the primordial paragon of the "Mediterranean diet." Sadly, *nemo propheta in patria* (no one's a prophet in his own land), so eloquently demonstrated by Italian youth thronging to American-style fast-food restaurants and sinking their teeth into greasy, overcooked hamburgers. Americans themselves in the meantime are praising the "Mediterranean diet" as the ultimate safeguard against high cholesterol and evil triglycerides—and what better example can there be of the genuine "Mediterranean diet" than that of ancient Rome?

The idea for this book actually originated during a casual meal in a restaurant near the coast of Sorrento. I had happened to overhear some foreign tourists who, fresh from the obligatory tour of Pompeii, were praising their pizzas steaming before them as "an ancient Roman specialty, so simple yet so good." After smiling inwardly at the idea of an ancient Roman consuming pizza with tomato sauce (furnished no doubt by some prescient ancestor of Christopher Columbus), I found myself lost in thought. Meanwhile my husband, who heartily enjoys a good meal, pondered aloud: "But how could they live without tomatoes? Or potatoes, peppers, eggplant, spaghetti, risotto—not even a cup of coffee to top off a meal?! All the food that comes to mind when one thinks of the Mediterranean arrived here from America or other faraway places hundreds of years after the end of the Roman Empire!"

This is indisputably true; but since every epoch typically presumes that there is no better way of eating than its own, I decided to determine just

1

what foodstuffs these "deprived Romans" had. Then, one step leading to another, after I learned what basic resources were available in the time of Julius Caesar, I went on to discover how they were combined, cooked, and consumed—in other words, how one dined in Rome two thousand years ago.

Italians still describe a particularly elaborate dinner as "a meal worthy of Lucullus," thus commemorating this Roman general and renowned epicure remembered more for the gastronomical fare he provided his guests than for his military career. This certainly suggests that the cuisine of the epoch must have been worthy of a populace that contributed so much to the course of history. And indeed, I found a wide variety of recipes—refined, like an appetizer of truffles in an herb vinaigrette; rustic, like a thick vegetable soup with ham hocks; unusual, like boiled or fried cucumbers; bizarre, like pickled peaches; rich, like stuffed chicken or capon; and outrageous, like flamingo or nightingale tongues. In sum, these recipes provide a general picture of how the ancient Romans ate, whether they were farmers and simple folk or members of the upper classes of society, including pockets of notoriously decadent eccentrics.

One of the most interesting discoveries is that eating habits and the general pace of living seem to have been closer to that of modern London or New York than to that of most of Italy today. Given the difficulty of illuminating their houses, Romans would rise and retire with the sun:

> Rise: already the baker is selling breakfasts to the
> children,
> and roosters crow everywhere with the first light of day.
> (Martial 14, 223)

Unlike today's Italian, the Roman would consume a fairly rich breakfast (*ientaculum*). For an adult this meal generally consisted of leftovers from the previous evening (olives, capers, eggs, a bit of cheese and bread, honey); while the children would have milk and sweet or salted focaccias. Then a long day of work would begin. A city resident would go perhaps to the Forum, to public offices, to the markets, to the courts if he was in litigation; and those living in the country would go about the various chores of field and farm.

At midday everyone would stop for a bite to eat. Lunch (*prandium*) in the city was always a kind of snack, even for those who returned home to eat. Most would simply stop in a tavern or buy something from any of the numerous street vendors. With the increasing level of well-being and the number of commodities to be had during the later years of the Roman Empire, thermal baths began to appear in all urban centers, large or small. People would frequent these "health clubs" as a matter of status, arranging their social calendars and laying the groundwork for business arrangements and agreements. They would gather there during a break or toward the end of the work day and eat something after a bath, exercise, and massage. Consequently, snack bars came to proliferate around the baths, and their enterprising owners would even send waiters inside to sell their wares.

At twilight the family gathered for dinner (*cena* or *coena*), the most abundant and complete meal of the day. In the earliest period Romans generally ate soups made from grains or dried legumes, milk, cheese, fresh or dried fruit, olives, and occasionally a bit of bacon. As new sources of food became available and tastes gradually grew more refined, the Roman dinner reflected these changes: soups and cooked cereals were replaced with bread, and meat—though always a luxury for the poor—became available to those who could afford it. Whatever the components of this meal, it brought the entire family together around the same table. In wealthier households, there were also frequent guests, for whom something more than the everyday meal was prepared. Dinner thus became a *convivium* (banquet), with a carefully prescribed order and number of courses. Here we can still find analogies with modern Italian custom: the dinner opened with various appetizers (collectively called the *gustum, gustatio*, or *promulsis*), followed by the main courses (*mensa prima* or *caput cenae*), and a dessert (*mensa secunda*) generally consisting of fruit and sweet confections.

A substantial number of people habitually entertained dinner guests for "business reasons." These were the rich and influential *patroni*, the political and financial leaders of their day. Their *clientes* were young aspiring politicians, social climbers, artists in need of a patron, or unemployed lawyers. A *patronus* was socially obliged to invite these *clientes* to dinner; if he did not desire their company and they were too poor to feed themselves, he instead offered them food to be taken away in a *sportula* or basket. Every dinner hosted by one of these important personages was a great banquet, abundant and perhaps often ostentatious, but full of fascinating dishes.

My presentation of these recipes includes a modern list of ingredients and procedures; nonetheless, a certain level of practical cooking experience and a knowledge of basic preparations are assumed on the part of the reader. Because it was surprising to discover how many ancient Roman recipes can still be found in the regional cuisines of Italy and other countries once part of the Roman Empire, I have also included several regional recipes for comparison with their probable progenitors.

I have chosen only those ancient recipes that can still be realized without significant changes or additions that would destroy their original character. In fact, my guiding principle has been not to modernize the original flavor but to attempt to reproduce it, even if it seems extremely unusual. Neither has it been my intention to produce a culinary treatise, but rather simply to tempt the reader to explore some appetizing dishes from forgotten historical sources, with their interesting sweet-and-sour juxtapositions, their masterful use of the many aromatic herbs we can still obtain today, their refined specialities truly worthy of Lucullus. These recipes are dedicated to those cooks who, with a bit of imagination and the desire to try something new, are fortunate enough to have family or friends willing to share and enjoy them.

› I ‹

ANCIENT SOURCES

How much food to provide for farm slaves
. . . for the slaves in chains, four *ponderi* of bread in winter; five when they begin to work the vineyard, until figs are available; then return to four.

(Cato, *De agricultura* 56)

Death of a glutton
Having consumed thousands of sesterces for food, Apicius, oppressed by debtors, was forced to review his accounts, and when he discovered that he only had a few hundred sesterces left, he poisoned himself for fear of dying of hunger.

(Seneca, *Epistulae ad Helviam matrem* 10, 8–9)

Anyone attempting to study ancient Roman nutrition and cooking must deal with countless sources that differ widely among themselves. Since the evolution of ancient Roman civilization spans more than a thousand years, it stands to reason that Roman eating habits and tastes also changed with the passing of time. Indeed, over the centuries Rome gradually passed from a self-contained and rather poor and limited agricultural economy to a significantly developed and diversified one that could offer an extensive variety of products from an immense amount of land on three continents.

Among all the available ancient sources reflecting the various periods of Rome's history, those that provide recipes, descriptions of the various courses of banquets, and information on the general rules of dining etiquette are of particular interest to us. Their authors are Cato, Columella, Apicius, Petronius, Martial, and Juvenal.

The first two, Cato and Columella, both wrote treatises on agriculture: Cato around 180 B.C., Columella more than two hundred years later, between A.D. 35 and 45. It may seem at first that there would be no connection between these treatises and cooking, especially because they deal predominantly with the raising of farm animals and the cultivation of grapevines and grafts of fruit plants. But they also contain instructions for the preparation of some basic, simple foods: for example, how to store and season olives, what to feed the slaves working the fields, what foods to preserve for the winter. They also have hearty rustic recipes for cooked grains, and tips for seasoning various cheeses and preserving fruits and vegetables.

Cato the Censor is a famous figure in the history of the Roman Republic, the man who relentlessly exhorted his fellow senators to destroy Carthage, Rome's greatest rival in the Mediterranean. As was traditional in ancient Rome, however, he was not only a politician but also a farmer. His character—severe, grim, hard-working, and parsimonious—was fairly typical of the period. As a youth he had worked in the fields of his family's modest estate, and even after he became wealthy he continued to maintain his agricultural activity along with his political career. His considerable experience is evident in *De agricultura,* where he instructs his reader how to manage the estate, what types of work to assign the slaves, what to feed them, even which breads to prepare for the ritual sacrifices to the gods.

Columella, military man and "agricultural industrialist," came from a wealthy Spanish family. His inherited property in Spain, already quite extensive, was supplemented with acquisitions in Latium. He personally ran what was apparently a very successful business selling plants, in addition to his military and political career.

Columella's treatise, *De re rustica,* is more complex and specialized than that of Cato, consisting of thirteen books, each dedicated to a different subject. The twelfth volume is of specific interest to us, containing numerous recipes for preserving fruits and vegetables and instructions for the preparation of wine, vinegar, and mustard.

Two other contemporaries of Columella, Apicius and Petronius, provide between them the most extensive information on ancient Roman cuisine. Both belonged to the "high society" of their day, but they were quite different from each other and their writings reflect these personal contrasts. Apicius left us the foundation of the most famous cooking treatise of all antiquity, containing around five hundred recipes, while Petronius used the timeless technique of satire to skewer a parvenu's banquet for our delighted inspection. His *Cena Trimalchionis* is an entertaining mine of information about the exceedingly elaborate types of meals that took place among the wealthy during the reign of Nero.

Marcus Gavius Apicius (first century A.D.) was a strange character who enjoyed living well and acquired considerable skill as a dilettante cook. He frequented the most exclusive social circles and organized sumptuous banquets, inventing extravagant dishes that he would cook himself. Flamingo and nightingale tongues, camel heels, roasted ostrich, and stuffed sow's womb are only a few of the dishes created by this eccentric gourmet who strove at any cost to *épater les bourgeois*.

Anecdotes of every kind abound about this man. It was his habit, for example, to attend the auctions held at the fish market, where he once reputedly bid an enormous sum of money for a gigantic mullet while the imperial family anxiously awaited news of the result. (For the record, the mullet was actually sold to another bidder for an astonishing five thousand sesterces.) On another occasion, having heard that the shrimp caught near the coast of Libya were particularly large, he promptly outfitted a ship and sailed off to buy them. But when he discovered even before disembarking that they were in fact no larger than those available in Rome, he immediately had the ship return home without making a purchase.

The famous naturalist Pliny the Elder credited Apicius with the idea of force-feeding figs to geese in order to enlarge their livers (*Naturalis historia* 8, 209). This would mean that the origins of *foie gras* are not French, as is widely believed, but Italian. Apicius also devised delicate sauces and sophisticated entrees with skill and taste. His writing was addressed to his social peers; indeed, they were the only ones to whom he could suggest many of the extravagances found therein.

Very few ancient recipes have come down to us with proper names attached to them, but among those as many as seven cite Apicius. Another indication of his influence lies in the wide adoption of certain names he gave to particular dishes: an egg-based dish from then on became a *patina*, a bean or pea dish became a *concicla*, a fricasee a *minutal*, stew meat became *ofellae*, a ground meat patty an *isicia*. Two hundred years after Apicius's death, it was said that only the famous emperor Elagabalus was able to surpass Apicius in organizing sumptuous and magnificent meals (*Historia Augusta, Heliogabalus* 24); two hundred years later still, during the period of Saint Jerome, a good cook had come to be called an "Apicius."

Unfortunately, Apicius met a tragic if deliberated end. After squandering a patrimony over the years in order to maintain his expensive habits, he came one day to realize that his financial distress would not allow him to continue to live in the same fashion and committed suicide by swallowing poison.

It is presumed that Apicius himself was responsible for two books of recipes: the first, *De condituris,* was dedicated to sauces; the second contained recipes for complete dishes and even included illustrations. Over the ensuing centuries, however, recipes from other sources, including many of Greek origin, were integrated with those of Apicius to become a single volume, *De re coquinaria,* and divided into ten books by subject. The collection has come down to us in various editions from two ninth-century manuscripts, which in turn probably derived from a fourth- or fifth-century compilation, datable by the style of Latin.

The *Cena Trimalchionis* (Trimalchio's Feast), centerpiece of the *Satyricon* by Petronius, is as famous as its spirited author and deserves a special place among our sources.

There are no better words than those of Tacitus to describe Petronius's life and personality:

> His days were entirely spent sleeping, while at night he looked after the necessities and pleasures of life. Having attained through indolence a level of fame that others gained only through toil, he was not considered a glutton and a spendthrift like so many others who fritter away their wealth, but rather a refined pleasure-seeker. . . . Proconsul of Bithynia and then consul, he proved himself to be a man of energy and ability. Then, having returned to a life that was hedonistic in appearance if not in substance, he was brought into the circle of the emperor's favorite few and became the arbiter of good taste in Nero's reign, the person who, amid such wealth, determined what was beautiful and delicate.
>
> (Tacitus, *Annales* 16, 18)

It was this Roman Beau Brummel, then, who so wonderfully depicted in his *Cena Trimalchionis* all the excesses of bad taste, all the ridiculous things a boor-become-millionaire could do and say. His satire is a priceless if distorted reflection of what had become a truly decadent society, allowing us to discern the features of current etiquette and tastes even through this obviously exaggerated description of a Roman feast.

Always the gentleman, so intolerant of the throngs of enterprising parasites (most of them wealthy ex-slaves like Trimalchio himself) who filled the imperial court, Petronius ultimately fell into Nero's disfavor. A certain Tigellinus, the most powerful of these freedmen and one whom Petronius had mocked in the *Satyricon,* succeeded through false accusations in convincing Nero to condemn Petronius to death. In keeping with his estimable and gentlemanly image, Petronius chose to execute the sentence himself:

> The emperor had recently departed for Campania, and Petronius, who had been with him in his entourage, was detained. He allowed himself no delay out of fear or hope; but neither did he wish to expire too quickly. He cut his veins, which he then closed and reopened; and he passed the time in conversation with his friends. . . . He wished to feast and to sleep, so that even though death was imposed upon him it would look natural. Unlike most others in their dying moments, he did not praise Nero or Tigellinus or other powerful individuals in his will.
>
> (Tacitus, *Annales* 16, 19)

Martial and Juvenal provide a pleasant close to this chapter with their perspectives of everyday life in ancient Rome. These two first-century poets left us many useful bits of information.

Martial, a Spanish poet who came to Rome in search of success and a wealthy patron, was the typical *cliens,* a person who was forced by economic circumstances to call someone often less learned than himself his *patronus* or *dominus* in order to secure a donation or an invitation to dinner. His lively epigrams provide pictures of his rather difficult life placed in stark contrast to that of the wealthy whom he frequented. We find many descriptions of meals and popular foods scattered throughout his *Epigrams;* but the two closing books of this collection, *Xenia* and *Apophoreta,* are the most useful to us. The first consists of verses attached to gifts of food that the Romans would traditionally exchange for the Saturnalia, their most important annual holiday; the second is a group of epigrams describing the mementos that guests would receive from their host at banquet's end.

Little is known of Juvenal, who wrote a collection of *Satires* ridiculing the faults and vices of imperial society. Born at Aquinum, he lived and wrote in Rome first under the perfidious Domitian (81–96), then under the more tranquil reigns of Nerva, Trajan, and Hadrian (96–138). The most interesting among the *Satires* for our study are the fifth, which describes the public humiliation to which a patron would subject his *cliens* at dinner, and the fourth, wherein Juvenal wrote of the time Domitian called the Senate together to debate which pot and preparation were most suitable for cooking a huge turbot he had received as a gift.

A TASTE OF ANCIENT ROME

›II‹

FOOD SOURCES IN
ANCIENT ROME

Food and drink are useful not only to cure every type of
disease, but also to guarantee good health. Therefore it is
necessary to understand their properties, so that healthy
people know how to use them, and that in the event of
illness one knows which should be consumed.

(Celsus, *De medicina* 2, 18, 1)

The emperor Tiberius gave 200,000 sesterces to Asellius
Sabinus for a dialogue in which mushrooms, figpeckers,
oysters, and thrushes competed for honors as the best
food.

(Suetonius, *De vita Tiberii* 42, 2)

When we learn just what foods were consumed by the ancient Romans
and other populations living along the Mediterranean coast and in conti-
nental Europe, our first reaction may well be one of surprise. In fact, many
foods that we consider intrinsic to Italian cooking were simply not available to them.

For example, we think immediately of the tomato, a basic ingredient in
modern Italian cuisine, and of the potato, the primary means of survival
for many generations of northern Europeans. Both of these foods came to
Europe only after the discovery of America, together with eggplant, sweet
and hot peppers, corn (and consequently corn polenta, the nutritional
staple for many inhabitants of the Italian Alpine regions up to fifty years
ago), and turkey. All these foods have become closely identified with Mediterranean cooking—corn (*granturco*) and turkey to the point that their
names, the first in Italian and the second in English, are indissolubly (if
inaccurately) tied to such a typically Mediterranean country as Turkey.

Another item conspicuously missing is pasta, which made its appearance as we know it much later. Rice, though imported from India by the Romans, was used in cooking simply as a starch for its thickening property. The only "exotic" fruits they had were dates, and almost no citrus was available. Oranges were not introduced into Sicily until the tenth century by the Arabs. Only lemons and citrons were grown. The lemon, apparently discovered in the Orient and brought to Greece by Alexander the Great, was called in Rome *malum medicum* (the fruit or apple of the Medes). During the Empire it was carefully acclimatized, first through hothouse cultivation and then in the open air. Butter, though available, was not used in cooking; one finds it cited only in medical treatises of the time. Tea, coffee, and cocoa were unknown, and sugar came to Europe only in the Middle Ages.

At first glance this seems a bleak picture indeed, with the absence of so many staples that we have long taken for granted. However, as we examine the recipes and study the relevant literature, we gradually find that this ancient cuisine is still quite appealing.

The Mediterranean was richer with fish than it is today, providing every imaginable sort of seafood; bonito, sardines, anchovies, mackerel, gilthead, snapper, numbfish, sole, tuna, red mullet, sea bream, scorpion fish, striped mullet, monkfish, halibut, lamprey eel. Lobster, squid, cuttlefish, and octopus were then as now the delight of every gourmet. Industrial-scale breeding farms of oysters and mussels furnished these popular items on a daily basis to urban markets.

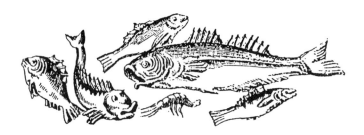

Meat lovers would encounter no great hardship if they were to find themselves traveling back in time. The only unusual factor would be the scarcity of beef. Cattle were used to work the fields; consequently their meat, toughened by toil, was undesirable to eat. In compensation there were pigs, lambs, goats, chickens, geese, ducks, pigeons, and doves to grace banquet tables, along with wild fowl and furry game: hare, boars, partridges, pheasant, deer, roebucks, thrushes, and figpeckers were in great demand. Frogs and snails were also a popular specialty, snails among the Romans and frogs largely in Gaul.

Even goose liver, an appetizing item that we associate with French cuisine, is actually of Greek and Roman origin, as mentioned above. Goose breeders fattened these unfortunate birds on figs, then killed them by force-feeding them large amounts of honeyed wine (*mulsum*), which, according to the imaginative Apicius, gave their meat a special flavor. The liver thus enlarged was called *iecur ficatum* (fig-flavored liver), from which *ficatum* became the direct source for the modern Italian word for liver, *fegato*.

Bacon, all types of sausage, and hams plumped out the Roman diet. The most popular sausage, *lucanica*, though now traditionally considered a northern Italian specialty, actually came from the district of Lucania, in the southern region of the peninsula. "I am a Lucanian sausage, the daughter of a Picenum-bred sow; I provide a delightful wreath with which to garnish white polenta" wrote Martial (13, 35) in a note accompanying a gift of these sausages to a friend. Here we learn that the idea of combining polenta (though made from spelt and not corn) and sausage was already well established many centuries ago.

Vegetables, often served as appetizers, were available in great variety, including asparagus, beets, leaf cabbage, carrots, cardoons, rutabagas, onions, leeks, squash, and cucumbers. Lettuce, watercress, chicory, endive, and mallow were popular leafy greens, either raw or cooked. Fava beans, lupines, lentils, peas, and chick peas were the bases of soups and side dishes.

Mushrooms and truffles were as highly prized then as they are today. "It is easy to send a gift of silver or gold, a cloak or toga; but it is difficult to send mushrooms," warned Martial (13, 48), with whom mushroom hunters will no doubt agree.

Cheeses were also present in abundance. Made mostly from the milk of goats and sheep, they were long a basic source of nutrition during the Republic, and they continued to be so in the rural areas and among the poorer segments of the population during the Empire. Martial has left us the names of several cheeses, including those from Vestino and Trebula, an Etrurian cheese from Luni, and a smoked cheese from the Velabrum—all areas in or around the city of Rome. Another precious source of information comes down to us from the pleasant Roman custom of sending gifts of food to friends for the seasonal festivities of the Saturnalia, accompanying them with a short note in verse. "We are won either by a gentle fire or by water," Martial (13, 33) wrote of Trebula cheeses, thus indicating that they were eaten hot, warmed perhaps in an oven or on a grill. Cheeses could also be mixed with water and cracked wheat to make delicious cakes, or simply flavored with herbs. One colorful country scene describes a farmer in the early morning as he prepares his evening meal consisting of a round focaccia together with some cheese blended with herbs and garlic (*Appendix Vergiliana, Moretum*). This recipe can be found in chapter 5 on appetizers, pages 54–55.

Many types of fruit could always be found on Roman tables. It was eaten at the end of the meal just as in modern Italy: *ab ovo usque ad malum* was the saying, or "from the egg [a favorite appetizer] to the fruit" (the equivalent of the English "soup to nuts"). A variation of this motto, *cominciare ab ovo* (to begin from the very beginning) is still a popular Italian expression.

Romans commonly enjoyed apples, pears, pomegranates, azaroles, quinces, plums, blackberries, and mulberries. From the first century B.C. there were cherries that the wealthy general Lucullus brought from the distant Black Sea. And from the first century A.D. there were peaches and apricots: the apricot (*malum armeniacum* or *praecox* or *praecoquium*) came from Armenia, the peach (*malum persicum*) from Persia, as their Latin names suggest. But the most prevalent fruits, those that had always been grown and gathered in the Mediterranean region, were figs and grapes. Muskmelons and watermelons quenched summer thirst, and in the winter there were walnuts, hazelnuts, almonds, and pine nuts, and dates imported from Palestine and Ethiopia. Finally, the olive, most typical of Mediterranean products, was consumed both as an appetizer and as a fruit at meal's end.

This brief exploration of Roman food must also include the various grains. The Romans were unacquainted with pasta as we know it, but they made flavorful soups and appetizing porridges with all the grains at their disposal, and they also ate bread and cakes. It is important to remember that their grains were not processed and refined, hence their nutritional value was superior to that of many grain products we use today.

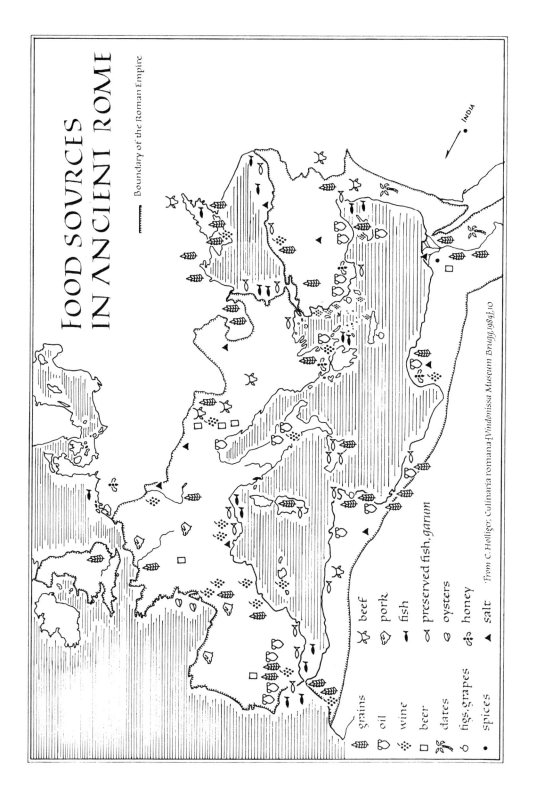

FOOD SOURCES
IN ANCIENT ROME

‒‒‒‒‒ Boundary of the Roman Empire

INDIA

🦌	beef		
🐖	pork		
🐟	fish		
	preserved fish, garum		
🦪	oysters		
🐝	honey		
▲	salt		

grains		
oil		
wine		
beer	□	
dates		
figs, grapes		
spices	•	

From C. Hölliger, Culinaria romana [Vindonissa Museum Brugg, 1984], 10

The earliest grains to be grown by the Romans were barley, spelt, rye, oats, millet, and panicum. Because of its adaptability and resilience, barley was perhaps the first of these. Its usefulness as a basis of military rations caused it to be most popular during the Republican period of expansion and conquest; afterward, during the Empire, its consumption was greatly reduced.

Spelt, which was too hard to be ground into a fine flour, was cracked and cooked for *puls,* or porridge, and polenta. But the introduction of dehusked wheat (*triticum*) in the fifth century B.C. permitted the production of flour and therefore of bread and cakes.

Romans considered oats to be suitable only for animals, while millet and panicum were commonly used for porridge. Millet continued to figure as a staple for the poor up through the Middle Ages, usually in soups. Rye was thought to be little more than a weed, at best occasionally mixed with spelt for *puls.*

Rice was originally imported as a luxury item from India and used as a starch to thicken certain dishes and in medicine. It has been discovered in archaeological excavations of Roman-age remains even north of the Alps. European cultivation of rice as a food began only in the eighth century by the Arabs in Spain. Once again it is curious that a food long considered an important part of regional cooking in many areas of Italy is not of Italian origin at all.

The Romans made fine white bread, black bread, leavened bread, flatbread for sailors, and breads variously flavored with poppy, anise, fennel, celery, and caraway seeds. The baker (called *pistor* or *triticarius* or, when he also made pastries, *placentarius*) used three types of flour distinguished by the degree of sifting: fine flour (called *siligo* or *pollen*), an intermediate type (*simila* or *similago*), and a whole-grain flour (*cibarium*) "from which nothing has been removed," commented Celsus (*De medicina* 2, 18, 4), hence not sifted at all. The baker could also choose to make leavened or unleavened bread. A type of yeast (*fermentum*) made in Gaul and Spain from the froth produced during the fermentation of beer (Pliny, *Naturalis historia* 18, 68) made leavened bread particularly soft and delicate. But according to the *Geoponica* (a sixth-century compilation of agricultural literature), the best yeast was made with millet: "If a year's supply of yeast is desired, let us mix the froth that rises to the surface in containers of fermenting must with millet flour, blend thoroughly, and form portions of the mixture to dry in the sun. Then we preserve them in a moist place" (*Geoponica* 2, 23).

The favorite beverage of ancient Rome was wine, but there were also *mulsum* (wine mixed with honey), *aqua mulsa* (hydromel), and beer. See chapter 12 for further information on this subject.

We turn in conclusion to a discussion of the food shops. Those Roman citizens who lived in rural areas or who owned large estates made few purchases of either food or clothing. As described by Cato and Columella, their objective was complete self-sufficiency. But city dwellers in general, obviously unable to cultivate crops, relied more and more, as time went on, upon an increasing number of shops for their needs. Rome itself, whose importance grew steadily through the duration of the Empire, witnessed the development of large marketplaces. For example, the various shops originally established around the Forum were brought together in 179 B.C. in the *Macellum,* a single building that embraced this diversified selection like an Oriental covered bazaar. It was demolished for urban expansion during the reign of Augustus and rebuilt on the Esquiline Hill (*Macellum Liviae*).

The most magnificent, forward-looking "shopping center" of antiquity was the Market of Trajan, whose ruins suggest a remarkably modern organization. The edifice was built on a semicircular plan and housed 150 individual shops on six floors rising a total of some one hundred feet. The emperor Trajan (98–117) entrusted the realization of the impressive urban complex containing this market to the greatest architect of the day, Apollodorus of Damascus. The other components were the piazza (*Forum*), courthouse (*Basilica Ulpia*), two libraries (one housing Latin volumes and the imperial records, the other Greek volumes), and the famous Column of Trajan. This ambitious project, which required cutting away an entire spur of stone that extended from the Quirinal Hill toward the Capitoline, was quickly completed between 109 and 113.

The finished market was a majestic structure in brickfaced concrete, with the various shops distributed according to the merchandise they offered. The ground floor had cool, shallow rooms for the sale of fruit and flowers, and the second floor had large halls for merchants of wine and olive oil. Pepper and spices (*pipera*), which were rare merchandise and more expensive, could be found on the third and fourth floors. (The memory of this important area of the market endured through the Middle Ages in the name of a steep and twisted road behind the edifice called the Via Biberatica.) The fifth floor was given over to imperial offices responsible for the periodic distribution of *congiarii*: these were subsidies available to the populace in the form of grain, olive oil, and wine. On the top floor there were large tanks of fish (either in salt water brought from nearby Ostia or in fresh water that arrived through a technically advanced plumbing system) placed on display like the acquariums of certain fashionable restaurants today. This last floor was level with the top of the Column of Trajan; thus, to an observer in the piazza, the column served as a measure of the exact height of the market, providing a sense of the sheer audacity of its construction.

So we see that even our largest supermarkets are nothing new. With the appearance of each of these complexes such as the *Macellum* or the Market of Trajan, we can easily imagine someone shaking his head and saying, "This marks the demise of the small family business," or "You can never find what you want in these enormous places!"

A TASTE OF ANCIENT ROME

›III‹

THE BANQUET AND ITS PREPARATION

Grill and spit
Let the bars of your grill drip the juices of a round cutlet;
let a sizzling boar smoke upon the long spit.
(Martial 14, 221)

Semicircular triclinium
Accept as a gift this semicircular triclinium
decorated with crescents of inlaid tortoise shell.
It is large enough for eight: let anyone come who is your
friend.
(Martial 14, 87)

Trimalchio's toothpick
. . . then with a silver toothpick
he picked his teeth . . .
(Petronius 33, 1)

The common Roman kitchen was not particularly large, nor was it well equipped or well ventilated. The earliest homes (and the poorest ones even later) did not have a room designated specifically for cooking: the hearth was in the *atrium,* the room of most daily activity when family members were not away or sleeping in their tiny *cubiculi* (bedrooms).

Urban residences and most wealthier homes, however, had a real kitchen. From the excavations of Pompeii and Herculaneum we have an idea of the average size and layout of these rooms: generally small, lacking windows, with a packed dirt floor (that could therefore not be cleaned) and no exhaust channel for the smoke to escape, these rooms were undoubtedly dirty, impractical, and rather dangerous. Horace described one of the frequent outbreaks of fire that resulted from these conditions: "In fact, once the fire began, the flame spread through the ancient kitchen and quickly reached high enough to lick the ceiling" (*Satires* 1, 5, 73–74).

The furnishings of an average kitchen consisted of a small oven for bread and cakes, a water basin, and a few burners inserted in a brick base placed up against one wall. Foods were kept in pantries and storage rooms. They were cooked over burners using wood or, more frequently, charcoal, which produced less smoke. There were few utensils: knives, spatulas, spoons (made of wood, metal, or bone), whisks, sifters, skewers, grills, mortars, and all types of pots in terracotta or bronze.

The large earthenware amphoras containing wine, oil, must, and *garum* (see pp. 27–29) were stored in pantries along with jugs and jars containing olives, dried fruit, and legumes. Fruits and vegetables were also stored in jugs. Preserved fish arrived prepacked in earthenware containers from Spain, Greece, and the Black Sea, and it was bought and stored in this condition.

A TASTE OF ANCIENT ROME

There were cooking pots called *ollae*, usually made of clay (or, rarely, of bronze), with their *opercula* (lids), and *patinae*, round or oval pans of varying depths used to cook egg-based dishes and fish and meat patties in embers. The most common serving dishes were the *acetabulum*, used for sauces, the *calix*, for fruit, the *lanx*, a general-purpose platter, the *catinus* or *catillus*, for meat or fish, and the *ciatus* and the *simpulum*, large ladles for pouring wine into goblets. Different types of spoons (even special varieties for oysters and seasoned egg yolks), containers, dishes, and cups completed the everyday battery of kitchenware.

Slaves did the cooking (everyone but the poorest Romans had at least one or two), leaving the mistress of the house free to oversee the acquisition of supplies and the state of stock on hand. The richest people even had well-paid cooks (*coci*); those unable to afford a regular cook hired one when needed for a banquet.

As we have seen, the kitchens were usually rather small, but there were certainly exceptions. No doubt those houses capable of holding banquets such as the one described by Petronius in the *Cena Trimalchionis* (see chapter 13) necessarily had kitchens that were much larger and better equipped to prepare complicated dishes for many guests. Considerable space was needed for the various chefs, cooks, and attendants that were present on such occasions. We know, in fact, that sumptuous receptions organized by such figures as Lucullus were prepared by troops of cooks directed by a head chef, called the *archimagirus*. Seneca described one suggestive scene in a letter: "Observe our kitchens, and the cooks who run back and forth among many stoves" (*Epistulae morales ad Lucilium* 114, 26).

Those areas of distinguished homes in which dinner was eaten, the *triclinia*, were large, richly furnished and elaborately decorated rooms, full of light and luxury. Prior to the advent of the *triclinium*, Romans ate in the uncovered *atrium*; later they used covered *triclinia* in both summer and winter.

These *triclinia* were always very inviting. If they were outside, there were mosaics on the pavement, fountains, ornamental waterworks, pools stocked with fish, plants, beds and tables of fine inlaid marble, all combined in an attractive and engaging atmosphere. When they were enclosed, there were frescos (often depicting convivial occasions but also hunting and fishing scenes or gardens with fruit and flowers), mosaics, fresh flowers, wooden beds with cushions and covers, and wooden tables inlaid with bronze and silver, for an atmosphere of elegance and refinement. Sometimes flowers and perfumes were lightly showered from the ceiling upon the gathering as the meal progressed.

Beginning in the first century, tablecloths (*mappae*) appeared; prior to that time slaves would clean and dry the wood or marble surface during the meal.

The dishes and serving plates of the rich were beautiful, made of terracotta with decorations in bronze, silver, even *electrum* (an alloy of gold and silver) and pure gold. In the house of Menander in Pompeii, 118 pieces of table silver were found, with a total weight of more than 50 pounds. Even north of the Alps, at Augusta Raurica (today Kaiseraugst, near Basel), archaeologists discovered a beautiful set of silver tableware from the epoch of Julian the Apostate.

The guests for the *convivium* arrived at sunset, after visiting the thermal baths, in evening dress (*vestis cenatoria*). Some brought several changes of clothing in a show of ostentation; while others, *clientes* too poor to obtain the proper attire, were furnished clothing by the *patronus*. Upon entering the *triclinium* (beginning "with the right foot," warns one of Trimalchio's slaves in the *Cena Trimalchionis* [Petronius 30]), each guest was accompanied to a position indicated by the host.

The room was arranged thus: the beds, called *triclinia* (whence the name of the room itself), were set on each of three sides of the table. Every *triclinium* accommodated three people (the Greek word *triclinos* means a bed with three places); if there were more than nine at the meal, another table with three *triclinia* was set up, and so on.

The upper classes ate in a reclining position, following a custom adopted from the Greeks; only the common people ate in a seated position. (For family meals, however, the father reclined, while the mother and offspring sat.) The distribution of places on the *triclinia* followed a precise order, according to which the guest of honor was put next to the host. The illustration defines this arrangement.

A guest could also bring along his own guest, who sat behind him on the *triclinium;* thus the second person was called, amusingly, an *umbra* (shadow). If further uninvited guests could obtain no room on the beds, they were forced to take chairs.

On particularly festive occasions the *nomenclator* would announce what dishes were to be served. This individual was only one of many slaves at work that evening. The *cellarius,* or wine steward, supervised the beverages, ordering that *mulsum* be served as aperitif and pouring the wines that accompanied the *mensa prima* and *mensa secunda*. The delicate process of decanting the wine from the amphora into an *authepsa* to filter it, flavor it with herbs, and cool it in summer or warm it in winter (see chapter 12) was performed in the same room before the diners.

The slave responsible for cutting the meat (the *structor* or *scissor*) prepared it in bite-size pieces, which the *ministratores* then served to the din-

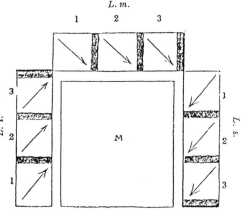

L.i. lectus imus
  (last bed)
L.m. lectus medius
  (middle bed)
L.s. lectus summus
  (first bed)

1 *locus imus*
  (last place)
2 *locus medius*
  (middle place)
3 *locus summus*
  (first place)

Every bed had space for three people, each of whom would recline (with the left elbow resting on a cushion, illustrated by the thin dark bars) in the direction indicated by the arrows.
L.i. 3 was the place for the master of the house.
L.m. 1 was the *locus consularis,* or place of honor.

(*Source:* Guhl and Koner, *La vita dei Greci e dei Romani* [Loescher: Turin, 1875], 510.)

ers. If there were few guests and the meal was not strictly formal, the serving dishes, sauces, and bread were left on the table, but during large banquets the numerous *ministratores* busily replenished the diners' plates.

Reclining on the left arm, each diner held a plate in the left hand and took the food from the plate with the right. Forks had not yet come into use, but spoons of all types were available. Knives were used only to carve and cut meat.

Etiquette required that small amounts of food be taken each time and that one should always remain clean. Ovid admonished: "Take the food with your fingers, this is the usual way to eat; but do not soil your face with your dirty hand" (*Ars amatoria* 3, 755–56). Toothpicks of bone or ivory were available in case of necessity. Trimalchio predictably betrayed his coarseness by cleaning his teeth with a *pinna argentea*—even his tooth-pick was silver—while casually conversing with his guests. However, these operations must have tended to be anything but discreet if Martial (14, 22) called the toothpick a *dentiscalpium* (tooth chisel).

For the larger banquets the courses were quite elaborate, nothing less than *pièces montées* worthy of Louis XIV. These examples come from the *Cena Trimalchionis:* for appetizers there were olives served in saddle bags straddling an artistic bronze donkey, and a wooden hen perched on a tray of imitation peahen eggs made of pastry, each of which contained a roasted figpecker; then the main dish, a roasted pig stuffed with warm sausages; and finally a fruit-laden figure of Priapus in pastry, a magnificent center-piece for dessert.

All this refinement, however, was not reflected in Roman table manners. It was usual for the diners to toss any remnants of food on the ground, leaving them for the slaves to remove periodically. There are "unswept floor" mosaics that depict the colorful variety of refuse to be found beneath a table at banquet's end.

Sometimes amid this festive atmosphere there was what would seem to us to be a decidedly macabre note, though evidently the Romans did not consider it such. Sculpted silver goblets were often decorated with skele-tons, and mosaics in the *triclinium* would depict skulls or skeletons, like that from Pompeii with a skeleton and the maxim γνῶθι σαυτον (know thyself).

ΓΝѠΘΙ·ϹΑΥΤΟΝ

A serving table survives with the decoration of a skull on its surface; and two *modioli* (drinking goblets) decorated with skeletons of philosophers and poets are among the silver found at Boscoreale. We also know that frequently in the middle of the banquet the host called for the *larva convi-vialis,* a small articulated skeleton made of ivory or wood. This strange custom of Egyptian origin (Herodotus, *Historia* 2, 78) was both an invitation to partake of the ephemeral joys of life and a warning to remember that this same life is brief. In the *Cena Trimalchionis,* the presentation of the *larva convivialis* (again made of silver, as we might have expected) by a slave was only an excuse for Trimalchio to deliver a bit of his own pseudo-philosophical verse (Petronius 34). (Interestingly enough, a small silver *larva* that closely matches the description of the one in this passage from Petronius has been recovered at Pompeii.)

During the course of a banquet various types of entertainment were also offered: music, dance, juggling and acrobatic acts, and recitations of poetry. Finally the guests departed, taking with them the most appetizing leftovers wrapped in a napkin brought from home for this specific purpose. Some guests exceeded the limits of good taste, as did Caecilianus in one of Martial's epigrams:

> You rifle through every dish that's served: sow's paps, pig's ear,
> enough woodcock for two, half a mullet and an entire pike,
> fillet of moray eel, a pullet thigh, a dove dripping with sauce.
> When it is all wrapped well between the corners of
> > an oil-soaked napkin,
> you pass it to your servant who carries it home;
> while we remain seated there and can do nothing.
> Give us back our meal, if you have even the slightest shame.
> I did not invite you for tomorrow, Caecilianus.
> > (Martial 2, 37)

The most generous hosts either randomly distributed or individually presented gifts of all kinds and worth, called *apophoreta,* to the guests as they left. Martial dedicated an essay to this custom in the last book of his epigrams. In this "convivial lottery" the host gave out food, lamps, musical instruments, pins and combs, dice and table games, small jewel boxes, vases with gold friezes, gold goblets, even flyswatters and ivory back scratchers in the form of a small hand.

With that the guests returned home; but sometimes the group would linger, reluctant to depart, whereupon the host would invite them to a second *triclinium.* There, while the slaves cleaned the first room, he began the *commissatio,* a libation of wine similar to those described in certain nineteenth-century Russian novels. The drinking was led by a participant chosen at random, who prescribed how many goblets had to be emptied in a single breath. By the time this "ceremony" ended, no doubt it remained the servants' final responsibility to see their masters safely home.

›IV‹

SAUCES

Garum
I confess that I am only the product of tuna from Antibes;
if I were made from mackerel I would not have been sent
    to you.

                      (Martial 13, 103)

Vinegar
I hope this amphora of Egyptian vinegar does not seem
        contemptible to you;
as wine it was even worse.

                      (Martial 13, 122)

Garum sociorum
Accept this exquisite *garum,* a precious gift
made with the first blood spilled from a living mackerel.
                      (Martial 13, 102)

Sauces are the war-horses of all great cooks. Apicius made them his specialty, writing a book dedicated completely to them and entitled *De condituris* (absorbed in later centuries into *De re coquinaria*). These sauces were for domestic meats, fish, all types of game (furry or fowl), vegetables, eggs, or exotic flights of fancy such as camel heels, flamingos, or ostriches.

There are sauces that we would call marinades, vinaigrette sauces, sauces made with raw or cooked egg, white sauces that derived their color from ground nuts. Even with butter noticeably missing, these sauces provide an appealing range of choice.

The principal sauces are presented here, but many others can be found in subsequent chapters where their preparation is included in recipes for the foods they accompany.

The following are the basic ingredients for these sauces:

Aromatic herbs, berries, and spices were always present: the most important ones were pepper, ginger, clove, saffron, mustard, cardamom; poppy, fennel, cumin, anise, celery, and sesame seeds; myrtle, bay, and juniper berries; mint, thyme, rue, savory, oregano, parsley, lovage, chervil, dill, coriander, and lavender.

The most important liquid ingredients were wine, reduced must (*defrutum*) or wine (*caroenum*), raisin wine (*passum*), fermented fish sauce (*garum*), olive oil, vinegar, and water.

Thickeners for the sauces were mainly starch (*amulum*), eggs, and sometimes crumbled bread or dried dough (*tracta*).

Ground walnuts, pine nuts, hazelnuts, and chopped dates and prunes were also mixed into sauces.

Salt was seldom used; but there was *garum*, which was already sufficiently salty in flavor. Because *garum* was prevalent not only in sauces but in the entire range of Roman cuisine, it merits a separate and more detailed discussion here.

GARUM

Inherited from the Greeks and initially considered a luxury for only the wealthiest Romans, *garum* was a common item throughout the Mediterranean region by the epoch of the Roman Empire. There were large *garum*-producing manufacturers all along the coast—at Pompeii, at Leptis Magna (in Libya), in southern Spain, at Clazomenae (Asia Minor), wherever saltworks and shops for preserving fish were located.

Naturally, as for any product, there were various qualities of *garum*. But everyone, from emperor to slave, used this fish sauce as prevalently as soy sauce is used in Oriental cuisine.

Ancient sources contain countless recipes for the preparation of *garum*, also known as *muria* or *liquamen*. The most complete is provided by Gargilius Martialis, a writer from the third century A.D.

> Use fatty fish, for example sardines, and a well-sealed (pitched) container with a 26–35 quart / liter capacity. Add dried aromatic herbs possessing a strong flavor, such as dill, coriander, fennel, celery, mint, oregano, and others, making a layer on the bottom of the container; then put down a layer of fish (if small leave them whole, if large use

pieces); and over this add a layer of salt two fingers high. Repeat these three layers until the container is filled. Let it rest for seven days in the sun. Then mix the sauce daily for twenty days. After that time it becomes a liquid (*garum*).

(Gargilius Martialis,
De medicina et de virtute herbarum, 62)

This sauce must have been very salty, very strong and aromatic, certainly appealing to fish-lovers.

The most expensive *garum* was the so-called *garum sociorum* (*garum* for friends), made exclusively from mackerel and produced in southern Spain. The residue after any first-quality *garum* was obtained was then used to produce a secondary type called *allec;* and for the slaves there was a *garum* made from whatever entrails remained of the fish prepared for the household meal.

The fact that the Romans sometimes used fish entrails, and the idea that the containers were left for days in the sun for the fish to decompose, have encouraged a long-standing prejudice against the quality of Roman cuisine in general. Many later texts claim that the Romans enjoyed a sauce made of rotted fish organs, a description one would hardly consider appetizing. But in reality the fish were usually whole and the brine in which they were preserved apparently prevented them from putrefying. Instead the fermentation produced bacteria that gradually caused the fish to dissolve. This same process of fermentation is still in use for the preparation of many foods and beverages (such as wine, beer, vinegar, cheese, and yogurt), where it is hardly synonymous with putrefaction.

Garum was usually purchased in large pre-packed amphoras and later mixed with other ingredients: thus there was *oenogarum* (*garum* with wine), *hydrogarum* (*garum* with water), and *oxygarum* (*garum* with vinegar). There was also a *garum castimoniale* for Jews, in deference to biblical dietary prescription, made only from "animals with both fins and scales living in water" (Leviticus 11:9–12); thus it was guaranteed to have used no mollusks, eels, and such, for its production. We know that Jews living on the Italian peninsula could obtain this particular *garum,* as is evidenced by fragments of amphoras found in Italy carrying inscriptions of their contents (cf. *Corpus Inscriptionum Latinarum* 4, 2569 and 2609).

Since nearly every recipe in Apicius contains *garum,* it is necessary for us either to make it or to find a suitable surrogate. However, readers who do not like fish need not be dismayed: even then there were those, such as Pliny, who disliked this sauce.

Obviously we would prefer to prepare *garum* without having to leave it to ferment in the sun. One alternative is this quick recipe:

> If you wish to use *garum* immediately, that is, not to expose
> it to the sun but instead to cook it, do this: prepare a brine
> salty enough that an egg will float in it . . . Put the fish in
> the brine in a new earthenware pot, add oregano, and place
> it over a flame sufficient for the liquid to reduce gradually
> (some people also add *defrutum*). Then let it cool, and filter
> it several times until it becomes clear.
>
> (*Geoponica* 20, 46, 5)

If this recipe still seems too complicated, try the following: Cook a quart / liter of grape juice, reducing it to one tenth its original volume. Dilute two tablespoons of anchovy paste in this concentrated juice, and mix in a pinch of oregano.

Still another solution could be to use the Oriental sauce called *nuoc mam,* whose basis is fish extract. It can be purchased in some supermarkets and all Oriental food shops. I suggest, however, that you make your own *garum,* adjusting the amount of fish or fish extract to match your desire for saltiness and strength of flavor.

DEFRUTUM or SAPA

Wine was an extremely popular ingredient for all types of dishes. Though today we, too, make use of it in cooking, we generally add it in small portions, either directly during cooking and then boiling down the liquid, or for marinating meat (especially game). The Romans instead almost always used reduced wine or must. According to the degree of concentration and whether wine or must was used, this was called *caroenum* or *defrutum* (*sapa*).

Two descendants of *sapa* can be found in the Emilia and Sardinia regions of Italy. Both consist of reduced must and both retain the ancient name, *sapa* or *saba.*

Sardinian recipe for *sapa*

Use the must from the first pressing of white Nuragus grapes. Cook it until it is reduced to one tenth its original volume.

Emilian recipe for *sapa*

Use the must of red grapes and reduce it to one third its initial volume. This *sapa* is used to prepare a popular sauce called *savor* by cooking it together with a fruit of your choice (pears, apples, quinces, peaches) and a bit of squash pulp. The resulting dense sauce can be preserved for many months and used to accompany boiled meats, to serve with polenta, or to add to the filling of squash ravioli.

It was also once popular to make a delicious flavored ice during the winter by filling a cup with snow, packing the center down, and pouring some *sapa* over it.

If you live in a region where wine is produced it should be easy to procure fresh must and prepare your own *sapa*. Use a copper pot to boil it down to the concentration you desire, either Sardinian or Emilian. Let it cool, then store it in a bottle that closes tightly. It will last for years.

AMULUM

Amulum (starch), used as a thickener for sauces, was derived from such grains as rye or wheat (Cato 87) or, in a more refined variety, from rice. It can be easily replaced today with cornstarch or potato starch if necessary.

Other thickening agents were *buccelli* (pieces of bread), *tracta* (a dough made of flour and water, rolled or flattened out and dried or baked, then broken into pieces), and eggs.

SILPHIUM

Silphium (in Greek, τὸ σίλφιον; the Romans also used the names *laserpicium* and *laser*) was a precious herb that often appears in ancient recipes. It belonged to the fennel family, and its stem, roots, and resinous liquid were used. Only the smallest amount was sufficient to flavor food.

This plant was the first exotic spice to arrive in Rome. It came from Cyrene (in Libya), where it was so important for the economy that its image was stamped on all the coins of the region from the sixth century B.C. This was undoubtedly effective as a form of publicity, since money enjoyed such wide circulation and its imagery was consequently a powerful message. Thus the cultivation of silphium was a measure of the wealth of Cyrene and its territory. But already by the time of Nero the plant had become mysteriously extinct. An inferior quality was still imported from Persia and Armenia; and dishonest vendors sold products based on the resin of other plants (even with ground beans occasionally mixed in), peddling them as silphium.

This spice was so expensive that the Apician manual advised its rich and sophisticated readers how to make each portion last longer:

> To have an *uncia* of silphium always ready: put the silphium in a sufficiently capacious glass container with around twenty pine nuts; every time you want to use some silphium, grind some of the pine nuts and you will be surprised by the flavor it gives the food; every time replace the number of pine nuts you have used in the container.
>
> (Apicius 14)

Botanists think that *laser parthicum,* which replaced silphium when it disappeared, is *ferula asafoetida;* the gum resin, extract of asafetida, was present for many years in European pharmacology and is still used in the Middle East. If you are unsuccessful in procuring it, try using a few drops of garlic juice instead, since the asafetida extract apparently provides an unusual flavor that is rather bitter and garlicky.

Two final bits of advice before you approach the recipes. First: Roman cooking made extensive use of many herbs. However, if you are unable to find a particular type, it will not be critical to the success of the recipe. The important thing is to have a representative sample of the herbs indicated, possibly availing yourself of useful substitutions when necessary (such as mint for pennyroyal, lemon balm for coriander, celery leaves for lovage). Second: If you do not like *garum* and prefer not to add it to a dish, remember to use salt in its place.

WHITE SAUCE FOR BOILED MEAT
(APICIUS 276)

Ius candidum in elixam: Piper, liquamen, vinum, rutam, cepam, nucleos, conditum, modicum de buccellis maceratis unde stringat, oleum. Cum coxerit, ius perfundis.

White sauce for boiled meat: Pepper, *garum*, wine, rue, onion, pine nuts, *conditum*, a few pieces of soaked bread to thicken, and oil. When [the meat] is cooked, pour the sauce over it.

Serves 4
4 slices whole-wheat bread
2 small onions (or 1 large onion)
3 oz. (100 g.) pine nuts
1 cup *conditum* (spiced wine)
1 cup dry white wine (both wines can be replaced with
 vermouth)
½ cup olive oil
pinch each of pepper and rue
1 tsp. *garum*

(For discussions of *conditum* and vermouth, see chapter 12.)

This sauce is not cooked. Remove the crust from the bread and soak the remainder in the wine. Meanwhile, chop the pine nuts and the onion. Mix all the ingredients together.

NUT SAUCE FOR SCALOPPINE
(APICIUS 281)

Ius album in copadiis: Piper, ligusticum, cuminum, apii se-
men, timum, nucleos infusos, nuces infusas et purgatas,
mel, acetum, liquamen et oleum.

Clear sauce for scaloppine: Pepper, lovage, cumin, celery
seeds, thyme, soaked pine nuts, shelled and soaked walnuts, honey, vinegar, *garum*, and oil.

Serves 4
7 oz. (200 g.) pine nuts
7 oz. (200 g.) shelled walnuts
1 Tbs. *garum*
pinch each of pepper, lovage, cumin, celery seeds, and thyme
1 Tbs. vinegar
1 Tbs. honey
2 Tbs. olive oil

Soak the pine nuts and walnuts overnight in the *garum*. Then crush them in a mortar, moistening the mixture with a teaspoon of the *garum* used to soak the nuts. You can also obtain this result with a blender. Add the other ingredients and mix together. Serve this sauce cold (or slightly warmed in a bain-marie) as an accompaniment to veal scaloppine, veal steaks, or chicken breasts.

This sauce is similar to that in the following popular Turkish recipe:

MODERN TURKISH RECIPE
Circassian Chicken

Boil a chicken; when it is cooled, cut it into pieces and arrange it on a plate. Prepare a sauce with 1 lb. (500 g.) walnuts, pepper, salt, and oil. Add a bit of broth and 1 tablespoon of paprika (obviously a later addition to the other, traditional, elements). Pour the sauce over the chicken and serve.

The following Piedmontese sauce is also a close descendant of the Roman white sauce, but, unlike the Turkish sauce, it uses only ingredients that were available to the Romans:

REGIONAL ITALIAN RECIPE
(Piedmont)
Honeybee sauce

Take shelled walnuts and crush them in a mortar. Add meat broth and mustard and mix well. Add honey and mix again. Proportions: for every 1/2 cup of crushed walnuts, use 1 tablespoon of broth, 1 teaspoon of mustard, and 1 or 2 tablespoons of honey.

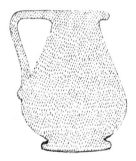

HARD-BOILED EGG SAUCE FOR SCALOPPINE
(APICIUS 284)

Ius in copadiis: Ova dura incidis, piper, cuminum, petroselinum, porrum coctum, mirtae bacas, plusculum mel, acetum, liquamen, oleum.

Sauce for scaloppine: Chop hard-boiled eggs; [add] pepper, cumin, parsley, cooked leek, myrtle berries, a generous portion of honey, vinegar, *garum*, and oil.

Serves 4
3 hard-boiled eggs, coarsely chopped
1 bunch fresh parsley, minced
2 small leeks, boiled and chopped
4–5 pitted myrtle berries
pinch each of pepper and cumin
1 tsp. honey
1 Tbs. *garum*
1 Tbs. vinegar
½ cup olive oil

This is another uncooked sauce that is used to accompany scaloppine. Put the coarsely chopped eggs, minced parsley, and boiled, drained, and chopped leeks in a blender. Add the other ingredients, blend well, and serve. (To accommodate modern tastes I have limited the amount of honey.)

DATE SAUCE FOR SCALOPPINE
(APICIUS 282)

Ius in copadiis: Piper, apii semen, careum, satureiam, cneci flos, cepullam, amigdala tosta, careotam, liquamen, oleum, sinapis modicum. Defrito coloras.

Sauce for scaloppine: Pepper, celery seeds, caraway, savory, safflower, onion, roasted almonds, dates, *garum*, oil, and a bit of mustard. Add color with *defrutum*.

Serves 4
ca. 10 pitted dates
2 oz. (50 g.) roasted almonds
3–4 small onions (or one large red onion)
pinch each of pepper, celery seeds, caraway, summer savory,
  and safflower
1 Tbs. *garum*
½ tsp. mild mustard
1 cup *defrutum*
1 Tbs. olive oil

Finely chop the onion, almonds, and dates. Add the spices and mustard. Mix in the *garum*, oil, and *defrutum*, and serve.

PRUNE SAUCE FOR SCALOPPINE
(APICIUS 278)

In copadiis ius album: Piper, cuminum, ligusticum, rutae semen, damascenas, infundis vinum, oenomeli et aceto temperabis. [Agitabis] timo et origano.

Clear sauce for scaloppine: Pepper, cumin, lovage, rue seeds, and damsons; pour on wine and mix it with *mulsum* and vinegar. [Stir with] thyme and oregano.

Serves 4
10 oz. (300 g.) pitted prunes
pinch each of cumin, lovage, and rue seeds,
ca. 2 tsp. pepper
1 cup dry white wine
½ tsp. vinegar
½ cup *mulsum*
1 bunch each, fresh thyme and oregano

Plump the prunes (any kind is acceptable) in water; cook them with the wine and herbs (be fairly generous with the pepper). When the prunes start to disintegrate, add the vinegar and *mulsum*. The curious instruction "stir with thyme and oregano" refers to the practice of tying together a bouquet of fresh herbs and using it like a spoon to mix the sauce, thus flavoring it at the same time.

As with the previous recipes, the preparation of the scaloppine is not explained. I believe that the best result is obtained by adding the scaloppine or chicken breasts to the sauce at the same time you add the vinegar and *mulsum,* and letting them cook over a low heat. You can serve the scaloppine thus in the same cooking dish.

COOKED SAUCE FOR ROAST
(APICIUS 270)

Assaturas: Mirtae siccae bacam extenteratam cum cumino, pipere, melle, liquamine, defrito et oleo teres et fervefactum amulas. Carnem elixam sale subassatam perfundis, piper aspargis et inferes.

For roasted meat: Crush dried, pitted myrtle berries with cumin, pepper, honey, *garum, defrutum,* and oil; heat and thicken with starch. Boil the meat and then roast it slightly with salt; pour the sauce over, sprinkle with pepper, and serve.

Serves 4
5–6 pitted myrtle berries
1 tsp. cumin
½ tsp. pepper
1 tsp. honey
1 tsp. *garum*
1 cup *defrutum*
1 Tbs. olive oil
1 tsp. cornstarch

Put the myrtle berries, cumin, pepper, honey, *garum,* and oil in a casserole and crush these ingredients together with half of the *defrutum.* Cook the sauce for approximately 10 minutes, reducing it a bit. Meanwhile, dissolve the starch in the remaining *defrutum.* Add this to the sauce and cook a further 10 minutes.

The second part of the recipe deals with the way to cook the meat. When they did not roast the meat on a spit, the Romans often used a two-part cooking process: the meat was first partially boiled, then it was roasted in a casserole to brown nicely. Today it is preferable to cook the meat traditionally, because with the second method a good part of the flavor is lost in the cooking water, which does not have time to become a stock. Nonetheless, if you prefer to follow the recipe completely, boil the meat for around 30 minutes in water before roasting it.

DATE SAUCE FOR BOILED OSTRICH
(APICIUS 210)

In strutione elixo: Piper, mentam, cuminum assum, apii semen, dactilos vel careotas, mel, acetum, passum, liquamen et oleum modice, et in caccabo facies ut bulliat, amulo obligas, et sic partes strutionis in lance perfundis et desuper piper aspargis. Si autem in condituram coquere volueris, alicam addis.

For boiled ostrich: Pepper, mint, roasted cumin, celery seeds, dates or caryota dates, honey, vinegar, *passum, garum,* and a bit of oil, and cook them in a pot; thicken with starch and cover the pieces of ostrich on the serving plate with the sauce and sprinkle with pepper. If you wish instead to cook [the ostrich] in the sauce, add ground spelt.

Serves 4
ca. 20 pitted dates, chopped
pinch each of pepper, mint, roasted cumin, and celery seeds
1 tsp. honey
1 tsp. *garum*
1 cup *passum*
1 Tbs. vinegar
1 Tbs. olive oil
1 tsp. cornstarch

Put the chopped dates in a casserole with all the remaining ingredients but the starch. Cook for approximately 20 minutes. At this point add the starch, dissolved in a bit of water, and reduce the sauce.

The *careota* (caryota date) was a particularly sweet type of date that the Romans generally imported from Jericho. Naturally, common dates will be sufficient, if possible the fresh ones that can be found in many supermarkets.

This sauce works well with any type of fowl, whether domestic or wild. Obviously we can no longer use ostrich, but apparently even the Romans did not eat it regularly. Apart this recipe, the only other evidence that they ate ostrich comes from the biography of the emperor Elagabalus (famous for every sort of revelry and extravagance) contained in the *Historia Augusta* (*Heliogabalus* 30).

COLD SAUCE FOR FOWL
(APICIUS 218)

Piper, ligusticum, apii semen, mentam, mirtae bacas vel uvam passam, mel, vinum, acetum, liquamen et oleum. Uteris frigido.

Pepper, lovage, celery seeds, mint, myrtle berries or raisins, honey, wine, vinegar, *garum*, and oil. Use cold.

Serves 4
3 oz. (100 g.) raisins (or 5–6 pitted myrtle berries)
1 cup wine
pinch each of pepper, lovage, celery seeds, and mint
1 tsp. honey
1 Tbs. vinegar
1 Tbs. *garum*
1 Tbs. olive oil

Plump the raisins in the wine for one hour; then drain and mince them. Mix in the remaining ingredients. You can also mix all the ingredients together in a blender. The statement "use cold" could suggest that the sauce is cooked and then left to cool, but I have always prepared it without cooking.

The version with myrtle berries is much stronger and aromatic, while raisins provide a more delicate flavor. If you decide to make the version with myrtle berries, do not soak them but rather crush them completely in a mortar.

This and the following two recipes can be used for any type of fowl.

SAUCE FOR VARIOUS TYPES OF FOWL
(APICIUS 225)

Ius in diversis avibus: Piper, cuminum frictum, ligusticum, mentam, uvam passam enucleatam aut damascena, mel modice, vino myrteo temperabis, aceto, liquamine et oleo. Calefacies et agitabis apio et satureia.

Sauce for various birds: Pepper, roasted cumin, lovage, mint, seedless raisins or damsons, and a bit of honey. Mix with myrtle wine, vinegar, *garum,* and oil. Heat and stir with celery and savory.

Serves 4
pinch each of pepper, roasted cumin, lovage, and mint
5–6 pitted prunes (or a generous handful of raisins)
1 tsp. honey
1 Tbs. vinegar
1 Tbs. *garum*
1 Tbs. olive oil
1 cup wine

2 pitted myrtle berries
1 small bunch fresh savory
2–3 stalks leafy young celery

Boil the wine with the myrtle berries for several minutes. Plump the raisins in some wine for one hour (if you are using prunes, soak them in lukewarm water instead). Chop the fruit and put it in a casserole with the remaining ingredients. Cook for approximately 20 minutes. Tie the celery and fresh savory into a bouquet. Use this to stir the sauce, then leave it to sit in the sauce until you intend to serve. For a similar instruction elsewhere, see the Prune Sauce for Scaloppine (Apicius 278), above.

GREEN SAUCE FOR FOWL
(APICIUS 228)

Ius viride in avibus: Piper, careum, spicam indicam, cuminum, folium, condimenta viridia omne genus, dactilum, mel, acetum, vinum modice, liquamen et oleum.

Green sauce for birds: Pepper, caraway, spikenard, cumin, aromatic leaf, all varieties of fresh herbs, dates, honey, vinegar, *garum*, and oil.

Serves 4
1 large bunch parsley, minced
1 bay leaf
pinch each of pepper, caraway, cumin, and mixed aromatic
  herbs
1 sprig lavender (a relative of spikenard)
5–6 pitted dates
1 Tbs. vinegar
2 Tbs. olive oil
1 tsp. honey
1 tsp. *garum*
1 Tbs. wine

If you want a sauce that is very green, use a generous amount of parsley as in our modern green sauce. But while we use bread crumbs to thicken the sauce, here dates are used. You can use date flour instead if you can find it in a specialty shop. In this case, cook the sauce for around 20 minutes. Otherwise simply chop the dates, mix them together with the remaining ingredients in a blender, and serve cold.

SAUCE FOR ALL TYPES OF GAME
(APICIUS 351)

Ius in venationibus omnibus elixis et assis: piperis scripulos VIII, rutam, ligusticum, apii semen, iuniperum, timum, mentam aridam scripulos senos, pulei scripulos III. Haec omnia ad levissimum pulverem rediges et in uno commisces et teres. Adicies in vasculum melle quod satis erit, et his uteris cum oxigaro.

Sauce for all boiled and roasted game: Eight scruples of pepper, rue, lovage, celery seeds, juniper, and thyme, 6 scruples of dried mint, and 3 scruples of pennyroyal. Grind all these ingredients into a fine powder and mix them together. Add a sufficient amount of honey in the jar and when you want to use the mixture add *oxygarum*.

Serves 4
1 tsp. each, pepper, rue, lovage, celery seeds, thyme, mint, and
  pennyroyal
2–3 juniper berries
1 tsp. honey
1 cup *oxygarum*

This sauce, which can accompany all types of boiled or roasted meat, consists of a powder of herbs and spices that is prepared in advance and then mixed with honey and *oxygarum* to make a sauce just before serving. Use only dried herbs, crushing them together in a mortar.

You can also make a large quantity of the powder and store it with the appropriate amount of honey in a glass jar. One generous tablespoon of this mixture should be added to a cup of *oxygarum* to make the sauce when needed.

SAUCE FOR NUMBFISH
(APICIUS 405)

In torpedine elixa: Piper, ligusticum, petroselinum, mentam, origanum, ovi medium, mel, liquamen, passum, vinum, oleum. Si voles, addes sinape, acetum. Si calidum volueris, uvam passam addes.

For boiled numbfish: Pepper, lovage, parsley, mint, oregano, egg yolk, honey, *garum*, *passum*, wine, and oil. If desired, add mustard and vinegar. If you want the sauce warm, add raisins.

Serves 4
2 egg yolks
1 cup olive oil
1 tsp. *garum*
1 tsp. wine
½ Tbs. strong mustard (optional)
1 Tbs. vinegar
½ Tbs. honey (omit if using mustard)
1 tsp. *passum* (omit if using mustard)
1 Tbs. total, lovage, parsley, mint, and oregano
pepper to taste

This sauce is intended to accompany boiled numbfish, or electric ray, but it can be used for other varieties of fish as well. As with any mayonnaise-based sauce, you begin by beating the egg yolks, adding the oil first by drops and then gradually in a trickle. When you have beaten in all the oil, add the *garum* and the wine (both types), again very slowly. Mix in the remaining ingredients. The inclusion of mustard is very good; I often add it to mayonnaise. But if you do so, omit the *passum* and the honey.

The heated version of this sauce, which includes raisins, is similar to the one immediately below. See there for the procedure; however, remember to reduce the quantity of olive oil to 1 tablespoon.

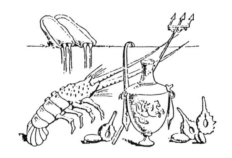

SAUCE FOR CUTTLEFISH
(APICIUS 411)

Sepias: Piper, ligusticum, cuminum, coriandrum viridem, mentam viridem, ovi vitellum, mel, liquamen, vinum, acetum et oleum modicum. Et, ubi bullierit, amulo obligas.

Cuttlefish: Pepper, lovage, cumin, fresh coriander, fresh mint, egg yolk, honey, *garum*, wine, vinegar, and a little oil. Once it boils, thicken with starch.

Serves 4
2 egg yolks
1 tsp. vinegar
1 tsp. *garum*
1 Tbs. olive oil
1 cup dry wine
1 Tbs. total, lovage, cumin, coriander, and mint
pepper to taste
1 tsp. cornstarch

Dissolve the starch in a bit of the wine and put aside. Beat the egg yolks with the liquid ingredients; add the herbs and the pepper and cook for about 10 minutes over a low heat. As soon as the sauce begins to bubble, add the starch, dissolved in water. Mix well.

SAUCE FOR GILTHEAD
(APICIUS 462)

Ius in pisce aurata: Piper, ligusticum, careum, origanum, rutae bacam, mentam, myrtae bacam, ovi vitellum, mel, acetum, oleum, vinum, liquamen. Calefacies et sic uteris.

Sauce for gilthead: Pepper, lovage, caraway, oregano, rue berries, mint, myrtle berries, egg yolk, honey, vinegar, oil, wine, and *garum*. Heat and use warm.

This sauce is a variation of the previous one; the principal difference is the addition of pitted and minced myrtle berries. Because the procedure for its preparation is otherwise the same, only the recipe is given here.

HERB SAUCE FOR FRIED FISH
(APICIUS 434)

Ius diabotanon in pisce frixo: Piscem quemlibet curas, lavas, friges. Teres piper, cuminum, coriandri semen, laseris radicem, origanum, rutam, fricabis; suffundes acetum, adicies careotam, mel, defritum, oleum, liquamen, temperabis; refundes in caccabum, facies ut ferveat. Cum ferbuerit, piscem frictum perfundes, piper asperges et inferes.

Herb sauce for fried fish: Clean, wash, and fry the fish of your choice. Grind pepper, crush cumin, coriander seed, silphium root, oregano, and rue. Moisten with vinegar;

add dates, honey, *defrutum*, oil, and *garum;* mix well. Pour into a pot and bring to a boil. When it boils, pour over the fried fish, sprinkle with pepper, and serve.

Serves 4
1 Tbs. total, cumin, coriander seeds, oregano, and rue
1 garlic clove, pressed for its juice
1 tsp. vinegar
5–6 pitted dates, minced
1 tsp. honey
1 tsp. *garum*
1 Tbs. olive oil
1 Tbs. *defrutum*

This sauce is excellent with both fried and baked fish. However, I think it should be served on the side in a separate bowl.

Mix the herbs with the garlic juice (replacing the silphium root) and put this in a saucepan with the vinegar; add the minced dates and the remaining ingredients. Cook for 15–20 minutes. Serve hot.

SAUCE FOR BONITO
(APICIUS 423)

Ius in sarda: Piper, origanum, mentam, cepam, aceti modicum et oleum.

Sauce for bonito: Pepper, oregano, mint, onion, a bit of vinegar, and oil.

This is a vinaigrette sauce made with herbs and minced onions. It is prepared cold: the ingredients are simply mixed together and left to stand for ½ hour. Since *garum* is missing here, you might add a pinch of salt.

The sauce can be used with baked fish, or hot or cold boiled fish.

CUMIN SAUCE FOR OYSTERS
AND MIXED SHELLFISH
(Apicius 31)

Cuminatum in ostrea et concilia: Piper, ligusticum, petro-
selinum, mentam siccam, folium, malabatrum, cuminum
plusculum, mel, acetum et liquamen.

Cumin sauce for oysters and shellfish: Pepper, lovage, parsley, dried mint, aromatic leaf, malabathrum, ample cumin,
honey, vinegar, and *garum*.

Serves 4
1 Tbs. total, lovage, parsley, mint, bay, malabathrum, and
  cumin
pepper to taste
1 tsp. honey
½ cup vinegar
1 Tbs. *garum*

This is another vinaigrette sauce, a variety to serve with or over cooked
oysters. Grind the herbs and spices in a mortar, using enough cumin so
that it is the predominating flavor; mix with the honey, vinegar, and
garum. Let stand ½ hour before serving.

SAUCE FOR OYSTERS
(Apicius 413)

In ostreis: Piper, ligusticum, ovi vitellum, acetum, liqua-
men, oleum et vinum. Si volueris, et mel addes.

For oysters: Pepper, lovage, egg yolk, vinegar, *garum*, oil,
and wine. If you wish, add honey.

This is another type of mayonnaise sauce, a relative of the French *rémou-*
lade, which is nothing more than mayonnaise with herbs. In contrast to
the Sauce for Numbfish (Apicius 405, pp. 40–41), this sauce uses only one
herb, lovage, and it does not contain *passum*. Even the honey is optional.
Follow the instructions for Apicius 405 to prepare this sauce, which is also
good with any type of boiled fish or vegetable.

SAUCE FOR WILD MUSHROOMS
(APICIUS 311)

In fungis farneis: Piper, carenum, acetum et oleum.

For ash tree mushrooms: Pepper, *caroenum*, vinegar, and oil.

This seems to be a sauce used to dress mushroom salad. It can be used with boletus, *amanita Caesarea*, and even cultivated mushrooms.

The quantities of the ingredients depend upon the amount of mushrooms you use, but the proportions should be the following: one part wine, two parts vinegar, two parts oil. Add a dash of salt (not mentioned in the recipe), and use a generous amount of pepper.

VINEGAR MARINADE
(APICIUS 84)

Cucumeres: Piper, puleium, mel vel passum, liquamen et acetum. Interdum et silfi accedit.

Cucumbers: Pepper, pennyroyal, honey or *passum*, garum, and vinegar. Sometimes silphium is added.

2–3 large garlic cloves
1 cup vinegar
1 tsp. *garum*
1 tsp. honey or *passum*
1 handful of fresh mint
pepper to taste

This marinade is good with vegetables that have been boiled (carrots, string beans) or fried (squash slices, zucchini sticks). Use either the juice of the garlic cloves or the cloves themselves, lightly crushed, to replace the silphium in the recipe. Place them in the bowl that you will use to serve the vegetables. The mint is a satisfactory substitution for fresh pennyroyal, which is fairly difficult to find.

Put the vinegar, *garum*, and honey or *passum* in a saucepan and bring to a boil. Mince the fresh mint. Place the vegetables in the serving bowl, sprinkle with pepper and the mint, and pour the hot marinade over. Let stand at least 3–4 hours before serving.

If you are using string beans, you can replace the mint with savory; for zucchini, use 4–5 bay leaves instead.

This vinegar marinade is only one of many that were used to accompany raw and cooked vegetables. Fulvio Uliano, author of *L'antica Roma a tavola* (Naples, 1985), suggests a fanciful but fascinating interpretation for the name of this sauce: he calls it *esca Apicii* (seasoning of Apicius), and infers that this expression is the basis of *a scapece*, a Neapolitan term referring to vegetables in a marinade of vinegar, garlic, and herbs (p. 36). Since there doesn't seem to be any more plausible explanation for the term, I am happy to include this curiosity in the hope that such an ingenious theory may actually be true.

COOKED SAUCE FOR BOILED ARTICHOKE BOTTOMS
(APICIUS 117)

Aliter: Sfondilos elixos perfundes amulato infra scripto: apii semen, rutam, mel, piper teres, passum, liquamen et oleum modice, amulo obligas, piper asperges et inferes.

Another recipe: Cover boiled cardoon bottoms with a starch sauce prepared thus: Grind celery seeds, rue, honey, and pepper; [add] *passum, garum*, and a little oil. Thicken with starch, sprinkle with pepper, and serve.

1 cup wine
1 Tbs. olive oil
1 tsp. *garum*
1 tsp. honey
1 Tbs. total, ground celery seeds and rue
1 tsp. cornstarch

Dissolve the starch in a little of the wine. Cook all remaining ingredients together. When the mixture has started to amalgamate, add the starch and thicken further. Total cooking time should be around 20 minutes.

The recipe calls for cardoon bottoms (*sfondili*), for which we can substitute artichoke bottoms. See page 154 for a discussion of the artichoke.

SAUCE FOR HARD-BOILED EGGS
(APICIUS 328)

Ova elixa: Liquamine, oleo, mero vel ex liquamine, pipere, lasere.

Boiled eggs: *Garum,* oil, and pure wine; or with *garum,* pepper, and silphium.

4 hard-boiled eggs, sliced
1 tsp. *garum* or *oenogarum*
2 garlic cloves, pressed for their juice
2 Tbs. olive oil
pinch of pepper

This rendition is a combination of the two alternatives given in Apicius, and it seems to work nicely. Mix the *garum* or *oenogarum,* garlic juice, oil, and pepper together. Pour over the sliced eggs and serve.

PINE NUT SAUCE FOR MEDIUM-BOILED EGGS
(APICIUS 329)

In ovis apalis: Piper, ligusticum, nucleos infusos. Suffundis mel, acetum, liquamine temperabis.

For medium-boiled eggs: Pepper, lovage, and soaked pine nuts. Pour on honey and vinegar; mix with *garum.*

4 medium-boiled eggs
ca. 2 oz. (50 g.) pine nuts
3 Tbs. vinegar
1 tsp. honey
pinch each of pepper and lovage

Soak the pine nuts 3–4 hours beforehand in the vinegar. Then mix all the sauce ingredients thoroughly in a blender.

This exquisite sauce should be presented in a sauceboat so that each person can serve himself or herself, since the eggs cannot be sliced and placed on a dish in advance.

CHEESE SAUCE FOR LETTUCE
(APICIUS 38)

Hypotrimma: Piper, ligusticum, mentam aridam, nucleos pineos, uvam passam, cariotam, caseum dulcem, mel, acetum, liquamen, oleum, vinum, defritum aut carenum.

Hypotrimma: Pepper, lovage, dried mint, pine nuts, raisins, dates, sweet cheese, honey, vinegar, *garum,* oil, wine, and *defrutum* or *caroenum.*

3 oz. (100 g.) fresh soft cheese (e.g., ricotta)
1 cup olive oil
1 tsp. honey
1 tsp. *garum*
1 Tbs. vinegar
1 Tbs. *defrutum* or *caroenum*
pinch of pepper
1 Tbs. total, lovage and mint
1 handful of pine nuts and raisins, mixed
4–5 pitted and chopped dates

Place all ingredients but the pine nuts, raisins, and dates in a blender, and mix thoroughly. Mix in the nuts and fruit afterward by hand.

This is a tasty and unusual sauce, a kind of ancestor of the delicate French salad dressing based on Roquefort cheese. It goes well with raw or cooked leafy lettuce or Belgian endive.

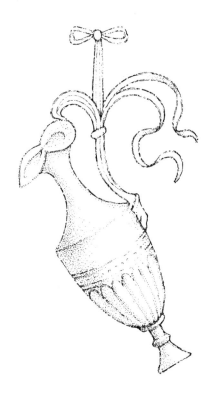

› V ‹

APPETIZERS

GUSTUM

Goose liver
Behold how this liver is larger than the largest goose.
You will say in astonishment: "This liver, I ask, where did
    it grow?"
(Martial 13, 58)

Figpeckers
Since the fig nourishes me, but I also feed on sweet
    grapes,
why did the grape not give me my name?
(Martial 13, 49)

Eggs
If a white wave surrounds the yellow yolk,
let a sauce of Spanish mackerel season the eggs.
(Martial 13, 40)

Oysters
I am a shellfish freshly arrived, drunk with the Lucrine
    Lake near Baiae;
A lover of luxury, now I thirst for noble *garum*.
(Martial 13, 82)

The Romans served many different appetizers to begin their banquets. The most popular items were seasoned eggs and egg-based dishes, vegetables, salad, mushrooms and truffles, assorted shellfish, cheese with herbs, olives, sausages, and even more filling dishes, such as complicated fricassees and casseroles, which today would be considered complete meals in themselves. You should select at least two or three different dishes from among the choices in this chapter to serve together—variety was very important—and accompany them with chilled *mulsum*.

EGGS

Hard-boiled eggs (*ova elixa*): Garnish with the sauce described in Apicius 328, pp. 46–47.
Medium-boiled eggs (*ova apala*): Garnish with the delicate pine nut sauce in Apicius 329, p. 47.
Fried eggs (*ova frixa*): Fry the eggs in *garum* mixed with wine (Apicius 327).

Salad with eggs and tuna: Prepare a bed of washed and dried lettuce. Place albacore tuna on it, then cover with slices of hard-boiled eggs. I suggest serving both *garum* and olive oil on the side. This is an appetizer based on a description in Martial (11, 52; see chapter 13, p. 199).

Eggs and artichokes: See Apicius 112, pp. 141–42.

EGG-BASED DISHES, CHEESES, AND PÂTÉS

CONCICLA À LA COMMODUS
(APICIUS 198)

Concicla Commodiana: Pisam coques. Cum despumaverit, teres piper, ligusticum, anetum, cepam siccam, suffundis liquamen, vino et liquamine temperabis. Mittis in caccabum ut combibat. Deinde ova IIII solves, in sextarium pisae mittis, agitas, mittis in cumana, ad ignem ponis ut ducat, et inferes.

Concicla à la Commodus: Cook peas. When they begin to put out a froth, grind pepper, lovage, dill, and dried onion, moisten with *garum,* and mix with wine and *garum.* Put it in the pot [with the peas] so that it can be absorbed. Then add 4 beaten eggs for every *sextarius* of peas, stir, put it in a baking dish, place in the oven so that it sets, and serve.

Serves 4
4½ lb. (2 kg.) fresh peas in the shell
4 eggs

For the sauce:
  1 tsp. each of pepper, lovage, and dill
  1 Tbs. dried onion
  1 tsp. *garum*
  1 Tbs. wine

Shell and boil the peas, drain them, and then put them through a vegetable grinder. Mix the herbs and dried onion together with the wine and *garum* to make a sauce, and add to the ground peas.

Beat the eggs well; if you desire a soufflé, separate the eggs, beat the yolks, and stiffly whip the whites. Combine the eggs with the pea mixture. Place in an ovenproof dish, bake 20–25 minutes in a hot oven (400°F.) and serve.

This delicate dish was apparently dedicated to the emperor Commodus Antonius (161–92), son of and successor to Marcus Aurelius. For a discussion of the term *concicla,* see the Glossary.

ASPARAGUS AND FIGPECKER *PATINA*
(Apicius 132)

Patina de asparagis frigida: Accipies asparagos purgatos, in mortario fricabis, aqua suffundes, perfricabis, per colum colabis. Et mittes ficetulas curatas, teres in mortario piperis scripulos sex, adicies liquamen, fricabis, vini ciatum I, passi ciatum I, mittes in caccabum olei uncias III. Illic ferveant. Perungues patinam, in ea ova VI cum oenogaro misces, cum suco asparagi impones cineri calido, mittes inpensam supra scriptam. Tunc ficetulas compones. Coques, piper asparges et inferes.

A cold asparagus *patina:* Take cleaned asparagus, crush them in a mortar, pour on water, crush thoroughly, and strain. Put plucked and cleaned figpeckers [in a pot]. Grind 6 scruples of pepper in a mortar; add *garum* and grind; add 1 *cyathus* of wine, 1 *cyathus* of *passum,* and put this in a pot with 3 *unciae* of oil. Bring to a boil. Grease a pan, mix 6 eggs together with *oenogarum* in it, add the asparagus puree, and place it in embers. Put in the ingredients described above. Then add the figpeckers. Cook, sprinkle with pepper, and serve.

Serves 4
4 quail (or chicken breasts)
4½ lb. (2 kg.) asparagus
6 eggs
For the sauce:
ample pepper corns
1 Tbs. *garum*
1 Tbs. wine
1 Tbs. *passum*
2 Tbs. olive oil

Figpeckers, songbirds with thin beaks, were considered particularly delicious fare by the Romans. Because they are obviously hard to find today, you can use quail or chicken breasts in their place.

The recipe assumes that the plucked and cleaned birds have been half cooked before they are arranged on the bottom of an ovenproof dish.

Prepare the sauce as described above: grind the pepper, add the *garum* and mix; follow with the wine, *passum,* and olive oil, and heat.

Boil, drain, and strain the asparagus. Beat 6 eggs well and mix with the asparagus. Then add the sauce and mix well. Pour this mixture over the birds and bake at 375°F. for 25–30 minutes.

This dish may also be served cold, as its Latin title suggests.

For a discussion of the term *patina,* see the Glossary.

ASPARAGUS *PATINA* WITH HERBS
(Apicius 133)

Aliter patina de asparagis: Adicies in mortario asparagorum praecisuras quae proiciuntur, teres, suffundes vinum, colas. Teres piper, ligusticum, coriandrum viridem, satureiam, cepam, vinum, liquamen et oleum. Sucum transferes in patellam perunctam et, si volueris, ova dissolves ad ignem, ut obliget. Piper minutum asparges.

Another asparagus *patina:* Put asparagus ends, which are usually cut away, in a mortar, grind, pour wine over them, and strain. Grind pepper, lovage, fresh coriander, savory, onion, wine, *garum,* and oil. Transfer the sauce into a greased pan and, if you wish, beat in eggs when it is over the fire to thicken. Sprinkle with finely ground pepper.

The following recipe is traced to an ancient people living in the region of Apulia. The quantities here can serve as a point of reference for the Apician recipe above.

REGIONAL ITALIAN RECIPE
(Apulia)
Daunian Asparagus Frittata

Serves 4
2 lb. (1 kg.) wild asparagus
5 eggs
1 Tbs. grated pecorino cheese
1 handful of fresh parsley, minced
salt and pepper to taste

Clean, boil, and chop the asparagus. Beat the eggs in a large bowl; mix in the grated cheese, parsley, salt, pepper, and asparagus. Cook this mixture like a frittata and serve hot.

LETTUCE *PATINA*
(APICIUS 130)

Aliter patina: Tyrsum lactucae teres cum pipere, liquamine, careno, aqua, oleo. Coques, ovis obligabis, piper asparges et inferes.

Another *patina:* Grind lettuce stalks with pepper, *garum, caroenum,* water, and oil. Cook, thicken with eggs, sprinkle with pepper, and serve.

Serves 4
3 bunches romaine lettuce
1 Tbs. *garum*
ca. ¼ cup *caroenum*
1 Tbs. olive oil
sufficient water
4 eggs

Coarsely chop the lettuce and heat it in a pan with the pepper, *garum, caroenum,* olive oil, and water. Do not begin with too much liquid; you can add more if necessary while it cooks. Meanwhile, beat the eggs. Add them to the mixture and finish cooking either on the stove or in the oven, as you prefer. The recipe does not specify which cooking method to use, and it can in fact be successfully realized both ways.

PATINA WITH BRAIN
(APICIUS 128)

Patina cotidiana: Cerebella elixata teres cum pipere, cumino, lasere. Cum liquamine, careno, lacte et ovis ad ignem lenem vel ad aquam calidam coques.

An everyday *patina:* Grind boiled brain with pepper, cumin, and silphium. Cook over a low fire or over hot water with *garum, caroenum,* milk, and eggs.

Serves 4
2 lamb brains (or 1 veal brain)
pinch of pepper
pinch of cumin
1 garlic clove, pressed for its juice
4 eggs
1 Tbs. *garum*
1 Tbs. *caroenum*
½ cup milk

Boil the lamb or veal brain. Grind it in a mortar together with a bit of pepper and cumin and the garlic juice. In a bowl beat the eggs, then combine them with the brain mixture. Add the *garum, caroenum,* and milk. Cook as for a frittata.

This dish is still very popular in Lebanon and Syria, where they consider lamb brain a delicacy.

CHEESE ROUND WITH HERBS
(APPENDIX VERGILIANA, MORETUM)

Quattuor alia, apius, ruta, coriandrum, salis micas, caseus.

Four garlic cloves, celery, rue, coriander, salt grains, and cheese.

In a mortar grind the garlic, then the fresh soft cheese, and finally the herbs (use celery leaf or parsley), so that these ingredients are thoroughly blended. The mixture can be moistened with olive oil, followed by a small amount of strong vinegar. Form the mixture into a round and chill.

Along with this herb cheese, the farmer protagonist of this poem *More-*

tum ate a kind of focaccia carefully prepared in the following manner: first wheat kernels were ground and the resulting flour was sifted; then the flour was mixed with water, aromatic herbs, and salt, and kneaded at length; finally the dough was formed into a flat round and the top surface was given a latticed decoration with the side of the hand. It was baked at the hearth in embers.

We can reproduce this same type of bread, baking it in the oven or cooking it in a nonstick pan so that no oil is needed.

CHEESE ROUND WITH HERBS
(APICIUS 41)

Moretaria: Mentam, rutam, coriandrum, feniculum, omnia viridia, ligusticum, piper, mel, liquamen. Si opus fuerit, acetum addes.

Condiment for a *moretum:* Mint, rue, coriander, fennel, all fresh, lovage, pepper, honey, and *garum.* If necessary, add vinegar.

Grind the herbs in a mortar; mix with the honey, *garum,* and olive oil. Blend with a fresh soft cheese, such as ricotta (not mentioned in the recipe, which lists only the ingredients used to season it).

This cheese is also good warmed: place it in a preheated oven (400°F.) for about 15–20 minutes. Serve with roasted sausage and seasoned olives.

A similar type of heated herb cheese is popular in Abruzzo, where the herbs are also used to cover the ricotta instead of being blended in with it.

CHILLED CHEESE AND
CHICKEN LIVER PÂTÉ
(APICIUS 125)

Sala cattabia: Piper, mentam, apium, puleium aridum, caseum, nucleos pineos, mel, acetum, liquamen, ovorum vitella, aquam recentem. Panem ex posca maceratum exprimes, caseum bubulum, cucumeres in caccabulo compones, interpositis nucleis. Mittes concisi capparis minuti . . . iocusculis gallinarum. Ius profundes, super frigidam collocabis et sic appones.

Sala cattabia: [Grind] pepper, mint, celery, dried penny-royal, cheese, pine nuts, honey, vinegar, *garum*, egg yolk, and fresh water. In a pot arrange bread that has been soaked in *posca* and squeezed to remove excess liquid, cheese made of cow's milk, and cucumbers, interspersed with pine nuts. Add finely minced capers, . . . chicken livers. Cover with the sauce, place it over a container of cold water to cool, and serve thus.

7–8 slices whole-wheat bread, crust removed
diluted vinegar (to soak the bread)
1 lb. (½ kg.) ricotta
2 Tbs. capers, minced (optional)
14 oz. (400 g.) chicken livers
2 large parboiled cucumbers (or 6 pickles), sliced
3 oz. (100 g.) pine nuts
For the sauce:
½ tsp. pepper
1 tsp. each, fresh minced mint and parsley
1 tsp. pennyroyal
1 Tbs. grated cheese
3 oz. (100 g.) pine nuts
1 tsp. honey
1 Tbs. vinegar
1 Tbs. *garum*
3 hard-boiled egg yolks
1 Tbs. water

This recipe, though surviving in fragmentary form, can still be realized with excellent results. The meaning of the name *sala cattabia*, which appears in this recipe and the two that follow, remains a mystery. Nonetheless, the result here is a dish similar to the French *terrine*.

Prepare a sauce from the ingredients listed above. Soak the bread in the diluted vinegar (*posca*: see the Glossary), squeeze, and mix it with the ricotta.

Fry the chicken livers in a bit of olive oil and then pass them through a meat grinder twice. Now begin to fill a casserole with layers of the various ingredients, distributing a tablespoon of the sauce over each: the first layer cucumbers or pickles, then pine nuts, then cheese and bread, a sprinkling of capers if desired, then chicken liver. Continue in this order, providing at least two layers of each. Chill for several hours before serving.

CHILLED CHICKEN, SWEETBREAD, AND CHEESE PÂTÉ
(Apicius 126)

*Aliter sala cattabia Apiciana: Adicies in mortario apii se-
men, puleium aridum, mentam aridam, gingiber, coriandrum viridem, uvam passam enucleatam, mel, acetum,
oleum et vinum, conteres. Adicies in caccabulo panis Pi-
centini frustra, interpones pulpas pulli, glandulas haedinas,
caseum Vestinum, nucleos pineos, cucumeres, cepas aridas
minute concisas. Ius supra perfundes. Insuper nivem sub
hora asparges et inferes.*

Another *sala cattabia* à la Apicius: In a mortar put celery
seeds, dried pennyroyal, dried mint, ginger, fresh coriander, seedless raisins, honey, vinegar, oil, and wine. Grind
together. In a pot put small pieces of Picentine bread, alter-
nated with chicken meat, kid sweetbreads, Vestine cheese,
pine nuts, cucumbers, and minced dried onion. Pour the
sauce over this. Then sprinkle with snow [over the cover to
chill] and serve.

3 chicken breasts
1 veal sweetbread
2 large parboiled cucumbers (or 6 pickles), sliced
14 oz. (400 g.) grated Parmesan or mild pecorino cheese
7–8 slices whole-wheat bread, crust removed
diluted vinegar (to soak the bread)
1 lb. (½ kg.) ricotta
2 Tbs. capers, minced (optional)
14 oz. (400 g.) chicken livers
2 large parboiled cucumbers (or 6 pickles), sliced
3 oz. (100 g.) pine nuts
For the sauce:
½ tsp. pepper
1 tsp. each, fresh minced mint and parsley

Prepare the sauce with the herbs, raisins, honey, vinegar, wine, and oil.
Soak the bread in the diluted vinegar and squeeze out the excess liquid.
Boil the chicken breasts and cut into small pieces; boil the sweetbread and
slice. Place the cucumbers, bread, cheese, chicken, and sweetbread slices in
alternating layers in a casserole, beginning with the cucumbers or pickles,
and covering each layer with a tablespoon of the sauce. Chill for several
hours before serving.

Picenum was a region to the northeast of Rome, corresponding in part to modern-day Marches. The bread of Picenum was a type of sweet, dry flatbread consisting of flour kneaded with grape juice, which was soaked in milk before it was eaten (cf. Pliny, *Naturalis historia* 18, 106, and Martial 13, 47).

The Vestines inhabited a region to the east of Rome, along the Aterno River (in what is now Pescara). The cheese they produced was among those most in demand by the Romans. Although we do not know what type of milk was used, it would appear that Vestine cheese was dry, thus it was grated for use.

HERBAL BREAD AND CHEESE
(APICIUS 127)

Aliter sala cattabia: Panem Alexandrinum excavabis, in posca macerabis. Adicies in mortarium piper, mel, mentam, alium, coriandrum viridem, caseum bubulum sale conditum, aquam, oleum. Insuper nivem et inferes.

Another recipe for *sala cattabia:* Cut out the center of Alexandrian bread and soak it in *posca.* In a mortar put pepper, honey, mint, garlic, fresh coriander, salted cheese made from cow's milk, water, and oil. Put snow over [the cover to chill] and serve.

1 lb. (½ kg.) coarse-textured bread, crust removed
diluted vinegar (to soak the bread)
1 lb. (½ kg.) ricotta (or other fresh cheese)
pepper to taste
1 Tbs. honey
1 Tbs. total, minced fresh mint and coriander
2 cloves garlic, minced
sufficient water
sufficient olive oil

Soak the bread in the diluted vinegar (*posca*), then squeeze the excess liquid from it. Put the bread in a bowl and mix it thoroughly with the remaining ingredients, adjusting the water and oil to maintain a reasonably firm consistency. Chill before serving.

For a discussion of Alexandrian bread, see Sweet Buns with Must (Apicius 297), page 158.

LIVER PÂTÉ
(Apicius 430)

*Iecur coques, teres et mittes piper aut liquamen aut salem,
addes oleum—iecur leporis aut haedi aut agni aut pulli—
et, si volueris, in formella piscem formabis. Oleum viridem
supra adicies.*

Cook liver, grind it, add pepper or *garum* or salt, add oil—
use the liver of hare, kid, lamb, or chicken—and, if you
wish, mold it in a fish-shaped pan. Pour green oil over.

Serves 4
1 lb. (½ kg.) liver (possibly a mix of chicken, lamb, and veal)
pepper to taste
garum to taste
sufficient olive oil

Fry the liver, flavoring it with a bit of pepper and *garum,* and then pass it
twice through a meat grinder. Adjust the consistency with oil; taste and
add more *garum* and pepper if necessary. Put it in a form and chill for
several hours.

This pâté is included in a small group of recipes entitled *salsum sine
salso* (salted fish without the salted fish), referring to the Roman custom
of disguising certain dishes so that their ingredients could not be distinguished; hence the option here of forming the pâté to resemble a fish. Obviously, you can use any form you choose.

OLIVE PASTE OR *EPITYRUM*
(Cato 119)

*Epityrum album, nigrum, varium sic facito. Ex oleis albis,
nigris variisque nucleos eicito. Sic condito. Concidito ipsas,
addito oleum, acetum, coriandrum, cuminum, feniculum,
rutam, mentam. In orculum condito, oleum supra siet. Ita
utito.*

Make green, black, or varicolored *epityrum* in this way. Pit
the green, black, or varicolored olives. Season them thus:
Chop them, and add oil, vinegar, coriander, cumin, fennel,
rue, and mint. Put them in a small jar, with oil on top, and
they are ready to use.

Pit the olives, then mix them in a blender with the herbs, olive oil, and vinegar. Avoid the temptation to add any salt, since the olives we buy today are already sufficiently salted.

The Greeks and Romans ate this olive paste together with cheese, whence the derivation of its name (*epityrum* = over cheese). Varro (*De lingua latina* 7, 86) described it as a Greek recipe, and Columella (12, 49, 9) suggested that the olives be seasoned with salt, lentiscus, rue, and fennel.

Olive paste is available for sale today, so you can purchase it instead if you are pressed for time. However, it is far more aromatic and flavorful if you make it from scratch.

You can serve this olive paste following ancient custom, that is, as an appetizer together with ricotta or other fresh cheese; or you can spread it on small slices of toast. In this latter case, you should offer both green and black olive paste to make a more attractive presentation. In Umbria, where olives and olive oil are particularly good, *epityrum* is still used to dress even such "modern" dishes as spaghetti.

Here is a delicious specialty from Perugia for comparison:

REGIONAL ITALIAN RECIPE
(Umbria)
Black Spaghetti with Olive Paste

Sauté a large garlic clove in ½ cup olive oil without allowing it to turn brown. Remove from the heat and add 4 tablespoons of olive paste and a generous amount of minced parsley. This is sufficient for 1 lb. (½ kg.) of spaghetti.

Olive paste is also used today in tomato sauce for pasta and for stewed chicken.

SALADS

The Romans also offered salad as an appetizer, a custom that still survives in Switzerland and Germany. You can follow the Roman practice, serving romaine lettuce, endive, and chicory, mixed with mallow and lavender, and seasoned with the Cheese Sauce for Lettuce (Apicius 38) on pp. 47–48. Or you can use the following recipes: the first one is popular throughout the Middle East, especially Turkey, and the second one is Romanian.

MODERN TURKISH RECIPE
Arugola and Watercress Salad

Serves 4
1 large bunch arugola (garden rocket)
1 bunch watercress
2 garlic cloves, pressed for their juice
salt and pepper to taste
olive oil to taste
vinegar to taste

The Romans widely believed that the extremely aromatic and bitter arugola was an aphrodisiac. Perhaps this summer salad green continues to be similarly regarded by those populaces who consume it.

MODERN ROMANIAN RECIPE
Salad with Bread and Olives

Pit and chop around 30 olives. Put them in a salad bowl, and add 3–4 slices of coarse-textured bread that have been soaked in vinegar and broken into small pieces. Add a few sprigs of lavender and some olive oil. When the flavors have had sufficient time to blend, add washed and dried salad greens (preferably watercress) and toss.

Although the Romans used lavender for food purposes, modern Italians no longer generally do so. However, this recipe demonstrates the fact that it continues to be consumed in the Middle East and the Balkan peninsula. The common Italian word for lavender, *lavanda,* is nothing more than a corruption of *levantica,* meaning "from the Levant."

VEGETABLES AND SEAFOOD

SWEET-AND-SOUR TURNIPS OR RUTABAGAS
(APICIUS 100)

Rapas sive napos: Elixatos exprimes, deinde teres cuminum plurimum, rutam minus, laser parthicum, mel, acetum, liquamen, defritum et oleum modice. Fervere facies et inferes.

Turnips or rutabagas: Once they are boiled, squeeze the excess liquid from them, then grind a generous amount of cumin, a smaller amount of rue, silphium, honey, vinegar, *garum, defrutum,* and a bit of oil. Bring to a boil and serve.

Serves 4
2 lb. (1 kg.) turnips or rutabagas
ample cumin
1 tsp. rue
2 garlic cloves, pressed for their juice
1 tsp. honey
½ cup vinegar
1 Tbs. *garum* or *oenogarum*
1 Tbs. *defrutum*
1–2 Tbs. olive oil

Peel and boil the turnips or rutabagas. Drain, slice, and arrange in a casserole with a sauce consisting of the cumin, rue, garlic juice (in place of the silphium), honey, vinegar, *garum, defrutum,* and olive oil.

Heat for several minutes to steep, then serve.

Vinegar and honey mixed together in a vegetable recipe was fairly common in Roman cooking. Italians still enjoy baby onions cooked with vinegar and sugar, and the inhabitants of the region of Trentino typically cook turnips with the same mixture.

SQUASH APPETIZER
(APICIUS 73)

Gustum de cucurbitas: Cucurbitas coctas expressas in patinam compones. Adicies in mortarium piper, cuminum, silfi modice (id est laseris radicem), rutam modicum, liquamine et aceto temperabis, mittes defritum modicum ut coloretur, ius exinanies in patinam. Cum ferbuerint iterum ac tertio, depones et piper minutum asparges.

Squash appetizer: Arrange cooked, squeezed, and drained squash in a pan. Put pepper, cumin, a bit of silphium (that is, *laser* root), and a bit of rue in a mortar; mix with *garum* and vinegar, and add a bit of *defrutum* to color; empty the sauce into the pan. When it has boiled a second and third time, remove from the heat and sprinkle with ground pepper.

Serves 4
2 lb. (1 kg.) squash, cut into pieces
1 Tbs. total, pepper, cumin, and rue
1 garlic clove, pressed for its juice
1 Tbs. *garum*
1 cup vinegar
1 cup *defrutum*

Boil (or, even better, bake) the squash, squeeze out the excess liquid, and arrange in a pot. Make the sauce by combining the remaining ingredients. Pour the sauce over the squash, reheat and steep for several minutes, and serve.

SEASONED MELON
(APICIUS 85)

Pepones et melones: Piper, puleium, mel vel passum, liquamen, acetum. Interdum et silfi accedit.

Cantaloupe and melons: Pepper, pennyroyal, honey or *passum, garum,* and vinegar. Sometimes silphium is added.

Modern Italians continue to offer cantaloupe as an antipasto, but certainly not with this herb vinaigrette. You may be put off at first by the unusual flavor, but it grows on you quickly. Remember to use garlic juice as a substitute for silphium.

OYSTERS AND MIXED SHELLFISH SALAD

Use the sauce recipes Apicius 31 and Apicius 413, which you can find on p. 44, to season oysters and mixed shellfish. The Romans ate oysters both raw and cooked.

FRIED ANCHOVY *PATINA*
(APICIUS 147)

Patina de apua fricta: Apuam lavas, ova confringes et cum apua commisces. Adicies liquamen, vinum, oleum, facies ut ferveat et cum ferbuerit, mittes apuam. Cum duxerit, subtiliter versas. Facies ut coloret, oenogarum simplex perfundes, piper asparges et inferes.

A *patina* of fried anchovies: Wash anchovies, break eggs, and mix with the anchovies. Take *garum*, wine, and oil, and bring to a boil. When it has boiled, put in the anchovies. When one side sets, turn carefully. Let them brown, pour *oenogarum* made from common wine over them, sprinkle with pepper, and serve.

Serves 4
1¼ lb. (600 g.) anchovies or other small fish
1 egg
1 Tbs. *garum*
1 Tbs. wine
1 cup olive oil
pepper to taste
1 Tbs. *oenogarum*

Clean and gut the fish. Dip them in the beaten egg and fry in a sauce of *garum*, wine, and olive oil. Brown quickly on both sides, no more than 10 minutes total cooking time. Season with pepper and serve with *oenogarum*.

MUSHROOMS AND TRUFFLES

Mushrooms and truffles have long been considered a culinary luxury. The Romans ate both white and black truffles in delicate salads, as you can see from the two recipes included here. They also ate mushrooms raw in salads, boiled and covered with sauce, or cooked directly in a sauce or on a grill. There was even a special serving dish called a *boletarium* or *boletar*.

Although it is not always possible to determine what varieties of mushrooms they ate from the names they used, undoubtedly there were boletus or cepes (which the Romans called *suilli*), morels (*morchellae*), different edible agarics (including meadow mushrooms and the *amanita Caesarea*), and ash tree mushrooms (*fungi farnei*), which seem to be a variety of those mushrooms the Italians today call *polipori*. The Greeks and perhaps the Romans even attempted to cultivate mushrooms, but they were unsuccessful.

TRUFFLE SALAD
(APICIUS 35 AND 36)

Oenogarum in tubera: Piper, ligusticum, coriandrum, rutam, liquamen, mel, [vinum] et oleum modice.

Oenogarum for truffles: Pepper, lovage, coriander, rue, *garum*, honey, [wine], and a bit of oil.

Aliter: Timum, satureiam, piper, ligusticum, mel, [vinum], liquamen et oleum.

Another recipe: Thyme, summer savory, pepper, lovage, honey, [wine], *garum*, and oil.

Slice the truffles and season them with either of these sauces. You can use *oenogarum* instead of *garum* and wine in both recipes.

MUSHROOM CAPS
(APICIUS 314)

Boletos: Caliculos eorum liquamine vel sale aspersos inferunt.

Mushrooms: The caps are served sprinkled with *garum* or salt.

Use the caps from large, firm boletus mushrooms. Grill them and serve sprinkled with *garum*.

SEASONED MUSHROOM STEMS
(APICIUS 315)

Boletos aliter: Tirsos eorum concisos in patellam novam perfundis, addito pipere, ligustico, modico melle; liquamine temperabis; oleum modice.

Another recipe for mushrooms: Put the chopped stems in a clean pan, add pepper, lovage, and a bit of honey; mix with *garum;* [add] a bit of oil.

Serves 4
1 lb. (½ kg.) mushroom stems (or whole mushrooms)
1 handful of fresh lovage or parsley
2 Tbs. olive oil
pepper to taste
¼ tsp. honey
1 Tbs. *garum*

Apparently a sensible gourmet, the author included a recipe for mushroom stems, since the caps were to be grilled separately.

Finely chop the lovage or parsley. Cut the stems into small pieces and sauté in a pan with the olive oil, pepper, lovage or parsley, honey, and *garum*. Naturally, you can use the entire mushroom for a better flavor.

The Romans used this method to cook large wild meadow mushrooms; it is also good for both boletus and cultivated mushrooms.

OTHER APPETIZERS

APRICOT APPETIZER
(APICIUS 178)

Gustum de praecoquis: Duracina primotica pusilla. Praecoquia purgas, enucleas, in frigidam mittis, in patina componis. Teres piper, mentam siccam, suffundis liquamen, adicies mel, passum, vinum et acetum. Refundis in patina super praecoquia, olei modicum mittis et lento igni ferveat. Cum ferbuerit, amulo obligas, piper aspargis et inferes.

Apricot appetizer: Clean the apricots (young clingstone), remove the pits, and put them in cold water. Then arrange them in a pan. Grind pepper and dried mint, moisten with *garum,* and add honey, *passum,* wine, and vinegar; pour into the pan over the apricots, add a bit of oil, and cook over a low fire. When it boils, thicken with starch, sprinkle with pepper, and serve.

Serves 4
4½ lb. (2 kg.) apricots
1 Tbs. mint

1 Tbs. honey
½ cup wine
½ cup *passum*
1 tsp. *garum*
1 tsp. cornstarch
1 Tbs. pepper

Clean the apricots and remove the pits, then cook in the sauce consisting of all the remaining ingredients but the starch (dissolved in water) and pepper, which should be added at the last minute.

I have omitted the vinegar from the list of ingredients only because it made the dish inedible for me. You may, of course, find it perfectly appropriate and appealing, in which case 1 teaspoon should suffice.

APRICOT FRICASSEE
(Apicius 170)

Minutal ex praecoquiis: Adicies in caccabo oleum, liquamen, vinum, concides cepam Ascaloniam aridam, spatulam porcinam coctam tessellatim concides. His omnibus coctis teres piper, cuminum, mentam siccam, anetum, suffundis mel, liquamen, passum, acetum modice, ius de suo sibi, temperabis. Praecoquia enucleata mittis, facies ut ferveant, donec percoquantur. Tractam confringes, ex ea obligas, piper aspargis et inferes.

Fricassee with apricots: In a pot put oil, *garum*, and wine; chop dried Ascalonian onion, and dice cooked pork shoulder. When all these things are cooked, grind pepper, cumin, dried mint, and dill; moisten with honey, *garum, passum,* a bit of vinegar, and the cooking juice; mix. Add pitted apricots, bring to boil, and heat until cooked. Thicken with crumbled *tracta,* sprinkle with pepper, and serve.

Serves 4
10 oz. (300 g.) single slab raw bacon
1 lb. (½ kg.) apricots
1 lb. (½ kg.) onions (or scallions)
1 Tbs. olive oil
1 Tbs. *garum*
½ cup wine
For the sauce:
1 Tbs. total, pepper, cumin, mint, and dill
1 tsp. honey
1 cup *passum*
1 Tbs. *garum*
1 Tbs. pork drippings
¾ cup semolina or couscous

Cut the bacon into cubes. Mince the onion or scallions ("Ascalonian onions") and sauté until golden in the oil, *garum,* and wine. Add the bacon and continue to cook.

Meanwhile, prepare the sauce with the first five ingredients listed. Pit the apricots and cut them into quarters. Add them to the bacon along with the sauce and cook until the apricots are soft. Thicken with semolina or couscous, which replaces the *tracta* in the recipe (see the Glossary). Total cooking time should be approximately 50–60 minutes.

ONION APPETIZER
(Apicius 176)

Gustum de holeribus: Condies bulbos liquamine, oleo et vino. Cum cocti fuerint, iecinera porcelli et gallinarum et ungellas et ascellas divisas, haec omnia cum bulbis ferveant. Cum ferbuerint, teres piper, ligusticum, suffundis liquamen, vinum et passum ut dulce sit, ius de suo sibi suffundis, revocas in bulbos. Cum ferbuerint, ad momentum amulo obligas.

Vegetable appetizer: Season bulbs with *garum,* oil, and wine. When they are cooked, [take] pork liver and chicken wings and thighs cut up, and cook everything with the bulbs. When they are boiled, grind pepper and lovage; pour on *garum,* wine and *passum* to sweeten it, and cooking broth, and pour it over the bulbs. As soon as they are boiled, thicken with starch.

Serves 4
7 oz. (200 g.) pork liver
2 each, chicken thighs and wings
2 lb. (1 kg.) onions
2 Tbs. olive oil
2 Tbs. *garum*
2 Tbs. wine
For the sauce:
½ cup wine
½ cup *passum*
1 Tbs. *garum*
pepper to taste
1 Tbs. lovage
1 tsp. cornstarch

This recipe calls for bulbs, perhaps flower bulbs. The Romans would sometimes cook gladiolus or asphodel bulbs, but the bitter bulbs of today's cultivated flowers are inedible. Thus our only available substitution is the common everyday onion.

Cut the pork liver into pieces; do the same with the chicken wings and thighs (or better, have it done by your butcher). Slice the onions and let them cook in the olive oil, *garum,* and wine to blend the flavors; add the meat and cook for 30 minutes. Meanwhile, prepare the sauce by mixing together the first five ingredients listed. Add this sauce and continue to cook for another 30 minutes. Thicken with dissolved cornstarch before serving.

The name of this recipe belies the fact that it is a rather substantial dish of meat and onions.

CONCICLA À LA APICIUS
(APICIUS 196)

Conciclam Apicianam: Accipies cumanam mundam ubi coques pisum. Cui mittis lucanicas concisas, esiciola porcina, pulpas petasonis. Teres piper, ligusticum, origanum, anetum, cepam siccam, coriandrum viridem, suffundis liquamen, vino et liquamine temperabis. Mittis in cumanam, cui adicies oleum, pungis ubique et combibat oleum. Igni lento coques ita ut ferveat et inferes.

Concicla à la Apicius: Take a clean earthenware pot to cook peas. Add chopped Lucanian sausages, small pork patties, and shoulder meat. Grind pepper, lovage, oregano, dill, dried onion, and fresh coriander; moisten with *garum*, and mix with *garum* and wine. Put this in the pot, add oil, and puncture [the meat] all over so that it absorbs the oil. Cook over a low fire and serve.

Serves 4
4½ lb. (2 kg.) fresh peas in the shell
7 oz. (200 g.) pork rind or shoulder
7 oz. (200 g.) mild sausage
14 oz. (400 g.) pork ribs, individually separated
1 pig's foot (optional)
2 Tbs. olive oil
For the sauce:
1 tsp. each, lovage, oregano, anise, dried onion, and coriander
1 Tbs. *garum*
1 cup wine
salt and pepper to taste

Shell the peas, parboil them in salted water, and put aside. Boil the pork shoulder and cut into cubes. Cut the sausage into slices.

Prepare the sauce by mixing together the ingredients indicated above. Then place the various pieces of pork in an earthenware (*cumanam* = made of Cumaean clay) pot with the sauce and the oil and cook. When the meat is almost done, add the peas. Finish cooking, add salt to taste, season generously with pepper, and serve.

Although here we have peas rather than the traditional cabbage, this mixture of various cuts of pork with vegetables is similar to the popular Milanese dish called *cassoeula* or *bottaggio*. Undoubtedly the cooking methods must also be similar. Those pork parts that require a longer cooking time should be boiled first; this way they lose much of their fat as well. The sausage and ribs, on the other hand, can be cooked directly in the pot. (For a discussion of Lucanian sausage, see page 13.)

UNUSUAL APPETIZERS

The following recipes further broaden this panorama of ancient appetizers by demonstrating the Roman attraction to culinary eccentricity.

ROSE PATINA
(APICIUS 136)

Patinam de rosis: Accipies rosas et exfoliabis, album tolles, mittes in mortarium, suffundes liquamen, fricabis. Postea mittes liquaminis ciatum unum semis et sucum per colum colabis. Accipies cerebella IV, enervabis et teres piperis scripulos VIII, suffundes ex suco, fricabis. Postea ova VIII frangis, vini ciatum unum semis et passi ciatum I, olei modicum. Postea patinam perunges et eam impones cineri calido, et sic inpensam supra scriptam mittes. Cum cocta fuerit in termospodio, piperis pulverem super asparges et inferes.

A *patina* of roses: Take roses and detach the petals, cut away the white part, put in a mortar, moisten with *garum*, and grind. Then add 1½ *cyathi* of *garum* and pass the sauce through a strainer. Take 4 brains, remove the membranes; grind 8 scruples of pepper, pour in the sauce, and grind. Then break 8 eggs with 1½ *cyathi* of wine and 1 *cyathus* of *passum*, and a bit of oil. Then oil a dish and place it in embers, and put in the mixture indicated above. When it is cooked in the *termospodio*, sprinkle with finely ground pepper and serve.

Serves 4
30 roses
1 tsp. *garum*
3 lamb brains
6 eggs
1 cup white wine
½ cup *passum*
1 Tbs. olive oil
pepper to taste

Detach the petals from the roses and trim away the white part at the bottom. Grind the petals in a mortar, moistening with *garum;* then pass the mixture through a strainer.

Boil the lamb brains, then grind them in a mortar. Add the rose sauce and mix well. Then beat the eggs and mix them with the wine, *passum,* and olive oil. Pour into an ovenproof dish and bake at 350°F. until firm. Sprinkle with pepper before serving.

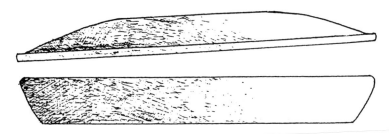

The *termospodio* or *testo* was a type of domed earthenware cover for a baking dish; embers could be placed over and under the dish thus covered, simulating a kind of oven on the hearth. For other recipes using this system, see pp. 163, 165–67, and 169 (dessert recipes from Cato).

APICIAN *PATINA*
(Apicius 141)

Patinam Apicianam sic facies: Frustra suminis cocti, pulpas piscium, pulpas pulli, ficetulas vel pectore turdorum cocta et quaecumque optima fuerint, haec omnia concides diligenter praeter ficetulas. Ova vero cruda cum oleo dissolvis. Teres piper, ligusticum, suffundes liquamen, vinum, passum, et in caccabum mittis ut calefiat, et amulo obligas. Antea tamen pulpas concisas universas illuc mittes, et sic bulliat. At, ubi coctum fuerit, levabis cum iure suo et in patella alternis de trulla refundes cum piperis grana integra et nucleis pineis ita ut per singula coria substernas diploidem, dein laganum similiter. Quotquot lagana posueris, tot trullas impensae desuper adicies. Unum vero laganum fistula percuties et super impones. Piper asparges. Ante tamen illas pulpas ovis confractis obligabis et sic in caccabum mittes cum impensam. Patellam aeneam qualem debes habere infra ostenditur.

Make an Apician *patina* thus: Pieces of cooked sow's paps, fish meat, chicken meat, figpeckers or cooked thrush breasts, and anything else that is good. Mince all these ingredients thoroughly, except the figpeckers. Beat raw eggs with oil. Grind pepper and lovage, and moisten with *garum*, wine, and *passum*; put into a pot to heat and thicken with starch. But first add the cut meats and bring to a boil. After it is cooked, remove [from the heat] with its juice and pour, one ladle at a time, in a pan, with peppercorns and pine nuts, so that every layer [of filling] has a sheet of pastry beneath and above. Alternate the pastry with ladles of the filling. Pierce a final layer of pastry with a reed and place on top. Sprinkle with pepper. But first thicken the meat with eggs and put it in the pot with the filling. The proper bronze pan to use is shown below.

Serves 6
1¾ lb. (800 g.) mixed ground meat and fish (for example, 7 oz. [200 g.] of chicken, 3 oz. [100 g.] of liver, 7 oz. [200 g.] of brains and sweetbreads, and 10 oz. [300 g.] of fish)
4 eggs
1 Tbs. olive oil
pepper to taste
1 tsp. lovage
1 Tbs. *garum*
1 cup strong red wine
1 cup *passum*
peppercorns
3 oz. (100 g.) pine nuts
For the pastry:
   2⅓ cups flour
   sufficient water
   2 Tbs. olive oil
   pinch of salt

For the meat mixture: Pass the various meats twice through a meat grinder. If you use giblets (brains and sweetbreads are best) in place of sow's paps, boil them first for several minutes. Use any type of fresh fish you choose (for example, tuna, salmon, or cod), and chicken breasts.

For the sauce: Beat the eggs with the olive oil, add the ground pepper, lovage, and *garum,* and dilute with the wine and *passum.*

Put the meat mixture in a pan with the sauce and heat. It should remain fairly moist so that you can later complete the cooking process in the oven. Add more wine if necessary.

For the pastry: Mix the flour, water, olive oil, and salt together; or prepare crepes if you prefer. In either case, try to form each layer of pastry or crepe in the same dimensions as those of the casserole.

Generously grease a casserole and begin to fill it, first with a layer of pastry and then the meat and sauce mixture, with 3 or 4 peppercorns and a bit of the pine nuts sprinkled over each time. Cover with a final layer of pastry and pierce its surface throughout with a fork. Cover with aluminum foil (so that the top layer of pastry does not burn) and bake at 400°F. for 20 minutes, then remove the foil and continue to bake for another 10 minutes.

Even though this recipe at first appears to be haphazardly put, it can be done with a bit of time and patience and is well worth the effort. Naturally, certain ingredients may require alternatives, such as the sow's paps and figpeckers; but remember that the recipe itself says to use any type of meat or fish you deem appropriate.

The last sentence of this recipe provides yet another interesting bit of information about the Apician manual, allowing us to deduce that it once contained illustrations to aid the reader.

This recipe is similar to the following Italian specialty:

REGIONAL ITALIAN RECIPE
(Marches)
Vincisgrassi

Boil brains, sweetbreads, and bone marrow for around 5 minutes. Chop chicken giblets, brain, marrow, sweetbreads, and ham or bacon. Mince onion and carrot and sauté them in butter and olive oil; when they are soft, add the chopped meat and cook, moistening from time to time with white wine. Dilute a bit of tomato concentrate (evidently a "recent" addition to the recipe) with stock and add to the meat. Salt and pepper to taste.

While this mixture is cooking, prepare the pastry: this is a rustic style of pastry, made with flour, semolina, eggs, and sweet red wine (such as *vin santo* or marsala). The sheets of pastry should be of the same size and form as the baking dish.

Prepare a béchamel. Then begin to fill a buttered baking dish, starting with a layer of pastry, then a thick layer of meat, then the béchamel and grated Parmesean cheese. Repeat until all the ingredients are used.

Cover the dish with a cloth and let it rest for several hours so that the pastry has a chance to absorb the flavor of the filling. Then bake for 30 minutes in a hot oven (400°F.) and serve.

In Macerata, where this recipe originated, anecdote has it that the curious title *Vincisgrassi* is a bastardized Italian pronunciation of Windisch-grätz. This Austrian general, who was active in Italy and other parts of the Austrian Empire during the period of the Napoleonic wars and the battles for Italian independence, reputedly was very fond of the dish.

STUFFED DORMICE
(Apicius 397)

Glires: Isicio porcino, item pulpis ex omni membro glirium trito, cum pipere, nucleis, lasere, liquamine farcies glires et sutos in tegula positos mittes in furnum aut farsos in clibano coques.

Dormice: Stuff dormice with pork filling, and with the meat of whole dormice ground with pepper, pine nuts, silphium, and *garum*. Sew up, place on a baking tile, and put them in the oven; or cook the stuffed [dormice] in a pan.

This particular recipe was by no means the whim of an extravagant cook; dormice were in fact raised on large farms (called *glirarii*) in great quantity, like chicken and rabbits. Because dormice normally fatten up during the winter, while they sleep in the hollows of trees, the breeders would keep them in containers that simulated this natural environment. They consisted of jars with inner rims that spiraled from bottom to top, and holes all around so the animals could breathe. The dormice would nestle within, receiving their food (acorns, chestnuts, and walnuts) from the top opening and fattening comfortably in the dark.

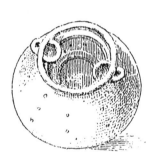 

The historian Ammianus Marcellinus (*Rerum gestarum* 28, 4, 13) noted that the weight of these rodents was checked periodically, and that the fattest dormice were in greatest demand. In 115 B.C., the consul Marcus Aemilius Scaurus issued a sumptuary law (against extravagance and excessive spending) that attempted to prohibit the consumption of dormice, but it was ineffective.

The Apician manual and the *Cena Trimalchionis* (in which dormice were served roasted and covered with honey and poppy seeds) provide testimony that these animals were still popular in the first century A.D. In fact, it is curious that in Apicius there is only one recipe for them. The most common method of cooking dormice was, as in the above recipe, to roast them on a baking tile in the oven.

›VI‹

SOUPS AND PORRIDGES

Porridge
I can send you porridge; the rich man, *mulsum*.
If the rich man does not want to send it to you, buy it.
(Martial 13, 6)

Fava beans
If the pale fava bean boils in your red earthenware pot,
you may often refuse the dinners of the rich.
(Martial 13, 7)

We have very few ancient recipes for soups and porridges, because our most prolific source, Apicius, is addressed to a rich and sophisticated public. However, we know that they were a nutritional mainstay for the masses, and that undoubtedly even the wealthy consumed them when they had no guests to impress. The abundance of grains, legumes, and vegetables undoubtedly encouraged the Romans to use them in their cooking.

Peasant porridges made with barley, chick peas, lentils, and beans, and various vegetable soups can still be found steaming on tables from the Alps to the islands of Italy, many carrying names that clearly reflect their ancient origins (such as the spelt porridges from Umbria and Lazio). You can also concoct some soup for your Roman dinner that is inspired by, but not necessarily found in, the ancient sources, as long as you use only those ingredients that the Romans had at their disposal.

The following are a few of those ancient recipes we do have, along with several regional Italian and other Mediterranean recipes for comparison.

CREAMED WHEAT
(CATO 86)

Graneam triticeam sic facito: Selibram tritici puri in mortarium purum indat, lavet bene, corticemque deterat bene, eluatque bene. Postea in aulam indat et aquam puram addat cocatque. Ubi coctum erit, lacte addat paulatim usque adeo, donec cremor crassus erit factus.

Make wheat porridge thus: One half *libra* of choice wheat is put in a clean mortar, washed well, dehusked well, and rinsed well. Then it is put in a pan, pure water is added, and it is cooked. When it is done, milk is added bit by bit, until it has become a thick cream.

Serves 4
10 oz. (300 g.) bulgur
1 quart (liter) water
1 quart (liter) milk
salt to taste

Bring the water to a boil and add the bulgur. When it is cooked (20–25 minutes), mix the milk in slowly and cook for another half hour. Salt to taste.

Obviously, it is no longer necessary to prepare the wheat for cooking, since it can already be purchased dehusked and ground as bulgur (a grind that provides a larger grain than does couscous).

MODERN LEBANESE RECIPE
Wheat Porridge

Place 2 pounds (1 kilo) of beef stew meat in 3 quarts (liters) of boiling water. Add 10 ounces (300 grams) bulgur and simmer for around 3 hours. Strain the mixture twice and serve the resulting porridge.

Spelt is still cultivated in Italy, especially in the mountainous zones of Lazio, Umbria, and Abruzzo, where spelt porridge remains popular. This is evidence of an uninterrupted tradition with its origins in the epoch of ancient Rome. Indeed, the Romans considered spelt (*far*) the symbol of life itself. In the most ancient Roman matrimonial rite (*confarreatio*), the bride and groom would offer a spelt loaf to Capitoline Jove.

(Umbria; Lazio)
Spelt Porridge from Umbria

Take a ham bone with some meat remaining on it and boil in around 5 cups unsalted water for one hour (some people add vegetables, such as carrots, onions, and celery). Strain the broth into a clean pot. Bring to a boil, add 7 ounces (200 grams) of spelt, and mix. Continue to cook for 20–25 minutes. Remove the pieces of ham from the bone and add to the porridge before serving.

Spelt Porridge from Lazio

This recipe uses pork rind and jowl. The rind (not more than 3 ounces, or 80–100 grams) should be boiled for around 20 minutes, then cut into small pieces and placed in 1½ quarts (liters) of fresh water to boil again. The jowl should be finely chopped and fried together with a garlic clove and a pinch of aromatic herbs. Then add a minced onion and 1 small can of peeled tomatoes (obviously tomatoes entered the recipe at a later period). When this mixture is cooked, add the pork rind pieces with the broth. Then add 10 ounces (300 grams) of spelt and cook for another 20 minutes. Serve with grated pecorino cheese on the side.

PORRIDGE À LA JULIANUS
(APICIUS 179)

Pultes Iulianae sic coquuntur: Alicam purgatam infundis, coques, facies ut ferveat. Cum ferbuerit, oleum mittis; cum spissaverit, lias diligenter. Adicies cerebella duo cocta et selibram pulpae quasi ad esicia liatae, cum cerebellis teres et in caccabum mittis. Teres piper, ligusticum, feniculi semen, suffundis liquamen et vinum modice, mittis in caccabum supra cerebella et pulpam. Ubi satis ferbuerit, cum iure misces. Ex hoc paulatim alicam condies, et ad trullam permisces et lias ut quasi sucus videatur.

Porridge à la Julianus is cooked thus: Soak cleaned spelt; bring it to a boil. When it boils add oil, and as it thickens carefully stir it smooth. Take two cooked brains and one half *libra* of meat, ground as though for patties, grind with the brains and put in a pot. Grind pepper, lovage, and fennel seeds, moisten with *garum* and a little wine, and put in the pot over the brains and meat. When this is sufficiently boiled, mix with broth. Season the spelt with this bit by bit, mixing in by the ladleful, and stir it smooth until it is like a cream.

Serves 4
2 lamb brains
7 oz. (200 g.) ground lamb (or beef)
1 Tbs. total, pepper, lovage, and fennel seeds
1 Tbs. *garum*
1 cup dry white wine
For the semolina:
   9 oz. (250 g.) durum semolina
   2 Tbs. olive oil
   sufficient water

In all probability this recipe is best realized with a semolina of durum wheat, indicated by the provision that any eventual lumps should be eliminated while it is cooked. Its preparation is rather complicated but well worth the trouble.

Boil the lamb brains (a delicacy for the ancient Romans just as they still are for Arabs and Turks), mince them, and then mix them with the ground lamb meat. Place this mixture in a pot, and cover it with a condiment of pepper and ground herbs. Moisten with *garum* and wine. Cook over a low heat for approximately 10 minutes, mixing well.

Prepare the semolina: Boil the water, add the semolina and olive oil, and cook. Add the meat slowly, one spoonful at a time, blending thoroughly. Continue to cook for 10 minutes. Serve.

We have no precise idea who the Julianus in the title for this *puls* would have been. Two emperors, Didius Julianus (193) and Julian the Apostate (360–63), and a usurper Julian of Pannonia (284–85) all came later than Apicius. Both emperors were notoriously parsimonious. The *Historia Augusta (Iulianus* 3) claims that, according to report, Didius Julianus "was so moderate in his ways . . . that he was content eating vegetables and legumes without meat." This recipe was not, in any case, an economical dish but rather an extremely rich porridge. Today we would consider it a meal in itself.

SOUP WITH *TRACTA* AND MILK
(APICIUS 181)

Pultes tractogalatae: Lactis sextarium et aquae modicum mittes in caccabo novo et lento igni ferveat. Tres orbiculos tractae siccas et confringis et partibus in lac summittis. Ne uratur, aquam miscendo agitabis. Cum cocta fuerit, ut est super ignem, mittis melle. Ex musteis cum lacte similiter facies, salem et oleum minus mittis.

Porridge of *tracta* and milk: Put a *sextarius* of milk and a bit of water in a clean pot and bring to a boil over a low flame. Dry three rounds of *tracta* and break into pieces, and drop the pieces into the milk. Stir so that it does not burn, mixing with water. When it is cooked, add honey while the pan is still on the fire. You can make this same recipe using sweet buns with must, without adding salt and oil.

This is a simple recipe similar to the traditional milk soup that was once popular for the very old and very young; thus it seems unnecessary to add any explanation or list of ingredients.

The variation with sweet buns and must requires the prior preparation of these ingredients, for which the recipe is given in chapter 10 (Apicius 297) on page 158. From the final phrase we may deduce that a little salt and olive oil should be added to the first version, but not to the second.

BARLEY SOUP
(APICIUS 173)

Tisanam sic facies: Tisanam lavando fricas, quam ante diem infundes. Impones supra ignem calidum. Cum bullierit, mittes olei satis et aneti modicum fasciculum, cepam siccam, satureiam et coloefium, ut ibi coquantur propter sucum. Mittes coriandrum viridem et salem simul tritum et facies ut ferveat. Cum bene ferbuerit, tolles fasciculum et transferes in alterum caccabum tisanam sic ne fundum tangat propter combusturam. Lias et colas in caccabulo supra acronem coloefium. Teres piper, ligusticum, pulei aridi modicum, cuminum et sil frictum, suffundis [mel], acetum, defritum, liquamen, refundis in caccabum, sed coloefium acronem ut bene tegatur. Facies ut ferveat super ignem lentum.

Prepare barley soup thus: Crush washed barley that has been soaked the day before. Place over a high flame. When it boils, add a generous quantity of oil, a small bouquet of dill, dried onion, savory, and a ham hock, and let it cook until it becomes a cream. Add fresh coriander and salt that have been ground together, and bring to a boil. When it has boiled well, remove the bouquet and transfer the barley into another pot, so that it will not stick to the bottom or burn. Stir out the lumps and strain it into the pot over the ham hock. Grind pepper, lovage, a bit of dried pennyroyal, cumin, and roasted seseli; moisten with [honey], vinegar, *defrutum*, and *garum*, and pour in the pot, so that the ham hock is covered well. Bring to a boil over a low flame.

Serves 4
9 oz. (250 g.) barley
1 ham hock
1 onion
1 bouquet fresh dill (or 1 tsp. dried dill)
1 tsp. savory
1 cup olive oil
For the sauce to add to the cooked barley:
    pinch of pepper
    1 Tbs. total, lovage, pennyroyal, and cumin
    1 Tbs. honey
    1 Tbs. vinegar
    1 Tbs. *defrutum*
    1 Tbs. *garum*

The recipe seems complicated at first, but it can be prepared in two stages. First the barley is boiled in water together with the herbs, the oil, and the ham hock until it becomes creamy; then the ham hock is transferred to a clean pot and the barley cream is poured over it through a strainer. In this way the herbs and any lumps are removed. In the second stage, a sauce is made of the pepper and remaining herbs, honey, vinegar, *defrutum*, and *garum*. When it is thoroughly blended, it is poured over the cream of barley to flavor it.

You can use pearl barley or ground barley. Because of the prolonged cooking time (a total of around 3 hours), either will produce a creamy texture.

BARLEY POLENTA

(PLINY, *NATURALIS HISTORIA* 18, 73)

Vicenis hordei libris ternas seminis lini et coriandri seli-
bram salisque acetabulum.

For each 20 *librae* of barley, 3 *librae* of linseeds and ½ *libra*
of coriander, in addition to an *acetabulum* of salt.

Serves 4
12 oz. (340 g.) ground barley
3 Tbs. linseeds
2 tsp. coriander
sufficient salt

Boil 1 quart (liter) of water, gradually add the ingredients, and leave to
cook for approximately one hour. Add more boiling water if the barley
consumes too much. A more flavorful polenta can be obtained by cooking
the barley in meat stock or vegetable broth instead of water.

The practice of adding linseeds to food survives in several regional Italian specialties, such as one of the many variations of the Lombard *pan-*
meíno (millet bread) that is prepared for the feast of St. George (23 April).

VEGETABLE SOUP

(APICIUS 174)

Tisanam farricam: Infundis cicer, lenticulam, pisam. De-
fricas tisanam et cum leguminibus elixas. Ubi bene bul-
lierit, olei satis mittis et super viridia concidis porrum, cor-
iandrum, anetum, feniculum, betam, malvam, coliculum
mollem; haec viridia minuta concisa in caccabum mittis.
Coliculos elixas et teres feniculi semen satis, origanum,
silfi, ligusticum. Postquam triveris, liquamine temperabis et
super legumina refundis et agites. Coliculorum minutas
super concidis.

Farrica barley soup: Soak [dried] chick peas, lentils, and
peas. Dehusk barley and boil with the legumes. When it
has boiled well, add sufficient oil and over this chop these
greens: leek, coriander, dill, fennel, beet, mallow, and tender young cabbage; put these finely chopped greens in the
pot. Boil young cabbage and grind a generous amount of
fennel seeds, oregano, silphium, and lovage. After you

have ground them, mix with *garum*, pour over the legumes, and stir. Over this add finely chopped young cabbage.

Serves 4–6
7 oz. (200 g.) each, dried lentils, chick peas, and peas
7 oz. (200 g.) barley
7 oz. (200 g.) beet greens
2 leeks
1 Tbs. total, coriander, dill, and fennel
½ cup olive oil
1 small savoy cabbage or broccoli
For the sauce:
    1 Tbs. total, fennel seeds, oregano, and lovage
    2 garlic cloves, minced
    1 Tbs. *garum*

This is a genuine minestrone, full of vegetables and legumes and further thickened by the addition of barley.

Soak the dried legumes for 24 hours; rinse and cook them along with the barley in salted water. After 3 hours, add the beet greens and leeks, cut into soup-size pieces, and the herbs. Then add the olive oil. On the side boil and chop the cabbage or broccoli, which should be added to the minestrone in the final half hour of cooking. Combine the sauce ingredients together and add only when the cooking is complete.

KALE SOUP
(APICIUS 70)

Betacios Varronis. Varro: "Betacios, sed nigros, quorum detersas radices et mulso decoctas cum sale modico et oleo vel sale, aqua et oleo in se coctas iusculum facere et potari, melius etiam si in eo pullus sit decoctus."

Beets according to Varro. Varro: "[Use] beets, but black ones, whose roots have been cleaned, and cook in *mulsum* with a bit of salt and oil—or in salt, water, and oil—to make a broth to drink. It is even better if a chicken is cooked in it."

Serves 4
½ chicken (or better still, ½ stewing hen)
1 bunch coarsely chopped kale or beet greens
2–3 Tbs. olive oil
salt to taste
2 cups *mulsum* (optional)

This broth is included in a group of digestive recipes, complete with the age-old suggestion to add a chicken to the pot if possible. You can first marinate the kale in *mulsum*, olive oil, and salt if you prefer.*

The attribution of this recipe to Marcus Terentius Varro (116–27 B.C.) is particularly interesting. It seems that someone using the Apician manual noted this recipe in the margin, whereupon it eventually became integrated into the text of later copies. Certainly it is fascinating to imagine that the habit of adding marginal annotations from other sources is a timeless one.

*For an alternative reading of this text, see André's translation and commentary—TRANS.

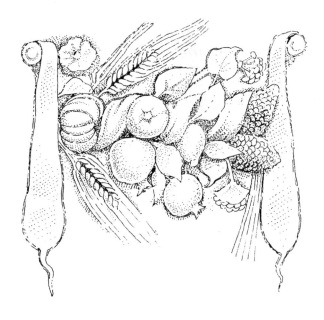

A TASTE OF ANCIENT ROME

Mosaic in Pompeii depicting an underwater scene of fish, mollusks, and crustaceans.

Still-life with birds, a plate of fish, and a goblet of black olives, in a fresco in Pompeii.

Silver objects from the treasure of the Casa del Menandro, Pompeii.

Bottles, pitchers, goblets, glasses, and perfume jars in blown glass, found in Pompeii.

Silver drinking vessels with embossed ornamentation from the treasure of the Casa del Menandro, Pompeii.

(Right)
Silver dipper, pitcher, and *phiale,* from the treasure of the Casa del Menandro, Pompeii.

A *gustum* of fried squash, olives, mushrooms, cheese, and breads.

Egg pudding with pine nuts.

Weighing bread at market, from a stone relief in Capua.

(Left)
Charred eggs, bread, figs, and walnuts discovered in ovens and taverns at Pompeii.

The interior of a tavern in Pompeii, with the marble-covered serving bar, drinking vessels, and bronze cauldrons.

(Left)
Bread shop, from a fresco in Pompeii.

Painted retail signs in a wine shop; prices (I, II, III, IV *asses*) are indicated beneath the pitchers according to quality.

›VII‹

DOMESTIC MEAT AND

GAME

MENSA PRIMA

Pig
There is no animal who furnishes more variety to the
tongue:
its meat provides nearly fifty flavors,
but that of the other animals only one.
(Pliny the Elder, *Naturalis historia* 8, 209)

Hen
The hen fattens readily on both sweet flour and darkness.
Appetite is full of resources.
(Martial 13, 62)

Peacock
You admire it whenever it spreads its feathers like
sparkling gems;
and then, cruel man, you can consign it to the heartless
cook?
(Martial 13, 70)

Flamingo
My pink feathers give me my name,
but my tongue among gourmands gives me my fame.
What would the tongue say if it could speak?
(Martial 13, 71)

The Apician manual contains a great many recipes based on meat from both domesticated and wild animals. This is not surprising, since it was largely directed to a rich and demanding public living in a period of unparalleled abundance and wealth in the history of Rome. The general predilection for extravagance, derived from the Greeks, had become part and parcel of Roman custom. Thus it is only logical that this manual would include all the various popular types of meat that made their way onto the dining tables of the epoch. Even bear, flamingo, and other unusual or exotic animals were slaughtered to satisfy the snobbery of rich hosts anxious to dazzle their guests.

Already during the last two centuries before Christ, meat began to appear with increasing frequency in the homes of Rome's wealthier citizens. Indeed, the demand reached such proportions that the Senate attempted to control the situation by issuing sumptuary laws limiting both the quantity and the types of meat served during banquets. But whenever a compliant host would follow these legal guidelines his guests were quick to complain. In a letter to his relatives, Cicero disappointedly wrote of attending a dinner that was almost completely vegetarian (*Epistulae ad familiares* 7, 26, 2).

The great generals of Republican Rome, Scipio Africanus, Metellus, and Caesar, were always careful to see that the troops were supplied with meat during their campaigns. There was free meat distribution to the populace beginning as early as 328 B.C. From Caesar and other Republican eminences up to the emperors of the fourth century, meat was given out on all sorts of occasions, including celebrating military victories or buying votes.

It was virtually everyone's aspiration to have meat on his table, though generally the urban residents were more privileged in this regard. The rare vegetarian, perhaps an adherent to a particular philosophical (Neoplatonic) or religious (Manichaean) group, was viewed with suspicion.

Naturally, there were serious problems in keeping the meat fresh, since mechanical refrigeration was unavailable. It was salted, smoked, and even preserved in honey, and there were cured hams and various types of sausages.

All meat was sold at the *Forum boarium* and the *Forum suarium* (beef and pork markets) and in shops handling eggs and poultry. Pork was the most popular type of meat. There were large herds of pigs in Cisalpine Gaul that supplied meat for Rome, and additional hams were imported from Transalpine Gaul and modern-day Belgium.

A significantly smaller quantity of beef was consumed. There is only one recipe in Apicius for beef or veal, and three others for veal alone. Oxen were generally considered work animals and they were usually butchered only when they were old or sick. Because their meat was consequently rather tough, it was logical to prefer suckling pig, kid, or lamb. All types of farmyard animals were bred in great quantities.

The Romans also raised all birds that could be kept in captivity: chickens, geese, ducks, doves, wood pigeons, thrushes, and peacocks. Various systems of raising, feeding, and breeding for the best quality of meat and, with regard to hens, egg-laying capacity, were painstakingly detailed by Columella in the eighth book of his treatise. Aquatic birds were raised in elaborate *nessotrophia* (from the Greek *nuxis* = swim and *trefo* = raise), complete with artificial ponds, reed beds, and small sheds for nesting. They were surrounded by walls that were very high (to prevent the birds from flying beyond them) and smooth (so that potential predators could not scale them).

The Romans also raised sheep and goats, mainly for the meat of their young, but sometimes for the adult meat as well. Finally, there was a wealth of game, since forests were far more plentiful on the Italian peninsula then than they are now. The infamous emperor Elagabalus (who emulated the most extravagant Apician inspirations and, according to the imaginative historian Lampridius, fed his dogs with goose liver and his horses with the highly prized grapes from Apamea of Phrygia) had an enormous number of wild sows slaughtered simply so that he could offer their paps and vulvas to his guests for ten consecutive days (*Historia Augusta, Heliogabalus* 21).

Meat was oven-roasted, spit-roasted, used in patties, stuffings, and stews, or (in the case of kid and lamb, pork liver and paps, sausages and brochettes) cooked on a grill. Tripe and variety meats were used in delicate recipes or they became stuffing for fish and meats. Pig's blood was essential for blood sausage, while the feet, head, and rind were used for soups.

It is important to remember that because meat was relatively tough and frequently salted to prevent spoilage, it was often necessary to rinse it in milk and boil it once or twice before using it in a specific recipe. Naturally, when we encounter such instructions we can skip them because our meat is always available tender and fresh.

The following multifarious series of recipes is characterized by the use of a wide choice of condiments and many more aromatic herbs than appear in modern Italian cooking. There is also many a pleasant surprise to be found in the juxtaposition of sweet and sour ingredients. Finally, you will find unusual, delicate stuffing recipes for various fowl, hare, boar, and suckling pig.

In addition to the recipes in this chapter, there are suggestions for the serving of boiled, roasted, grilled, and baked meats within various sauce recipes in chapter 4.

ROASTED MEAT
(APICIUS 268)

Assaturam: Assam a furno simplicem salis plurimo conspersam cum melle inferes.

Roasted meat: The meat is roasted plain in the oven, sprinkled generously with salt. Serve with honey.

This method of roasting gives a delicious flavor to any of various types of meat. Try it with beef, veal, pork, or lamb shanks. Take the piece of meat you have chosen and roll it generously in salt before placing it in the oven. Temperature and roasting times vary according to the type of meat and its weight. When it is done, remove from the oven and cover with around 2 tablespoons of liquid honey. Replace in the hot unlit oven for another 5 minutes, then slice and serve.

ROASTED MEAT WITH HERBS
(APICIUS 269)

Aliter assaturas: Petroselini scripulos VI, laser scripulos VI, gingiberis scripulos VI, lauri bacas V, condimenti, laseris radicem scripulos VI, origani scripulos VI, ciperis scripulos VI, costi modice, piretri scripulos III, apii seminis scripulos VI, piperis scripulos XII, liquaminis et olei quod sufficit.

Another way to roast meat: Six scruples of parsley, 6 scruples of silphium, 6 scruples of ginger, 5 bay berries, seasonings, 6 scruples of silphium root, 6 scruples of oregano, 6 scruples of cyperus, a bit of costusroot, 3 scruples of pyrethrum, 6 scruples of celery seeds, 12 scruples of pepper, sufficient *garum* and oil.

Serves 4
As a marinade:
2 Tbs. total, fresh minced parsley, oregano, mint, and chervil
1½ tsp. ginger

5 coarsely crushed bay berries
1½ tsp. celery seeds
1 Tbs. pepper
3 garlic cloves, pressed for their juice
1 Tbs. *garum*
2 Tbs. olive oil
As a baste:
2 large handfuls of fresh parsley
1 handful each of fresh oregano, thyme, and savory
1½ tsp. ginger
5 coarsely crushed bay berries
1½ tsp. celery seeds
1 Tbs. pepper
4 large garlic cloves, pressed for their juice
½ cup olive oil
½ cup *garum*

Today it is practically impossible to obtain all the ingredients listed in this recipe, whether the famous silphium, present as both a resin and a root; or the sweet tubers of cyperus or costusroot, a strong-smelling root that the Romans imported from distant India; or the African pyrethrum, no longer used in Western cuisine. Nonetheless, this roast can still be done with a few adjustments. The important thing is to use many herbs and spices, and naturally *garum*. The proportions given in the recipe (1 scruple is roughly equal to ¹⁄₂₄ ounce [1.13 grams]) are appropriate for 2 pounds (1 kilo) of the meat of your choice.

It is possible to approach this recipe as either a marinade or a baste. Prepare the marinade with the ingredients listed above. Mix well and brush onto the meat you want to roast. Let sit for 2 hours before cooking. Oven temperature depends upon the type and weight of meat you use.

If you choose instead to prepare a baste: Mince the parsley, oregano, thyme, and savory. Add the remaining ingredients and mix well. Baste the roasting meat frequently (this also works well with pot roast).

STUFFED MEAT PATTIES
(APICIUS 48)

Esicia omentata: Pulpam concisam teres cum medulla siliginei in vino infusi. Piper, liquamen, si velis, et bacam mirteam extenteratam simul conteres. Pusilla esicia formabis, intus nucleis et pipere positis. Involuta omento subassabis cum careno.

Ground meat patties in omentum: Grind chopped meat with the center of fine white bread that has been soaked in wine. Grind together pepper, *garum*, and pitted myrtle berries if desired. Form small patties, putting in pine nuts and pepper. Wrap in omentum and cook slowly in *caroenum*.

Serves 4
¾ lb. (400 g.) ground pork or beef
5 oz. (150 g.) white bread, crust removed
sufficient wine (to soak the bread)
pepper to taste
1 Tbs. *garum*
4–5 pitted myrtle berries
2 oz. (50 g.) pine nuts
1 cup *caroenum*
pork caul fat

This is one of the simplest and most flavorful Apician recipes to follow. Soak the bread in the wine, then add to the ground meat (pork if you want to remain close to the original flavor, otherwise you can use beef) in a mortar and grind together. Grind the pepper with the *garum* and the myrtle berries and add to the meat. Chop the pine nuts, then form the meat around them in small loaves so that they remain in the center like a filling. Wrap each loaf in caul fat, which will eventually cook away (soak the caul fat briefly in lukewarm water before use). Cook slowly in *caroenum*.

Within the section dedicated to recipes with ground meat, the Apician manual includes this curious rating: "The ground meat patties of peacock have first place, if they are fried so that they remain tender. Those of pheasant have second place, those of rabbit third, those of chicken fourth, and those of suckling pig fifth" (Apicius 54).

MEATBALLS WITH FAVA BEANS
(APICIUS 191)

Pisa sive faba: Ubi despumaverit, teres mel, liquamen, carenum, cuminum, rutam, apii semen, oleum et vinum. Tutunclabis. Cum pipere trito et cum esiciis inferes.

Peas or fava beans: When they have put out a froth, grind honey, *garum*, *caroenum*, cumin, rue, celery seeds, oil, and wine. Mix together. Serve with ground pepper and ground meat patties.

Serves 4
¾ lb. (400 g.) ground meat (pork would be an appropriate
   choice)
For the sauce:
   2 lb. (1 kg.) fresh unshelled fava beans or peas
   1 cup red wine
   1 Tbs. olive oil
   1 Tbs. *garum*
   1 Tbs. total, cumin, rue, and celery seeds
   1 tsp. honey

Form small meatballs (the recipe does not describe how they are prepared,
only that they are served together with the beans or peas). Shell and boil
the beans or peas. When they put out a froth, drain them and put them in
another pot together with the sauce made of the remaining ingredients.
Cook slowly. When done, coarsely crush the beans or peas with a fork,
then add the meatballs to this sauce and cook for another 15–20 minutes.

The following delicate fava bean sauce remains a favorite in the city of
San Remo:

REGIONAL ITALIAN RECIPE
(Liguria)
Marò

Take fresh, tender fava beans and grind them in a mortar together with a
bit of garlic and a few mint leaves. Then add grated pecorino cheese and
olive oil. Grind further so that all the ingredients blend together. Serve with
boiled or roasted meat.

VEAL OR BEEF STEW
(APICIUS 354)

*Vitulinam sive bubulam cum porris [vel] cidoneis vel cepis
vel colocaseis: Liquamen, piper, laser et olei modicum.*

Veal or beef with leeks [or] quinces or onions or colocasia:
Garum, pepper, silphium, and a bit of oil.

This is the only recipe in Apicius that calls for beef. As is often the case in
De re coquinaria, the principal ingredients are cited in the title, but the text
contains the ingredients for the condiment alone.

Brown the diced stew meat in a bit of olive oil. Add the fruit or vegetable you have chosen (cut into pieces), a tablespoon of *garum*, and the juice of 2 garlic cloves in place of the silphium.

Colocasia is a type of tuber, a sweet potato equivalent to the taro, or Chinese potato, consumed in the Orient. We can use the tubers of topinambours (Jerusalem artichokes), which came originally from America.

If you wish to use quinces in the recipe, you should first boil them for around 20 minutes, peel them, and then cut them into pieces before adding them to the meat.

Quantities and cooking times are those for a normal stew.

VEAL SCALOPPINE
(Apicius 353)

Vitellina fricta: Piper, ligusticum, apii semen, cuminum, origanum, cepam siccam, uvam passam, mel, acetum, vinum, liquamen, oleum, defritum.

Fried veal: Pepper, lovage, celery seeds, cumin, oregano, dried onion, raisins, honey, vinegar, wine, *garum*, oil, and *defrutum*.

1 Tbs. raisins, plumped in wine
1 Tbs. dried onion
1 Tbs. total, lovage, celery seeds, cumin, and oregano

pinch of pepper
½ tsp. honey
1 Tbs. *defrutum*
1 Tbs. olive oil
1 Tbs. wine
1 tsp. *garum*

The veal scaloppine are cooked in the sauce consisting of the ingredients listed above. Mix the raisins with the dried onion, mixed herbs, pepper, and honey in a bowl, gradually adding the *defrutum*, olive oil, wine, and *garum*.

Heat this sauce in a pan, then add the veal to cook. Quantities and cooking time are the same as those for veal scaloppine with marsala.

PORK STEW WITH APPLES
(APICIUS 168)

Minutal Matianum: Adicies in caccabum oleum, liquamen, cocturam, concides porrum, coriandrum, esicia minuta. Spatulam porcinam coctam tessellatim concides cum sua sibi tergilla. Facies ut simul coquantur. Media coctura mala Matiana purgata intrinsecus, concisa tessellatim mittes. Dum coquitur, teres piper, cuminum, coriandrum viridem vel semen, mentam, laseris radicem, suffundes acetum, mel, liquamen, defritum modice et ius de suo sibi, aceto modico temperabis. Facies ut ferveat. Cum ferbuerit, tractam confringes et ex ea obligas, piper asparges et inferes.

Fricassee à la Matius: In a pot put oil, *garum*, broth, chopped leeks, coriander, and small meat patties. Dice cooked pork shoulder with its rind. Cook everything together. When this is half-cooked, put in Matian apples that have been cored and cut into pieces. During the cooking, grind pepper, cumin, fresh coriander or coriander seeds, mint, and silphium root; pour in vinegar, honey, *garum*, a bit of *defrutum*, and cooking broth. Mix with a bit of vinegar. Bring to a boil. When it has boiled, break in pieces of *tracta* and thicken, sprinkle with pepper, and serve.

Serves 4–6
1 lb. (½ kg.) pork (or pressed ham)
¾ lb. (400 g.) ground meat
1 Tbs. olive oil
1 Tbs. *garum*
2 leeks, chopped
1 Tbs. minced fresh coriander
½ cup stock
1 lb. (½ kg.) cooking apples, cored and cut
For the sauce:
1 tsp. pepper
1 Tbs. total, cumin, coriander, and mint
1 garlic clove, pressed for its juice
1 Tbs. vinegar
1 tsp. honey
1 tsp. *garum*
½ cup *defrutum*
sufficient stock
1 Tbs. flour

This stew recipe is very good, an ancient relative of the German recipes for pork with apples.

You can use raw pork or pressed ham. If you use the latter, the cooking time should be greatly reduced. But if you follow the original recipe, you must first boil or roast the pork and then dice it as for a normal stew. The ground meat should be formed into small meatballs.

Heat the olive oil in a casserole, then add the *garum,* leeks, and coriander. Add the diced pork and the meatballs, letting it cook a while to flavor the meat, then moisten with a bit of stock and continue to cook. When the meat is half done, add the apple pieces. Shortly before the cooking time is complete, add the sauce composed of the first eight sauce ingredients listed above, and thicken with flour (replacing the *tracta* in the recipe: see the Glossary).

The recipe is attributed to Gaius Matius, a friend of Julius Caesar. Columella (12, 46, 1) wrote that he exercised consummate diligence in collecting recipes suitable for public dinners and banquets, and that he published three books entitled *Coci* (cooks), *Cetarii* (preparers of fish), and *Salgamarii* (preparers of preserves). Matius also gave his name to a type of apple, which Columella (5, 10, 19) considered very good and recommended cultivating.

PORK STEW WITH CITRON
(APICIUS 169)

*Minutal dulce ex citriis: Adicies in caccabo oleum, liqua-
men, cocturam, porrum capitatum, concides coriandrum
minutatim, spatulam porcinam coctam, esiciola minuta.
Dum coquitur, teres piper, cuminum, coriandrum vel semen, rutam viridem, laseris radicem, suffundis acetum, defritum, ius de suo sibi, aceto temperabis. Facies ut ferveat.
Cum ferbuerit, citrium purgatum intro foras, tessellatim
concisum et elixatum in caccabo mittes. Tractam confringes et ex ea obligas, piper aspargis et inferes.*

Sweet stew with citrons: In a pot put oil, *garum*, broth,
head of leek; finely chop coriander, cooked pork shoulder,
small meat patties. While this is cooking, grind pepper,
cumin, coriander or coriander seeds, fresh rue, silphium
root; pour on vinegar, *defrutum*, cooking broth, mix with
vinegar. Bring to a boil. When it boils, put into the pot
citron that have been cleaned inside and out, diced, and
boiled. Break in *tracta* and thicken, sprinkle with pepper,
and serve.

Serves 4–6
1 lb. (½ kg.) pork shoulder
¾ lb. (400 g.) ground meat, formed into small meatballs
1 Tbs. olive oil
1 Tbs. *garum*
2 leeks, chopped
1 bunch fresh coriander, minced
1 tsp. pepper
1 tsp. total, cumin and rue
2 Tbs. *sapa*
2 citrons
1 tsp. cornstarch
1 tsp. honey or sugar (optional)

This stew is very good, but one adjustment must be made: since, despite
its name, it is not at all sweet but actually rather sour, most modern palates
would probably prefer that the vinegar be completely omitted and that the
acidity of the citrons be corrected with a bit of sugar or honey.

Boil the pork shoulder, cut into cubes, and set aside. In a casserole heat
the olive oil and sauté the *garum*, leeks, and coriander. Then add the pork
shoulder and the meatballs. Prepare a sauce with the pepper, herbs, and

sapa, and add it to the cooking meat.

Peel the citrons, cut them into quarters, and then boil them for around 10 minutes in water. Add them to the meat and finish cooking. Thicken with a bit of dissolved cornstarch or crumbled bread, which replaces the *tracta* in the recipe (see the Glossary). Adjust the acidity if necessary with honey or sugar. Sprinkle with pepper and serve.

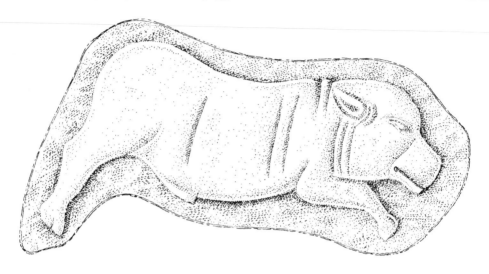

HAM IN PASTRY
(APICIUS 290)

Pernam, ubi eam cum caricis plurimis elixaveris et tribus lauri foliis, detracta cute tessellatim incidis et melle complebis. Deinde farinam oleo subactam contexes et ei corium reddis et, cum farina cocta fuerit, eximas furno ut est, et inferes.

After you have cooked the ham in water with many dried figs and three bay leaves, remove the skin, make reticulated incisions, and fill them with honey. Then work together flour and oil and replace the skin [with this pastry]. When the pastry is cooked, remove from the oven as it is and serve.

Serves 4
2–3 lb. (1–1½ kg.) boned ham
½ lb. (225 g.) dried figs

3 bay leaves
3 Tbs. honey
3½ cups flour
olive oil (sufficient for a moist pastry)
1 Tbs. salt

Boil the ham in water containing the dried figs and bay leaves. When it is done (approximately 2 hours cooking time), remove the skin, score the ham in a crosshatched pattern, and spread it with honey.

Make a sheet of pastry from the flour, oil, and salt. Wrap the ham in it, forming a new "skin," as the recipe says, and bake in the oven at 400°F. for around 30 minutes. When the pastry is cooked, remove from the oven and serve.

You may prefer to use a small vacuum-packed, pre-cooked ham. Score it as above, insert pieces of dried figs that have been plumped in a bit of *passum* or *defrutum*, and spread it with honey. You may also insert a few pieces of *mustacei*, or biscuits made with must (see Cato 121, p. 157): this variation can be found in Apicius 291. Wrap the ham in the pastry and bake as above.

This recipe is also good cold, so it is certainly no tragedy if you find yourself with leftovers for the next day.

STUFFED SUCKLING PIG
(Apicius 367)

Porcellum farsilem duobus generibus: Curas, a gutture extenteras, a cervice ornas. Antequam praedures, subaperies auriculam sub cutem, mittes impensam Terentinam in vescicam bubulam et fistolam aviarii rostro vesicae alligabis, per quam exprimes in aurem quantum ceperit. Postea carta praecludes et infiblabis et praeparabis aliam impensam. Sic facies: teres piper, ligusticum, origanum, laseris radicem modicum, suffundes liquamen, adicies cerebella cocta, ova cruda, alicam coctam, ius de suo sibi, [si] fuerit, aucellas, nucleos, piper integrum, liquamine temperas. Imples porcellum, carta obturas et fiblas, mittes in furnum. Cum coctus fuerit, exornas, perunges et inferes.

Suckling pig with two types of stuffing: Clean it, gut it from the throat, truss [the feet] to the neck. Before cooking it, open the ear under the skin. Fill an ox bladder with Terentian stuffing, and attach a bird's quill at the neck of the bladder; through this squeeze as much [stuffing] into the ear as it will hold. Then plug the hole with paper and close with fibulas, and prepare another stuffing. Make it thus: Grind pepper, lovage, oregano, a bit of silphium root; moisten with *garum*; add cooked brains, raw eggs, cooked spelt, cooking broth, small birds if available, pine nuts, peppercorns. Mix with *garum*. Stuff the pig, plug with paper, and close with fibulas. Place in the oven. When it is cooked, untruss, spread with oil, and serve.

For most of us it is impossible to prepare an entire suckling pig at home, unless a large spit is available. Otherwise, you might use the occasion of a catered banquet to request that this recipe be prepared for you.

The first stuffing mentioned in the recipe (Terentian stuffing: see Stuffed Leg of Boar à la Terentius, Apicius 339, pp. 117–18) is actually more of a sauce, consisting of pepper, bay berries, rue, silphium (we can use garlic juice instead), *garum, caroenum,* and olive oil. The Romans devised the sack described in the recipe to inject this stuffing into the animal through an incision in the ear. The main stuffing is made of boiled brain, mixed with raw egg, stock, pine nuts, the meat of small fowl, semolina, various herbs, pepper, garlic juice (again in substitution of silphium), and *garum*. Quantities depend upon the size of the pig.

For a buffet serving 12 people, a pig of around 15 pounds (6-7 kilos), should be prepared as a main course. If your guests like pork, you might also prepare the preceding Ham in Pastry (Apicius, 290). Otherwise the following recipe for lamb or kid makes an appropriate accompaniment.

The Romans frequently cooked entire pigs or hogs, often stuffed, when they had numerous guests to serve (this custom survives in central Italy). A recipe called *porcus troianus* dates from the second century B.C.: it was so named because the pig "was stuffed with other animals that were closed inside in the same manner that the Trojan horse was filled with warriors" (Macrobius, *Saturnalia* 3, 13). Another description of this spectacular dish for gala banquets appears in the *Cena Trimalchionis* (see page 203). The Italian word *troia*, or sow, is a colorful descendent of the name of this recipe.

ROASTED LAMB OR KID
(APICIUS 363)

Haedus sive agnus crudus: Oleo, pipere fricabis et asparges foris salem purum multo cum coriandri semine. In furnum mittis, assatum inferes.

For raw kid or lamb: Rub it with oil and pepper and sprinkle the surface with pure salt and a good quantity of coriander seeds. Place in the oven, serve when roasted.

This simple recipe can be used not only for whole lamb or kid, but also for parts of these animals, a more practical option for most situations. I recommend using fresh coriander instead of the seeds for its delicate perfume.

If you use the whole beast, clean it well, gut it, then slit the skin in various places and insert the coriander, salt, and pepper beneath. Grind a generous amount of coarse salt, press the meat in it to cover the surface, then bake in the oven or roast on a spit.

You can prepare a leg of approximately 2 pounds (1 kilo) (which serves 4), following the same procedure for preparation and baking it in the oven. One hour in a hot oven (400°F.) is sufficient. For juicier meat, bake it at 480°F. for the first 15 minutes, then lower the heat.

Keep in mind that ample coriander is needed to flavor the meat sufficiently. If you cannot find it fresh, be sure to mix the dry variety with olive oil so that it is easier to apply.

PARTHIAN KID OR LAMB
(APICIUS 365)

Haedum sive agnum particum: Mittes in furnum. Teres piper, rutam, cepam, satureiam, damascena enucleata, laseris modicum, vinum, liquamen et oleum. Fervens colluitur in disco, ex aceto sumitur.

Parthian kid or lamb: Put in the oven. Grind pepper, rue, onion, savory, pitted damsons, a bit of silphium, wine, *garum,* and oil. When [the sauce] is hot, it is poured [over the meat] on a round dish, and it is served with vinegar.

Serves 4–6
1 leg of lamb or kid (approximately 2–3 lb. [1–1½ kg.])
10 oz. (300 g.) pitted prunes (plumped in warm water)
3–4 large onions
1 tsp. *garum*
2 Tbs. olive oil
1 Tbs. total, rue and savory
pepper to taste
1 garlic clove, pressed for its juice

Roast a leg (or other appropriate cut) of lamb or kid without any condiment. Meanwhile, prepare the sauce: finely slice the onions and sauté in the olive oil and *garum*. Season with the pepper and herbs, and cook for around 15 minutes more. Add the prunes and a few drops of garlic juice. Continue to cook the sauce until the fruit has nearly disintegrated.

Remove the meat from the oven, moisten it with a bit of vinegar (which takes away the excess fat), and dry. Cover with the sauce, replace in the oven for another 10 minutes, then remove and serve.

If you want to simplify things when serving, slice the meat before you cover it with the sauce.

As I interpret the text, the name of this delicious sweet-and-sour recipe comes from the *laser parthicum* used to flavor it (for a more complete discussion of this herb, see pp. 30–31). Others have read *pasticum* instead of *particum*, thus "suckling kid or lamb"; this corresponds to the modern Roman *abbacchio*, the meat of a lamb that has been nourished exclusively with its mother's milk. But whatever the interpretation, the recipe itself is certainly worth trying.

GRILLED LIVER

(APICIUS 261)

Aliter: Ficatum praecidis ad cannam, infundis in liquamine, [teres] piper, ligusticum, bacas lauri duas, involves in omento et in craticula assas et inferes.

Another recipe: Cut the liver with a reed, and soak it in *garum*. [Grind] pepper, lovage, and two bay berries. Wrap in omentum, roast on a grill, and serve.

Serves 4
¾ lb. (400 g.) thickly sliced liver (either pork or veal)
2–3 Tbs. *garum*
pepper to taste
1 Tbs. lovage
2–3 bay berries
pork caul fat

Here liver is called *ficatum* and not *iecur* as in other recipes, an allusion to the liver of an animal that had been nourished on figs (see page 13). For our purposes either pork or veal liver works well.

Score the slices of liver with a knife and marinate them in *garum*. After 2 or 3 hours, remove the liver and season with the ground mixture of pepper, lovage, and bay berries. Then wrap in caul fat (see p. 90) and roast on a grill for around 10 minutes, turning the liver occasionally.

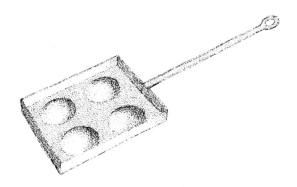

LIVER PATTIES
(APICIUS 45)

Omentata ita fiunt: Assas iecur porcinum et eum enervas. Ante tamen teres piper, rutam, liquamen, et sic superinmittis iecur et teres et misces, sicut pulpa omentata, et singula involuntur folia lauri et ad fumum suspenduntur quamdiu voles. Cum manducare volueris, tolles de fumum et denuo assas.

Patties in omentum are made thus: Roast pork liver and remove the veins and tissues. First grind pepper, rue, and *garum,* and put the liver in over this and grind and mix, as for ground meat in omentum. Wrap each [patty] in bay leaves, and hang to smoke for as long as desired. When you want to eat them, remove from the smoke and roast again.

Serves 4
1 lb. (½ kg.) pork liver
pepper to taste
1 tsp. rue
1 Tbs. *garum*
1–2 bay leaves per meat patty
pork caul fat

Cook the pork liver on a grill for around 10 minutes. Grind pepper, rue, and *garum* in a mortar, then add the liver and grind together. Mix thoroughly and form small patties. Wrap each one in bay leaves, then in the caul fat (see p. 90), and cook on a grill or in the oven at 400°F. for 10–15 minutes.

This method of cooking with bay leaves and pork caul fat is identical to that used in the following northern Italian recipe:

REGIONAL ITALIAN RECIPE
(Trieste)
Pork Liver, Trieste Style

Have the pork liver sliced not too thick. Place a bay leaf on each slice, then season with salt and pepper. Fold in half and wrap in pork caul fat. Place in a shallow pan, moisten with a cup of white wine, and bake at 325°F. for 20–30 minutes.

CHICKEN WITH SQUASH
(APICIUS 80)

Cucurbitas cum gallina: Duracina, tubera, piper, careum, cuminum, silfi, condimenta viridia, mentam, apium, coriandrum, puleium, careotam, mel, vinum, liquamen, oleum et acetum.

Squash with hen: Peaches, truffles, pepper, caraway, cumin, silphium, fresh condiments, mint, celery, coriander, pennyroyal, dates, honey, wine, *garum,* oil, and vinegar.

Serves 4
1 medium cleaned and gutted young stewing hen or chicken
  (around 2 lb. [1 kg.])
1½ lb. (700 g.) squash
1 Tbs. olive oil
1 Tbs. wine

1 tsp. *garum*
pepper to taste
For the sauce:
    4 peaches
    7–8 dates
    1–2 black truffles
    fresh aromatic herbs, minced, to taste
    1 cup white wine
    1 Tbs. olive oil
    1 tsp. *garum*
    1 tsp. honey
    dash of vinegar

As often happens in *De re coquinaria*, the recipe proper ignores the main ingredient, which appears only in the title. Perhaps for a reader of the epoch the missing procedures were obvious enough, but for us this is not necessarily the case. The following is one possible interpretation.

Cut the hen or chicken into pieces and cook for approximately 20 minutes in a pot with a bit of olive oil and wine. Meanwhile, clean the squash and dice. Add the squash to the chicken and continue to cook over a low heat until the squash has become completely soft. Flavor with *garum* and pepper.

For the sauce: Peel and cut the peaches into pieces, pit and chop the dates, and chop the truffles. Mix these ingredients together with the herbs, white wine, olive oil, *garum*, honey, and vinegar. Serve this sauce as an accompaniment to the cooked fowl.

STUFFED CHICKEN
(APICIUS 250)

Pullus farsilis: Pullum sicuti liquaminatum a cervice expedies. Teres piper, ligusticum, gingiber, pulpam caesam, alicam elixam, teres cerebellum ex iure coctum, ova confringis et commiscis ut unum corpus efficias; liquamine temperas et oleum modice mittis, piper integrum, nucleos abundantes. Fac impensam et imples pullum vel porcellum ita ut laxamentum habeat. Similiter in capo facies, ossibus eiectis coques.

Stuffed chicken: Gut the chicken from the neck, as for chicken with *garum* sauce. Grind pepper, lovage, ginger, ground meat, boiled spelt, brain cooked in broth. Break eggs and add, mixing everything to a uniform consistency.

Mix with *garum* and put in a bit of oil, peppercorns, abundant pine nuts. Make a stuffing [of these ingredients] and fill the chicken or a suckling pig, leaving some space. Use the same procedure with a capon, boning it before cooking it.

Serves 4

1 medium cleaned and gutted chicken (around 2 lb. [1 kg.])
¾ cup couscous
7 oz. (200 g.) brain (lamb or veal)
1½ quarts (liters) stock (to completely cover the chicken)
pepper to taste
1 tsp. ginger
1 tsp. lovage
7 oz. (200 g.) cooked ground meat of your choice
2 oz. (50–60 g.) pine nuts
2 eggs
1 Tbs. *garum*
1 Tbs. olive oil

Soak the couscous for 30 minutes, drain, and boil in water. Boil the brain in a bit of stock. Grind the cooked couscous and brain in a mortar, seasoning with the pepper, ginger, and lovage.

Place this mixture in a bowl, then grind the pine nuts together with the ground meat in the mortar. Add to the brain and couscous.

Beat the eggs and blend them into the mixture; season with *garum* and a bit of olive oil. Use this to stuff the chicken, being careful not to overfill. Sew it shut and cook in boiling water or stock.

For best results, you should enclose the stuffed chicken in a pork bladder before cooking. This system (recommended by the great French cook Bocuse for his chicken stuffed with greens) is the best for cooking chicken, capon, or other stuffed fowl in water or broth because it helps to seal in the flavor. Cooking time for a medium chicken is 90 minutes; the liquid should never reach a fast boil.

This recipe is also good with boned capon. Increase the quantities in proportion to the weight of the bird.

CHICKEN À LA FRONTO
(APICIUS 248)

Pullum Frontonianum: Pullum praedura, condies liquamine, oleo mixto, cui mittis fasciculum aneti, porri, satureiae et coriandri viridis et coques. Ubi coctus fuerit, levabis eum, in lance defrito perungues, piper aspargis et inferes.

Chicken à la Fronto: Brown a chicken, season with *garum* mixed with oil, to which you add a bouquet of dill, leeks, savory, and fresh coriander, and cook. When it is cooked, remove, coat it with *defrutum* on a serving plate, sprinkle with pepper, and serve.

Serves 4
1 medium cleaned and gutted chicken (around 2 lb. [1 kg.])
1 small bunch each, fresh dill, savory, and coriander (or lemon balm)
4 small tender leeks
2 Tbs. olive oil
1 tsp. *garum*
2 Tbs. *defrutum*
pepper to taste

Bundle together the dill, savory, coriander, and leeks into a bouquet that will not come apart when it is cooked. Brown the chicken, either whole or cut into pieces, without any oil or seasoning. Mix the *garum* with the olive oil, then add to the chicken with the bouquet of herbs and leeks. Continue to cook over a low heat. If you are cooking the chicken in pieces, the total time needed should be 45–50 minutes; if it is whole, add 15–20 minutes more. Arrange on a serving dish, pour on the *defrutum*, and sprinkle with pepper.

"À la Fronto" in this title is apparently a reference to the Roman author of a lost treatise on agriculture.

CHICKEN À LA ELAGABALUS
(Apicius 247)

Pullus Varianus: Pullum coques iure hoc: liquamine, oleo, vino, [cui mittis] fasciculum porri, coriandri, satureiae. Cum coctus fuerit, teres piper, nucleos ciatos duos et ius de suo sibi suffundis (et fasciculos proicies), lac temperas. Et reexinanies mortarium supra pullum, ut ferveat. Obligas eundem albamentis ovorum tritis, ponis in lance et iure supra scripto perfundis. Hoc ius candidum appellatur.

Chicken à la Varius: Cook the chicken in this sauce: *garum*, oil, wine, [to which you add] a bouquet of leek, coriander, savory. When it is cooked, grind pepper, two *cyathi* of pine nuts, moisten with cooking juice (and remove the bouquet of herbs), and mix with milk. Empty the mortar over the chicken, bring to a boil. Thicken with minced [boiled] egg white. Place on a serving dish and pour over it the sauce described above. This is called white sauce.

1 medium cleaned and gutted chicken (around 2 lb. [1 kg.]),
   cut into pieces
4 small tender leeks
1 bunch each, fresh coriander (or lemon balm) and savory
2 cups white wine
1 Tbs. olive oil
1 tsp. *garum*
For the sauce:
   ample white pepper
   3 oz. (100 g.) pine nuts
   1 cup milk
   3 hard-boiled egg whites, minced
   1 tsp. cornstarch (if necessary)

Gather the leeks, coriander, and savory into a bouquet, tying so that it does not come apart when cooked; place it in a pot with the olive oil, wine, and *garum*. Heat and add the chicken pieces to cook. When they are around three-quarters done, prepare the white sauce: Grind the pepper and pine nuts in a mortar, moistening with a bit of cooking juice from the chicken. Blend thoroughly with milk. Remove the herb bundle from the pot and cover the chicken with the white sauce. Cook a further 10 minutes to reduce the sauce, then add the minced boiled egg whites. If necessary, add cornstarch (dissolved in cold water) to thicken the sauce sufficiently.

This light, delicate recipe is generally attributed to the emperor Elagabalus (reigned 218–222). Inspired by his devotion to the sun god Elagabalus (of whom he had become a high priest while still a youth), he adopted the name we know him by today; his original name was Varius Avitus Bassianus.

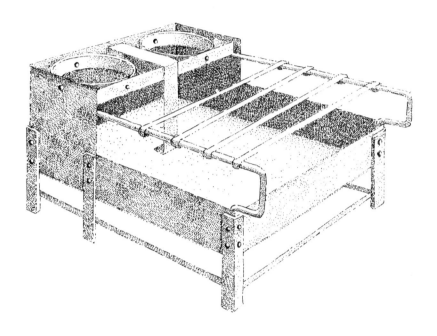

GUINEA HEN WITH
SWEET-AND-SOUR SAUCE
(APICIUS 240)

Pullum numidicum: Pullum curas, elixas, levas, laser ac piper [aspergis] et assas. Teres piper, cuminum, coriandri semen, laseris radicem, rutam, careotam, nucleos, suffundis acetum, mel, liquamen et oleum, temperabis. Cum ferbuerit, amulo obligas, pullum perfundis, piper aspergis et inferes.

Guinea fowl: Prepare a chicken, boil it, and remove it [from the water]. [Sprinkle with] silphium and pepper, and roast. Grind pepper, cumin, coriander seeds, silphium root, rue, dates, pine nuts; pour on vinegar, honey, *garum*, and oil, and mix. When it has boiled, thicken with starch and pour over the chicken; sprinkle with pepper and serve.

Serves 4
1 guinea hen
pepper to taste
1 garlic clove, pressed for its juice
For the sauce:
2 oz. (50–60 g.) pine nuts
10 pitted dates
pepper to taste
1 Tbs. total, cumin, coriander seeds, and rue
2 Tbs. olive oil
1 garlic clove, pressed for its juice
1 tsp. vinegar
1 tsp. *garum*
1 tsp. honey
1 tsp. cornstarch (if necessary)

Today we can skip the initial boiling because our meat is available fresh (see the discussion on page 87). Gut and clean the guinea hen, sprinkle with pepper and garlic juice, and roast. Meanwhile, prepare the sauce: Grind the dry ingredients together, moistening while you grind with the liquid ones. Heat in a small pan. When this sauce boils, add the dissolved starch if necessary to thicken. You can either serve the sauce apart or cut the hen into pieces and cover it with the sauce.

The guinea hen (*gallina numidica* or *africana*), which was introduced from Africa, appeared on the Roman table perhaps only after Carthage was taken (146 B.C.). In one of Martial's clever epigrams (13, 73) he described Hannibal, having had his fill of Roman geese but unable to enjoy the birds of his own region during his campaigns in Italy against the Romans.

BOILED GOOSE À LA APICIUS
(APICIUS 235)

Anserem elixum calidum ex iure frigido Apiciano: Teres piper, ligusticum, coriandri semen, mentam, rutam, refundis liquamen et oleum modice, temperas. Anserem elixum ferventem sabano mundo exsiccabis, ius perfundis et inferes.

Hot boiled goose with cold sauce à la Apicius: Grind pepper, lovage, coriander seeds, mint, and rue; pour on *garum*

and a bit of oil, and mix. Dry the steaming boiled goose
with a clean cloth, pour the sauce over it, and serve.

Boil the goose, skimming the surface of the liquid occasionally to remove the fat. Meanwhile, prepare the sauce with the pepper, herbs, *garum*,
and a bit of olive oil. When the goose is ready, wipe the fat from it with a
paper or cloth towel, cut it into pieces, and cover it with the sauce.

Cooking time depends upon the weight of the goose. Since most geese
weigh at least 4½ pounds (2 kilos), this recipe will serve a minimum of 6.

DUCK IN PRUNE SAUCE
(APICIUS 213)

*In grue vel in anate vel in pullo: Piper, cepam siccam, li-
gusticum, cuminum, apii semen, pruna Damascena enucleata, mulsum, acetum, liquamen, defritum, oleum et coques.*

For crane or duck or chicken: Pepper, dried onion, lovage,
cumin, celery seeds, pitted damsons, *mulsum*, vinegar,
garum, defrutum, and oil, and cook.

Serves 4
1 large duck, cleaned and gutted
1 Tbs. olive oil
1 tsp. *garum*
2 Tbs. *defrutum*
2 Tbs. dried onion
1 tsp. each, lovage, cumin, and celery seeds
pepper to taste
1 cup *mulsum*
10 oz. (300 g.) pitted prunes
1 Tbs. vinegar

Cut the duck into pieces (you can also cook it whole if you prefer). Brown
in the olive oil, *garum*, and *defrutum*. Add the onion, herbs, pepper, and
mulsum, and cook. When the duck is half done, add the prunes. If the
sauce is a bit fatty, add the vinegar.

This recipe also works extremely well for chicken.

The following is an exquisite north African recipe, which provides an
interesting comparison with the one above:

MODERN MOROCCAN RECIPE
Chicken with Prunes

Take a large chicken that has been thoroughly cleaned and washed and cut it into pieces. Brown it in a casserole with a little oil. Season with salt and crumbled hot red pepper and add a ladle of boiling water. Slice 2 large onions and add them to the chicken. Cook for 20 minutes over a low heat. Remove the pits from around ¾ lb. (400 g.) of prunes and add. Continue to cook for 40 minutes. Serve with couscous.

The hot red pepper (from America) in this recipe is the counterpart of the peppercorns in the ancient recipe.

DUCK WITH TURNIPS
(APICIUS 214)

Gruem vel anatem ex rapis: Lavas, ornas et in olla elixabis cum aqua, sale et aneto dimidia coctura. Rapas coque ut exbromari possint. Levabis de olla, et iterum lavabis et in caccabum mittis anatem cum oleo et liquamine et fasciculo porri et coriandri. Rapam lotam et minutatim concisam desuper mittis, facies ut coquatur. Modica coctura mittis defritum ut coloret. Ius tale parabis: piper, cuminum, coriandrum, laseris radicem, suffundis acetum et ius de suo sibi, reexinanies super anatem ut ferveat. Cum ferbuerit, amulo obligabis et super rapas adicies. Piper aspargis et adponis.

Crane or duck with turnips: Wash, truss, and boil in a pan with water, salt, and dill until half cooked. Cook the turnips so that they lose their bitterness. Remove the duck from the pan, wash again, and place in a pot with oil and *garum* and a bouquet of leeks and coriander. Over this put a turnip that has been well washed and cut into very small pieces, and cook. When it has cooked somewhat, add *defrutum* for color. Prepare this sauce: pepper, cumin, coriander, and silphium root, moistened with vinegar and cooking broth. Pour over the duck and boil. When it boils, thicken with starch and add over the [remaining] turnips. Sprinkle with pepper and serve.

Serves 4
1 large duck
1 Tbs. olive oil
1 tsp. *garum*
1 small tender leek
1 bunch fresh coriander (or lemon balm)
1½ lb. (700 g.) turnips
2 Tbs. *defrutum*
For the sauce:
   1 Tbs. total, cumin and coriander
   1 garlic clove, pressed for its juice
   1 Tbs. vinegar
   pepper to taste
   1 tsp. cornstarch (if necessary)

This recipe resembles the famous French *canard aux navets,* of which it is probably an ancient relative. However, here the turnips are boiled apart so that they do not give the duck too bitter a flavor.

As always, you can omit the initial boiling of the meat. Put the duck in a pot to brown with a little olive oil, *garum,* and a securely tied bouquet of the leek and coriander. Slice one turnip, add it, then mix in the *defrutum.* Cook over a low heat. Boil the remaining turnips (make sure you have chosen only those that are very fresh and firm) separately so that they lose their bitterness. Prepare a sauce with the herbs, garlic juice, vinegar, and pepper, and pour it over the duck. Mix well, thickening if necessary with dissolved starch. Slice the boiled turnips, add them to the duck, and serve.

ROASTED PIGEONS
(APICIUS 221)

In palumbis, columbis. In assis: Piper, ligusticum, coriandrum, careum, cepam siccam, mentam, ovi vitellum, cariotam, mel, acetum, liquamen, oleum et vinum.

For roasted pigeons and doves: Pepper, lovage, coriander, caraway, dried onion, mint, egg yolk, dates, honey, vinegar, *garum,* oil, and wine.

Serves 4
2–3 pigeons, depending upon their size
For the sauce:
  2 Tbs. dried onion
  pinch of pepper
  2 Tbs. total, lovage, coriander, caraway, and mint
  1 egg yolk
  5–6 pitted dates
  1 tsp. honey
  1 tsp. vinegar
  1 tsp. *garum*
  2 Tbs. olive oil
  1 cup white wine

Procure pigeons that are already cleaned and trussed and roast them in the oven at 400°F. for around 30 minutes. Meanwhile, prepare the cold sauce with the remaining ingredients (the dates should first be chopped and ground in a mortar) and serve it together with the pigeons.

STUFFED THRUSHES OR PIGEONS
(APICIUS 231)

Aliter avem: In ventrem eius fractas olivas novas mittis et consutam sic elixabis. Deinde coctas olivas eximes.

Another recipe for birds: Stuff the stomach with crushed fresh olives, sew up, and boil thus. Then remove the cooked olives.

Serves 4
4 thrushes or small pigeons
4 Tbs. ground olives
4 Tbs. crumbled bread without the crust (optional)
milk (to soak the bread)

This recipe is for birds in general, thus you can use any fowl you desire—for example, quail, thrushes, doves, or pigeons. I have tried it with thrushes and pigeons and found it to be very good.

  Soak the olives overnight so that they lose their bitterness, then grind them in a mortar or blender. (You can also use olive paste, or *epityrum,* as a stuffing; see the recipe on pp. 59–60.)

  Stuff the birds with the olive pulp, sew them up securely, and cook. The recipe suggests that they be boiled, in which case cooking time should be around 30 minutes. However, I think the result is far better if the birds are roasted instead. Should you decide to follow this latter method, put the stuffed birds in a pan and roast at 400°F. for 30 minutes, or broil for around 20 minutes.

If you want the stuffing to be a bit milder in flavor, you can mix the ground olives with an equal amount of bread that has been soaked in milk and then squeezed and drained. This stuffing can be left inside the birds; otherwise, you should remove and discard the olives before the birds are brought to table.

Thrushes were raised in captivity, as we know from Columella's manual. Their meat must have been considered quite a delicacy, since the Romans went to extraordinary lengths to feed these birds well. In fact, they were given a mixture of myrtle and other aromatic berries, fine flour, and dried figs that were softened by slaves who chewed them first. This fragrant sweet blend was so good that Columella (8, 10) added: "There is little convenience in adopting this system when a large quantity of thrushes is involved, because the slaves who are hired to chew the dried figs consume some of the feed for the thrushes." This situation would seem humorous were it not for the fact that it reveals the tragic condition of the *instrumentum vocale* (appliance that speaks), as a slave was legally defined in ancient Rome.

STUFFED HARE
(APICIUS 386)

Leporem farsum: Nucleos integros, amigdala, nuces sive glandes concisas, piperis grana solida, pulpam de ipso lepore; et ovis fractis obligatur, de omento porcino [involutum assatur] in furno. Sic iterum impensam facies: rutam, piper satis, cepam, satureiam, dactilos, liquamen, caroenum vel conditum. Diu combulliat donec spisset, et sic perfunditur. Sed lepus in piperato liquamine et lasere maneat.

Stuffed hare: Whole pine nuts, almonds, chopped walnuts or acorns, whole peppercorns, variety meats of the hare itself, and beaten eggs to thicken. [Wrap the hare] in pork omentum and [roast] in the oven. Separately, prepare this mixture: rue, sufficient pepper, onion, savory, dates, *garum*, and *caroenum* or *conditum*. Boil at length to thicken, and then pour it over [the hare]. But the hare must marinate in a pepper sauce with *garum* and silphium.

Serves 4
1 hare
For the marinade:
  2 cups *garum*
  10 peppercorns
  2 garlic cloves
  1 handful of fresh aromatic herbs as preferred
For the stuffing:
  7 oz. (200 g.) total, pine nuts, almonds, and walnuts
  1 tsp. peppercorns
  1 liver from the hare
  2–3 chicken livers (if necessary)
  2 eggs, beaten
For the sauce:
  1 cup strong red wine, *caroenum,* or *conditum*
  1 tsp. *garum*
  pinch of pepper
  1 Tbs. total, rue and savory
  5–6 pitted and minced dates
  1 onion, minced
  1 tsp. cornstarch (if necessary)

The last sentence of this recipe actually describes the first procedure: marinate the hare in *garum,* peppercorns, and silphium (substitute the cloves of garlic and add some fresh aromatic herbs) for at least 24 hours, turning occasionally, then remove.

Prepare the stuffing by grinding together the nuts, peppercorns, hare liver, and eggs. If the animal is large you may need to add a few chicken livers to the mixture. Stuff the hare, sew it shut or close with skewers, place in a baking dish, and roast in the oven for 2 hours at 350°F.

Meanwhile, prepare the sauce. Mix the listed ingredients together and cook over a low heat to thicken. If you prefer a sweet-and-sour flavor, use *caroenum* instead of the red wine or *conditum.* Use dissolved starch to thicken the sauce if necessary. You can pour this sauce over the hare when it is done, or serve it on the side.

ROASTED HARE WITH HERB SAUCE
(APICIUS 387)

*Ius album in assum leporem: Piper, ligusticum, cuminum,
apii semen, ovi duri medium. Trituram colligis et facies*

globum ex ea. In caccabo coques liquamen, vinum, oleum, acetum modice, cepullam concisam, postea globulum condimentorum mittes et agitabis origano vel satureia. Si opus fuerit, amulas.

Clear sauce for roasted hare: Pepper, lovage, cumin, celery seeds, yolk of hard-boiled egg. Grind, gather up, and make a ball of this. In a pot cook *garum*, wine, oil, a bit of vinegar, chopped onion; then add the ball of condiments and stir with oregano or savory. If necessary, thicken with starch.

Serves 4
1 hare
For the sauce:
    pepper to taste
    1 tsp. each, lovage, cumin, and celery seeds
    1 hard-boiled egg yolk
    1 cup red wine
    1 tsp. *garum*
    1 tsp. vinegar
    1 Tbs. olive oil
    1 Tbs. minced onion
    1 bunch fresh oregano or savory
    1 tsp. cornstarch (if necessary)

Procure a cleaned hare with the head and feet removed. Roast it in the oven for 90 minutes, or on a spit for 2 hours.

For the sauce, grind the pepper, herbs, and the hard-boiled egg yolk together, and press the mixture into a ball. Sauté the onion in the wine, *garum*, vinegar, and olive oil; then add the herb ball and blend thoroughly, stirring with the bunch of oregano or savory that has been tied into a bouquet. If the resulting sauce is too thin, add a bit of starch (dissolved first in a bit of cooled sauce) before removing from the heat. Serve on the side.

ROASTED LEG OF ROEBUCK WITH HERB SAUCE

(APICIUS 348)

Ius in caprea assa: Piper, condimentum, rutam, cepam, mel, liquamen, passum, oleum modice, amulum [cum] iam bulliet.

Sauce for roasted roebuck: Pepper, aromatic herbs, rue, onion, honey, *garum*, *passum*, and a bit of oil; starch, when it boils.

Serves 4
2 lb. (1 kg.) leg of roebuck
For the sauce:
　pepper to taste
　1 tsp. rue
　1 Tbs. minced fresh aromatic herbs as preferred
　1 onion, minced
　1 tsp. *garum*
　1 tsp. honey
　1 cup *passum*
　1 Tbs. olive oil
　1 tsp. cornstarch

The recipe indicates only that the meat should be roasted. As it cooks, grind together the pepper, rue, herbs (for example, mint, oregano, and lovage), minced onion, *garum,* and honey; then add the *passum* and olive oil, and heat it in a small pan. When it is cooked, thicken with dissolved cornstarch. Serve on the side.

ROASTED BOAR WITH COOKED SAUCE

(APICIUS 333)

In aprum assum iura ferventia facies sic: Piper, cuminum frictum, apii semen, mentam, timum, satureiam, cneci flos, nucleos tostos vel amigdala tosta, mel, vinum, liquamen acetabulum, oleum modice.

Prepare a heated sauce for roasted boar thus: Pepper, fried cumin, celery seed, mint, thyme, savory, safflower, roasted pine nuts or roasted almonds, honey, wine, an *acetabulum* of *garum*, and a bit of oil.

Serves 4

2 lb. (800 g.–1 kg.) boar tenderloin or shoulder butt, cut into
    large cubes
For the marinade:
    2 cups strong red wine
    ½ cup vinegar
    1 Tbs. *garum*
    1 Tbs. total, celery seeds, mint, thyme, and savory
For the sauce:
    1 tsp. cumin
    1½ oz. (35–40 g.) pine nuts
    2 oz. (50 g.) almonds
    1 Tbs. total, celery seeds, mint, thyme, and savory
    pinch of pepper
    ½ cup red wine
    1 tsp. *garum*
    1 tsp. honey
    1 tsp. olive oil
    1 Italian packet (.12 g.) or ¼ tsp. ground saffron

This is another recipe that lacks directions for cooking the meat, beyond
stating that it should be roasted. One good method would be to marinate
the pieces of boar for 24 hours in the same herbs you use for the sauce,
mixed with red wine, vinegar, and *garum*. Then drain the meat and roast
it in a moderately hot oven (350°F.) for around 2 hours.

For the sauce: Roast the cumin in a pan for a few minutes, and do the
same for the pine nuts and almonds. Chop together the herbs, pine nuts,
and almonds; add the pepper, wine, *garum*, honey, and olive oil, then finally the saffron. Heat. Serve on the side.

STUFFED LEG OF BOAR À LA TERENTIUS
(APICIUS 339)

*Perna apruna ita impletur Terentina: Per articulum pernae
palum mittes ita ut cutem a carne separes, ut possit condimentum accipere per cornulum ut universa impleatur.
Teres piper, bacam lauri, rutam; si volueris, laser adicies,
liquamen optimum, carenum et olei viridis guttas. Cum impleta fuerit, constringitur illa pars qua impleta est ex lino
et mittitur in zemam. Elixatur in aquam marinam cum
lauri turionibus et aneto.*

A leg of a boar is filled thus in the manner of Terentius: Pass a pointed stick along the joint of the leg to separate the skin from the meat, so that the seasoning can be poured through a small funnel and [the space between] can be completely filled. Grind pepper, bay berries, rue; if you wish, add silphium, fine *garum, caroenum*, and drops of green oil. When it is stuffed, the filled part is fastened with flax string and it is placed in a cauldron. It is boiled in sea water with bay twigs and dill.

Serves 6–8
4½ lb. (2 kg.) leg of boar (with the skin)
2–3 bay twigs
1 bunch fresh dill
For the stuffing:
  2 Tbs. *garum*
  ½ cup *caroenum*
  ½ cup olive oil
  7–8 garlic cloves
  4–5 bay berries
  pepper to taste
  2 handfuls of fresh rue

The initial preparation of the leg is rather difficult; if you can, have your butcher separate the entire skin in one piece like a pocket from the meat. Grind and mix the ingredients listed for the stuffing, and place this mixture between the skin and the meat; then close the opening securely with string so that the stuffing does not come out. Boil for 3 hours in heavily salted water (the Romans kept sea water in barrels and used it in the preparation of many dishes), to which you have added a few twigs of bay and some dill.

Terentius was a famous cook and gourmet, after whom a very popular dessert called *terentinon* was named. He is also mentioned in Apicius 166, on page 135.

MARINATED VENISON SADDLE WITH PRUNE SAUCE
(APICIUS 346)

In cervum assum iura ferventia: Piper, ligusticum, petroselinum, damascena macerata, vinum, mel, acetum, liquamen, oleum modice. Agitabis porro et satureia.

A heated sauce for roasted deer: Pepper, lovage, parsley, soaked damsons, wine, honey, vinegar, *garum,* and a bit of oil. Stir with leek and savory.

Serves 8–10
4½ lb. (2 kg.) venison saddle
For the marinade:
  2 cups red wine
  1 Tbs. *garum*
  10 peppercorns
  5–6 bay berries
  1 Tbs. total, savory and lovage
For the sauce:
  10 oz. (300 g.) pitted prunes, plumped in wine
  pinch of pepper
  1 Tbs. total, parsley and lovage
  1 cup red wine
  1 Tbs. honey
  1 Tbs. *garum*
  1 Tbs. olive oil
  1 Tbs. vinegar
  1 small tender leek
  1 bunch fresh savory

The sauce is an excellent accompaniment for either roasted saddle or leg of venison. I have chosen the version using the saddle, which you can prepare thus:

Make a marinade of the ingredients listed above and heat for around 10 minutes. Put the saddle in a casserole and pour the marinade over it. Cover securely and refrigerate for 2 days, turning the meat regularly so that it marinates uniformly. Remove the meat, put it in a clean casserole and roast in a moderately hot oven (350°F.) for 90 minutes, moistening occasionally with the marinade.

Prepare the sauce by mixing and heating the ingredients listed. Regarding the suggestion to stir the sauce with leek and savory, you can simply tie them into a bouquet, add it to the sauce as it cooks, and remove before serving.

This recipe is also good as a stew. For 4 servings, you can marinate 1¾ pounds (800 grams) of boned venison for 12 hours, then cook it in the sauce. Add the prunes only when the meat is half done. Total cooking time depends upon the cut of meat; ask your butcher for advice.

ROASTED FLAMINGO OR PARROT

(Apicius 232)

*Fenicopterum eliberas, lavas, ornas, includis in caccabum,
adicies aquam, salem, anetum et aceti modicum. Dimidia
coctura alligas fasciculum porri et coriandri ut coquatur.
Prope cocturam defritum mittis, coloras. Adicies in mortarium piper, cuminum, coriandrum, laseris radicem, mentam, rutam, fricabis, suffundis acetum, adicies careotam,
ius de suo sibi perfundis. Reexinanies in eundem caccabum, amulo obligas. Ius perfundis et inferes. Idem facies
et in psittaco.*

Pluck the flamingo, wash it, truss it, put it in a pot; add
water, salt, dill, and a bit of vinegar. When it is half
cooked, tie together a bouquet of leeks and coriander and
cook [together with the flamingo]. When it is almost
cooked, add *defrutum* for color. In a mortar put pepper,
cumin, coriander, silphium root, mint, and rue; grind,
moisten with vinegar, add dates, and pour on cooking
broth. Empty into the same pot and thicken with starch.
Pour the sauce over [the flamingo] and serve. Do the same
for parrot.

Obviously this is a recipe for us to read but not to realize. I include it here
as an example of the extreme self-indulgence that occurred among the rul-
ing classes during the decadent years of the Roman Empire. Even worse,
flamingos were said to have been slaughtered for their tongues or brains
alone (*Historia Augusta, Heliogabalus* 20, 6; Pliny, *Naturalis historia* 10,
133; and Martial 13, 71).

›VIII‹

FISH AND SHELLFISH

MENSA PRIMA

Gudgeon
Even in lavish banquets of Venetian lands,
the gudgeon usually opens the meal.

(Martial 13, 88)

Gilthead
Not every gilthead is worthy of its praise and price,
but only that which feeds on the mollusks of the Lucrine
Lake.

(Martial 13, 90)

"Culinary delicacies were held in high regard . . . and just as previously Numantinus [Scipio Aemilianus Africanus] and Isauricus [Servilius Vatia] adopted the names of the peoples they had conquered, so Sergius Orata [Gilthead] and Licinius Murena [Eel] proudly adopted the names of the fish they raised in captivity." This brief extract from Columella (8, 16, 5) gives us a striking sense of the passion that the Romans always had for fish, especially seafood. Because the daily deliveries from the *Forum piscarium,* or Fish Market, were not enough to meet the demand, the Romans built enormous ponds in order to keep all types of fresh fish available. Small lakes were used for industrial-scale breeding; Pliny wrote that a breeder named Gaius Hirrius was able to furnish Julius Caesar with six thousand moray eels for a victory banquet (*Naturalis historia* 9, 171).

When a particular species of fish became scarce in the local seas, the Romans immediately went elsewhere to replenish the supply. During the epoch of the emperor Claudius, the prefect of the navy was commanded to bring *scari,* an extremely popular fish, from the eastern Mediterranean to repopulate the western Mediterranean. The species was protected from fishing for five years, after which period it again filled the fish markets.

But no matter what the epoch or how plentiful the supply, fish were always very expensive. The highest recorded prices for any food were those paid for the larger specimens of fish. The Edict of Diocletian fixed a *libra* of the finest fish at double the price for a *libra* of pork, and triple that for a *libra* of beef or sheep.

Thus it is no surprise that those wealthy Romans who were able to do so always had *piscinae* (fishponds) on their estates. Columella went on in his *De re rustica* to give precise details for the construction of a *piscina*, how to feed the fish, and what species to raise.

When not eaten fresh, fish were pickled, salted by *salsamentarii*, or smoked. The flavor of fish was so popular that *garum*, as we have seen, was present in almost every Roman recipe.

Generally fish were grilled, fried, or boiled, and refined sauces frequently accompanied them. There were also recipes for stuffed tuna, cuttlefish, and squid, and for patties made with the meat of lobsters and other crustaceans. The Romans served this bounty from Neptune on beautiful ceramic fish platters made of clay from Apulia or Campania by skilled Greek artisans. Many of these platters have survived the centuries for us to admire today.

Among the ten books of the Apician manual (all of which carry Greek titles), two are exclusively concerned with fish: book 9, entitled *Thalassa* (the sea), and book 10, entitled *Alieus* (the fisherman); a few particularly refined recipes can be found among those for meat patties and fricassees in book 2, *Sarcoptes* (ground meats). From these recipes I have chosen to reproduce the ones I found most appealing. You can also prepare fish however you prefer and serve it with one of the appropriate sauces in chapter 4.

BAKED FISH WITH CORIANDER SEEDS
(APICIUS 437)

Ius in pisce elixo: Piscem curabis diligenter, mittes in mortarium salem, coriandri semen, conteres bene, volves eum, adicies in patinam, cooperies, gipsabis, coques in furno. Cum coctus fuerit, tolles, aceto acerrimo asperges et inferes.

Sauce for boiled fish: Clean the fish carefully. Put salt and coriander seeds in a mortar and grind well. Roll the fish in this, put it in a pan, cover, seal it with gypsum plaster, and cook in the oven. When it is cooked, remove, sprinkle with very strong vinegar, and serve.

The Latin title for this recipe is misleading: the fish is not, in fact, accompanied by a sauce, but rather it creates its own sauce as it cooks. This method can be used with such fish as bass, hake, or sea bream.

Grind salt and coriander seeds together, then roll the cleaned fish in this seasoning, making sure it adheres well.

Place the fish on an ovenproof dish, cover it with another dish of the same type, and seal them together with a thick paste of flour and water. This should harden quite quickly. Place the fish in a hot oven (400°F.) to bake. Total cooking time will be longer than that for poached fish: calculate 30 minutes for around 1¾ pounds (800 grams) of fish.

ROASTED RED MULLET
(Apicius 444)

Ius in mullos assos: Piper, ligusticum, rutam, mel, nucleos, acetum, vinum, liquamen, oleum modice. Calefacies et perfundes.

Sauce for roasted red mullet: Pepper, lovage, rue, honey, pine nuts, vinegar, wine, *garum*, and a bit of oil. Heat and pour over [the fish].

Serves 4
4 red mullet, around 5 oz. (150 g.) each
For the sauce:
    2 handfuls of pine nuts
    1 tsp. total, pepper, lovage, and rue
    ½ cup olive oil
    1 Tbs. *garum*
    1 Tbs. vinegar
    dash of wine
    ½ tsp. honey

Cook the red mullet in the oven or atop the stove in a pan, as you prefer.

For the sauce, grind the pine nuts, pepper, lovage, and rue together. Put the remaining ingredients in a sauce boat, add the ground mixture, and blend well.

Red mullet were particularly popular with the Romans. When an unusually large specimen was put on sale at the fish market, buyers would make exorbitant offers in an effort to compete for its purchase. You will recall that Apicius once participated in an auction for one of these enormous fish (chapter 1, pp. 7–8). Seneca, who recorded the episode (*Epistulae* 95, 42), wrote that the fish weighed 4½ *librae*, or around 3 pounds (1½ kilos). Apicius was also said to have smothered live red mullet in *garum* (Pliny, *Naturalis historia* 9, 66). This reminds one of the Venetian *moleche ripiene* (stuffed crabs): they are fed eggs beaten with salt in their last hours of life. It seems that this "last meal" gives their meat a special flavor.

TUNA STEAKS
(Apicius 425)

Ius in cordula assa: Piper, ligusticum, apii semen, mentam, rutam, careotam, mel, acetum, vinum et oleum. Convenit et in sarda.

Sauce for young roasted tuna: Pepper, lovage, celery seeds, mint, rue, dates, honey, vinegar, wine, and oil. This can also be used for bonito.

Serves 4
4 tuna steaks
flour

For the sauce:
    20 pitted dates
    1 cup wine
    2 Tbs. olive oil
    dash of vinegar
    ½ tsp. honey
    ample pepper, lovage, celery seeds, mint, and rue

Once again the recipe gives instructions only for preparation of the sauce. The tuna can be cooked in the sauce itself, or roasted or grilled first if you prefer.

Lightly coat the fish steaks with flour. Mince the dates and mix with the remaining ingredients. Heat this sauce in a pan for 10 minutes, then add the floured fish. Cook over a low heat, turning the fish once. For a steak about 1 inch (3 cm.) thick, 15 minutes cooking time should be sufficient.

STUFFED BONITO
(Apicius 421)

Sardam farsilem sic facere oportet: Sardam exossatur, et teritur puleium, cuminum, piperis grana, mentam, nuces, mel. Impletur et consuitur, involvitur in carta et sic supra vaporem ignis in operculo componitur. Conditur ex oleo, careno, allece.

Stuffed bonito are prepared thus: The bonito are boned. Pennyroyal, cumin, peppercorns, mint, walnuts, and honey are ground together. [The fish] is stuffed, sewn up, and wrapped in paper. It is placed in a covered container over the steam of the fire. It is seasoned with oil, *caroenum*, and *allec*.

Some say that the *sarda* of the Romans was a fish from the Thunnidae family. They enjoyed the meat of many of this species, such as pelamyd and tuna.

This recipe uses a cooking method that is the equivalent of the modern Italian *al cartoccio*, where the fish is wrapped in oiled paper to cook. It is an optimum way to cook stuffed fish and is well worth trying. Both this stuffing and cooking method can be used with many kinds of fish.

Take the fish of your choice and fill it with the stuffing (use a generous amount of walnuts in the mixture); then wrap it in oiled paper or aluminum foil and bake in the oven. Quantities and cooking times depend upon the size and number of the fish you use.

You can serve olive oil, *caroenum*, or *garum* as condiments if desired.

It is interesting to note here that, contrary to what is generally believed, the Romans had not only expensive papyrus and parchment, but also various kinds of "paper" distinguished by quality. The poorest grade of these was the so-called *charta emporetica* (from *emporium*), the ancestor of brown wrapping paper. It was produced from low-quality papyrus and used for packaging products for sale in the shops—or, as in this recipe, for cooking.

ROASTED SEA BREAM

(APICIUS 460)

Ius in dentice asso: Piper, ligusticum, coriandrum, mentam, rutam aridam, malum cidoneum coctum, mel, vinum, liquamen, oleum. Calefacies, amulo obligabis.

Sauce for roasted sea bream: Pepper, lovage, coriander, mint, dried rue, cooked quince, honey, wine, *garum,* and oil. Heat and thicken with starch.

Serves 4
4 sea bream fillets of ca. 5 oz. (150 g.) each
2 Tbs. total, lovage, coriander, mint, and rue
pepper to taste
flour
2–3 large quinces
1 tsp. honey (optional)
1 tsp. *garum*
½ cup wine
3–4 Tbs. olive oil

You can bake the sea bream whole and serve the sauce on the side; but I find it more flavorful to cook the fillets in the sauce.

Spread both sides of the fillets with olive oil, season them with half of the herb mixture and some pepper, and refrigerate for 2 hours. Meanwhile, boil the quinces and make a puree of the pulp. Add the honey (if desired), the remaining herbs, *garum,* wine, and 1 Tbs. olive oil to the puree and heat.

Remove the fillets from the seasoning. Lightly coat them with flour and fry in olive oil, 5 minutes per side. Then pour the sauce over the fillets and remove from the heat.

ROASTED MORAY EELS
(APICIUS 450)

Ius in morena assa: Piper, ligusticum, pruna Damascena, vinum, mulsum, acetum, liquamen, defritum, oleum, et coques.

Sauce for roasted moray eel: Pepper, lovage, damsons, wine, *mulsum*, vinegar, *garum*, *defrutum*, and oil. Cook.

Serves 4
1¾ lb. (800 g.) moray eels, cleaned and sliced
For the sauce:
    20 pitted prunes
    1 cup wine
    2 Tbs. olive oil
    1 Tbs. vinegar
    ¼ tsp. honey
    pepper to taste
    1 Tbs. lovage
    1 Tbs. *garum*
    ½ cup total, *mulsum* and *defrutum* (optional)

Buy your moray eels cleaned and ready to be cooked and, if possible, cut into large slices. Since eels are rather oily, I suggest you roast them on a spit so that the fat drains off.

Plump the prunes in tepid water for 2 hours, then cook them with the remaining ingredients. This sauce is ready when the prunes have disintegrated.

BOILED MORAY EELS
(APICIUS 453)

Ius in morena elixa: Piper, ligusticum, careum, apii semen, coriandrum, mentam aridam, nucleos pineos, rutam, mel, acetum, vinum, liquamen, oleum modice. Calefacies et amulo obligas.

Sauce for boiled moray eel: Pepper, lovage, caraway, celery seeds, coriander, dried mint, pine nuts, rue, honey, vinegar, wine, *garum,* and a bit of oil. Heat and thicken with starch.

Serves 4
1¾ lb. (800 g.) moray eels, cleaned and sliced
1 handful of pine nuts
1 tsp. honey
2 Tbs. vinegar
1 Tbs. wine
2 Tbs. *garum*
1 Tbs. olive oil
2 Tbs. total, pepper and mixed aromatic herbs
1 tsp. cornstarch (if necessary)

Boil the moray eels and serve with the sauce composed of the above ingredients mixed together and cooked. I use very little olive oil, since eels are already oily. Add dissolved starch to thicken if necessary.

GRILLED LOBSTER
(Apicius 399)

Locustas assas sic facies: Aperiuntur locustae, ut adsolet, cum testa sua et infunditur eis piperatum, coriandratum, et sic in craticula assantur. Cum siccaverint, adicies eis in craticula quotiens siccaverint quousque assantur bene, inferes.

Roast lobsters thus: They are opened in the usual manner, without the shell being removed, covered with a pepper and coriander sauce, and roasted thus on a grill. Whenever they start to become dry, moisten them on the grill [with the sauce], until they are well cooked; serve.

1 lobster
1 Tbs. coriander
⅓ cup *garum*
pepper to taste
⅔ cup vinegar

Break the lobster in half lengthwise and remove the bitter, grainy intestine. Make a sauce of the remaining ingredients by grinding them together in a mortar. Moisten the lobster with this sauce and grill. Baste it regularly so that the meat does not dry out. Cooking time depends upon the size of the lobster, 20–30 minutes on the average.

The *piperatum, cuminatum,* and *coriandratum* in Apicius were sauces that took their names from the flavor of the predominating herb or spice. They often contained a mixture of herbs ground in a mortar with *garum* and vinegar, and sometimes a touch of honey.

BAIAN STEW
(APICIUS 433)

Embractum baianum: Ostreas minutas, sfondylos, urticas in caccabum mittes, nucleos tostos concisos, rutam, apium, piper, coriandrum, cuminum, passum, liquamen, careotam, oleum.

Baian sauce: Into a pot put small oysters, mussels, jellyfish, chopped roasted pine nuts, rue, celery, pepper, coriander, cumin, *passum, garum,* dates, and oil.

Serves 4
20 oysters
20 Venus clams
40 mussels
For the sauce:
    1½ oz. (30–40 g.) roasted pine nuts
    2 celery stalks
    1 handful of fresh rue, minced
    1 cup dry white wine
    10 pitted dates, chopped
    1 Tbs. *garum*
    pepper, coriander, and cumin to taste
    1 Tbs. *passum*
    1 Tbs. olive oil

Soak the mollusks in a little salt water to force them to open and extract the meat. Meanwhile, prepare a sauce: Chop the pine nuts and celery, then mix with the remaining ingredients. Cook for around 10 minutes to blend the flavors thoroughly. Add the mollusks and continue to cook for 30 minutes.

The title of this appetizing recipe includes a reference to Baiae, a then-fashionable resort town near Naples. According to Tacitus (*Annales* 14, 3–5), one evening Nero gave a famous party at his villa there, after which he planned that the boat transporting his mother Agrippina home would founder and take her to her death. The boat did indeed sink, but Agrippina was able to swim to safety. We can imagine Nero offering this dish at that very party, hiding his murderous intentions behind a facade of gaiety and extravagance. Fortunately, we need not realize this recipe under the same circumstances in order to enjoy it. You can replace the jellyfish (which must be soaked for quite some time in vinegar to neutralize their irritating venom) with any mollusks you prefer—for example, any of the various types of clams.

SEASONED MUSSELS
(APICIUS 420)

In metulis: Liquamen, porrum concisum, cuminum, passum, satureiam, vinum. Mixtum facies aquatius et ibi mitulos coques.

For mussels: *Garum*, chopped leek, cumin, *passum*, savory, and wine. Dilute this mixture with water and cook the mussels in it.

Serves 4
40–50 mussels
2 Tbs. *garum*
½ cup wine
½ cup *passum*
1 leek, chopped
1 handful total, fresh cumin and savory, minced

Wash the mussels thoroughly to remove the sand, then boil them in sufficient water to cover, along with the remaining ingredients. They are eaten with no further seasoning, as in the Neapolitan *sauté* of clams and mussels.

STUFFED CUTTLEFISH
(APICIUS 409)

Sic farcies eam sepiam coctam: Cerebella elixa enerviata teres cum pipere, cui commisces ova cruda quod satis erit, piper integrum, esicia minuta, et sic consues et in bullientem ollam mittes ita ut coire impensa possit.

Stuff cooked cuttlefish thus: Grind boiled brain (with the membrane removed) with pepper. Mix in sufficient raw egg, peppercorns, and very small patties of ground meat.

Then sew up [the stuffed cuttlefish] and put in a pot of boiling water so that the stuffing becomes firm.

Serves 4
4 large cuttlefish
1 veal brain
pepper to taste
3 eggs, beaten
7 oz. (200 g.) ground meat or fish of your choice, shaped into small balls
peppercorns

Clean the cuttlefish, remove the bone and skin, and boil briefly (be careful not to overboil them, or they will be difficult to sew up later). Discard the outer membrane of the veal brain, then boil the brain and pound with pepper. Add the eggs, ground meat or fish, and peppercorns. Stuff the cuttlefish with this mixture. Sew them up so that the stuffing remains securely inside. Boil for around 20 minutes to firm the stuffing, and serve.

SQUID PATTIES
(APICIUS 43)

Esicia de lolligine: Sublatis crinibus in fulmento tundes, sicuti adsolet. Pulpa et in mortario et in liquamine diligenter fricatur, et exinde esicia plassantur.

Squid patties: After removing the tentacles, pound [the squid] on a board, in the usual manner. The meat is ground thoroughly in a mortar with *garum*, and then patties are formed from it.

Serves 4
1¾ lb. (800 g.) squid
1 Tbs. *garum*

Clean the squid (discard the membrane, sword, and beak), and remove and set aside the tentacles. Pound the body with a meat pounder. Then grind body and tentacles in a mortar or a meat grinder, adding *garum* or *oenogarum* to moisten. Form small patties and fry in olive oil or boil. If you boil them, try serving them with the Sauce for Cuttlefish (Apicius 411) on pp. 41–42.

SQUILL OR PRAWN PATTIES
(Apicius 44)

Esicia de iscillis vel de cammaris amplis: Cammari vel is-cillae de testa sua eximuntur et in mortario teruntur cum pipere et liquamine optimo. Pulpae esicia plassantur.

Patties of squills or large prawns: The prawns or squills are removed from their shells and ground in a mortar with pepper and the finest *garum*. Patties are formed with the meat.

Serves 4
1¾ lb. (800 g.) prawns, squills, or shrimp (shelled weight)
1 Tbs. *garum*
pepper to taste
pork caul fat

These seafood patty recipes are all fairly similar, differing mainly in the type of fish used. This recipe for squills or prawns (you can also use shrimp) is particularly delicate.

Scald the crustaceans in boiling water so that the heads and shells can be easily removed. Grind the meat in a mortar with the *garum* and pepper and form patties from this mixture. I suggest wrapping each of these in caul fat (see p. 90) so that the patties do not fall apart. Then boil or fry in a bit of olive oil.

SEAFOOD PATTIES
(Apicius 42)

Isicia fiunt marina de cammaris et astacis, de lolligine, de sepia, de lucusta. Esicium condies pipere, ligustico, cu-mino, laseris radice.

Seafood patties are made with prawns, shrimp, squid, cut-tlefish, lobster. Season the patties with pepper, lovage, cumin, and silphium root.

Serves 4
1¾ lb. (800 g.) mixed crustaceans and mollusks (shelled weight)
pepper to taste
1 Tbs. total, lovage and cumin
1 garlic clove, pressed for its juice
pork caul fat

Scald the crustaceans in boiling water, remove the meat from the shell, and mince or grind in a mortar. Season with the pepper, herbs, and juice from the garlic clove (in place of the silphium root). Form the mixture into pat-ties. I suggest wrapping them in caul fat so they do not fall apart (see p. 90). Boil them in water or fry them, if you prefer, in a bit of olive oil and minced parsley.

LOBSTER PATTIES

(Apicius 401)

Locusta. Esicia de cauda eius sic facies: Folium nocivum prius demes et elixas, deinde pulpam concides, cum li-quamine, pipere et ovis esicia formabis.

Lobster: Make patties from the tail thus: First remove the bitter intestine and boil, then chop the meat and form pat-ties with *garum*, pepper, and eggs.

Serves 4
2 lobster tails (3 lb. [1½ kg.] total)
2 Tbs. *garum*
2 eggs
pepper to taste
pork caul fat

If you decide to break the bank and try this recipe, scald the lobster tails, extract the meat, and grind it. Beat the eggs, add them to the lobster meat along with the *garum* and pepper, and mix well. Form small patties and fry them in a bit of olive oil; or wrap them in caul fat (see p. 90) and fry them without oil.

Lampridius credited the gluttonous emperor Elagabalus with the invention of various fish patties: "He was the first to prepare patties with the meat of fish, oysters and other shellfish, lobsters, prawns, and squills" (*Historia Augusta, Heliogabalus* 19).

MONKFISH *PATELLA*
(APICIUS 145)

Patellam esiciatam de tursione: Enervabis, concides minutatim. Teres piper, ligusticum, origanum, petroselinum, coriandrum, cuminum, rutae bacam, mentem siccam, ipsum tursionem. Isicia deformabis. [Adicies] vinum, liquamen, oleum, coques. Coctum in patellam collocabis. Ius in ea facies: piper, ligusticum, satureiam, cepam, vinum, liquamen, oleum. [In] patellam pones ut coquatur. Ovis obligabis, piper asparges et inferes.

A *patella* of *tursio* patties: Clean and bone, and chop finely. Grind pepper, lovage, oregano, parsley, coriander, cumin, rue berries, dried mint, and the *tursio*. Form patties. [Add] wine, *garum*, and oil, and cook. When it is cooked, put in a pan. Make a sauce for it as follows: pepper, lovage, savory, onion, wine, *garum*, and oil. Put in the pan and cook. Thicken with eggs, sprinkle with pepper, and serve.

Serves 4
2 lb. (1 kg.) monkfish steak
ample aromatic herbs (choose from among lovage, oregano, parsley, coriander, cumin, rue berries, and mint)
For the sauce:
pepper to taste
1 Tbs. total, lovage and savory
3–4 large onions or shallots, minced
½ cup white wine
1 Tbs. *garum*
1 Tbs. olive oil
1 egg, beaten

Though we are not sure what type of fish *tursio* was, it probably belonged to the family of sharks. Modern Italian cooking does not commonly use shark, although certain other cuisines include it as a specialty (for example, the Spanish *tiburòn*). Here I suggest using monkfish instead.

Prepare the fish steak for cooking: Arrange the herbs on the bottom of a fish kettle, place the steak over them, and close tightly. Begin the cooking process by steaming over a burner, then place the kettle in the oven. When the fish is done, remove, grind the meat and form patties.

Meanwhile, cook the sauce consisting of the pepper, lovage, savory, minced onion, wine, *garum,* and olive oil in a wide pan. When the ingredients have blended, place the fish patties in the sauce and cook for another 10 minutes. Just before serving, thicken the sauce with the egg and sprinkle with pepper.

I have adapted the recipe in the above manner because I find that the initial steaming renders the fish meat easier to use in patties.

FRICASSEE À LA TERENTIUS
(APICIUS 166)

Minutal Terentinum: Concides in caccabum albamen de porris minutatim, adicies oleum, liquamen, cocturam, esiciola valde minuta, et sic temperas ut tenerum sit. Esicium Terentinum facies—inter esicia confectionem invenies. Ius tale facies: piper, ligusticum, origanum, fricabis, suffundes liquamen, ius de suo sibi, vino et passo temperabis. Mittes in caccabum. Cum ferbuerit, tractam confringes, obligas. Piper aspergis et inferes.

Fricassee à la Terentius: In a pot finely chop the white of leeks; add oil, *garum,* cooking broth, very small patties of ground meat, and mix so that it becomes smooth. Make patties à la Terentius according to the recipe that you will find in the book on patties. Make the following sauce: grind pepper, lovage, and oregano, moisten with *garum* and cooking broth, mix with wine and *passum.* Put in the pot. When it boils, thicken with crumbled *tracta.* Sprinkle with pepper and serve.

Terentius is also mentioned in Apicius 339 (pp. 117–18). The recipe for patties à la Terentius is no longer included in Apicius, one indication of the manual's alterations over the centuries. You can nonetheless prepare them by making patties of fish meat, such as those in the previous recipe. Also, you can use boiled couscous or semolina (not too thick) instead of the pieces of *tracta* prescribed in the recipe.

The following Lebanese recipe is one of many popular dishes generically called *kibbé,* consisting of ground fish or meat cooked together with vegetables and couscous:

Fish *Kibbé*

Serves 4
2 lb. (1 kg.) umbrina (or other fish)
1½ cups couscous
¾ lb. (400 g.) minced onion
salt and pepper to taste
4 small bunches fresh coriander (or 2 Tbs. dried coriander)
1 Tbs. grated orange peel (or a pinch of saffron)
½ cup olive oil

Clean and bone the fish, and grind its meat in a mortar. Soak the couscous for 30 minutes, then wash it and squeeze out the excess water. Mince with a bit of salt. Grind the onion together with salt, pepper, coriander, and orange peel in a mortar. Mix this thoroughly with the fish and couscous. Grease a pan or baking dish, pour in the mixture, and smooth the surface. Then make a series of crosshatched incisions on the surface with a knife to produce a diamond pattern. Pour the olive oil over this and bake in a hot oven (400°F.) for 30–40 minutes. Serve with arrack.

FRICASSEE À LA APICIUS
(APICIUS 167)

Minutal Apicianum: Oleum, liquamen, vinum, porrum capitatum, mentam, pisciculos, esiciola minuta, testiculos caponum, glandulas porcellinas, haec omnia in se coquantur. Teres piper, ligusticum, coriandrum viridem vel semen, suffundis liquamen, adicies mellis modicum et ius de suo sibi, vino et melle temperabis. Facies ut ferveat. Cum ferbuerit, tractam confringes, obligas, coagitas, piper aspargis et inferes.

Fricassee à la Apicius: Oil, *garum*, wine, bulb of leek, mint, small fish, very small meat patties, rooster testicles, sweetbread of suckling pig. Cook everything together. Grind pepper, lovage, and fresh coriander or coriander seeds; moisten with *garum*, add a bit of honey and cooking broth, and mix with wine and honey. Bring to a boil. When it boils, thicken with crumbled *tracta*, stir, sprinkle with pepper, and serve.

Serves 4
7 oz. (200 g.) ground meat of your choice
8 small fish
1 sweetbread
10 oz. (300 g.) variety meats
3–4 leeks
1 bunch fresh mint
1 Tbs. olive oil
1 tsp. wine
1 tsp. *garum*
For the sauce:
pepper to taste
1 Tbs. total, lovage and coriander (or coriander seeds)
1 cup dry white wine
1 tsp. *garum*
1 Tbs. honey
3 oz. (100 g.) boiled couscous or crumbled coarse bread

This complicated recipe is the ancient ancestor of the Spanish *paella,* with its mixture of meat and fish; but here, instead of rice, we have crumbled dried dough (*tracta*), a frequent addition in these nutritious dishes of meat, fish, or vegetables.

Prepare the meat and fish of your choice (including small patties of ground meat, small mullet or anchovies, the sweetbread and rooster testicles or other variety meats you may prefer). Finely chop the leeks and the fresh mint, then sauté them in a pan with the olive oil, wine, and *garum.* When they have become soft, add the meat and fish and continue to fry for a few minutes.

Prepare the sauce with the pepper, lovage, coriander, wine, and a bit of the cooking broth, flavored with the *garum* and honey. Add this to the pan. Total cooking time to this point should be around 15 minutes. Then add the boiled couscous or pieces of bread and cook a further 15 minutes before serving.

SOLE *PATINA*
(Apicius 155)

Patina solearum: Soleas battues et curatas compones in patina. Adicies oleum, liquamen, vinum. Dum coquitur, teres piper, ligusticum, origanum, fricabis, suffundes ius, ova cruda, et unum corpus facies. Super soleas refundes, lento igni coques. Cum duxerit, piper asparges et inferes.

A *patina* of soles: Place the cleaned and beaten soles in a pan. Add oil, *garum*, and wine. While it cooks, grind pepper, lovage, and oregano together. Moisten with cooking broth and raw eggs and mix so that it is homogeneous. Pour over the soles and cook over a low fire. When it has set, sprinkle with pepper and serve.

Serves 4
4 soles of around 7 oz. (200 g.) each
1 Tbs. olive oil
½ cup dry white wine
1 tsp. *garum*
For the sauce:
4 eggs
pepper to taste
1 tsp. total, lovage and oregano

Scale the soles, remove the skins, and beat the fish briefly and very delicately with a meat pounder. Place them in a single layer in a pan with the olive oil, wine, and *garum* and poach over a medium heat. Meanwhile, beat the eggs with the pepper, lovage, and oregano. When the soles are almost done, pour this mixture over them and bake in a hot oven (400°F.) for around 15–20 minutes. You can also complete the cooking on the stove, in which case 10 minutes should be sufficient.

›IX‹

VEGETABLES

Leeks
Whenever you have eaten slices of strong-smelling
       Tarentine leeks,
you must kiss only through sealed lips!

                     (Martial 13, 18)

Lettuce
Lettuce once closed the dinners of our ancestors;
tell me, why today does it open ours?

                     (Martial 13, 14)

Turnips
These turnips I give you, which enjoy the winter cold,
Romulus is accustomed to eat in heaven.

                     (Martial 13, 16)

Squash
Caecilius, the Atreus of squash,
slices and cuts them into a thousand pieces
as if they were the sons of Thyestes.
You will eat them first as appetizer;
he will serve them in the first and second courses,
and place them before you again in the third;
then he will prepare dessert from them.
And afterward his baker will use them
to make insipid focaccias. . . .

                     (Martial 11, 31)

Vegetables (including salad greens, beans, and roots) were always present on the Roman table. In earliest times they were served at the end of the meal; while in the Imperial period they appeared as appetizers in banquets or as side dishes with everyday meals of meat or cheese, or sometimes they were integrated into single-course dishes.

The recipes in this chapter are primarily suited as accompaniments to the main course. Other vegetable recipes, especially those specifically described in the ancient sources as appetizers, are included in chapter 5. There are also several recipes in chapter 7 for single-course dishes that contain large quantities of vegetables, such as Chicken with Squash (Apicius 80, pp. 102–3) and Duck with Turnips (Apicius 214, pp. 110–11).

BEETS WITH MUSTARD
(APICIUS 98)

Betas elixas: Ex sinapi, oleo modico et aceto bene inferuntur.

Boiled beets: They are served nicely with mustard, a bit of oil, and vinegar.

Serves 4
2 large beets
1 Tbs. prepared mustard
2 Tbs. olive oil
1 Tbs. vinegar

Boil the beets, peel them, and slice. Cover with a sauce made with the mustard, olive oil, and vinegar.

Jacques André translates *betas* in this recipe as beet greens, which work equally well.

FRIED CARROTS
(APICIUS 122)

Carotae frictae oenogaro inferuntur.

Fried carrots are served with *oenogarum*.

Serves 4
2 lb. (1 kg.) baby carrots
2 cups white wine
1 Tbs. *garum*

Cut the carrots into thin strips, fry them, and cover with the mixture of wine and *garum*. Serve hot.

CARROTS WITH CUMIN SAUCE
(APICIUS 124)

Aliter: Carotas elixatas concisas in cuminato oleo modico coques et inferes. Cuminatum conciliorum facies.

Another recipe: Boil the carrots, cut them up, cook in cumin sauce with a little oil, and serve. Make the cumin sauce for shellfish.

Boil the carrots until they are just slightly undercooked. Slice them into rounds and return them to the pot. Add the cumin sauce described on page 44 (Apicius 31), and heat until the carrots are done.

CUCUMBER SALAD
(APICIUS 82)

Cucumeres rasos: Sive ex liquamine, sive ex oenogaro; sine ructu et gravitudine teneriores senties.

Peeled cucumbers: [Season them] either with *garum* or with *oenogarum;* you will find them more tender, and they will not cause belching or heaviness.

Wash the cucumbers and peel them so that they are more easily digested. Slice and season with *garum* or *oenogarum*. As with all salads, the quantities of the ingredients vary according to individual taste. The Romans also ate boiled or fried cucumbers, for which the seasoning works equally well.

ARTICHOKES WITH EGG
(APICIUS 112)

Carduos: Liquamine, oleo et ovis concisis.

Cardoons: *Garum,* oil, and chopped [hard-boiled] eggs.

Serves 4
8 artichokes
½ cup olive oil
1 Tbs. *garum*
4 hard-boiled eggs, chopped

In this recipe and the following two, the word *carduos* (thistled cardoon plants) can be interpreted for our purposes as artichokes. See the brief discussion of artichokes following the recipe for Lentils with Artichoke Bottoms, Apicius 183, page 154.

Remove the outer leaves from the artichokes, cut off the spiny tips, and remove the chokes if present. Dissolve the *garum* in the olive oil, and add to a deep pan containing sufficient water to cover the artichokes. Arrange the artichokes upright side by side in the pan, and close. Boil until cooked. When they are done, remove and sprinkle each with a spoonful of chopped boiled egg.

ARTICHOKES WITH HERBS
(APICIUS 113)

Aliter carduos: Rutam, mentam, coriandrum, feniculum, omnia viridia teres. Addes piper, ligusticum, mel, liquamen et oleum.

Another recipe for cardoons: Grind rue, mint, coriander, and fennel, all fresh. Add pepper, lovage, honey, *garum*, and oil.

Serves 4
8 artichokes
2 Tbs. total, rue, mint, coriander, fennel, and lovage
pepper to taste
1 Tbs. *garum*
1 tsp. honey
½ cup olive oil

Prepare the artichokes for cooking as in the preceding recipe. Mix the herbs and pepper with the *garum* and honey, and put some of this mixture inside the top of each artichoke. Place the artichokes upright in a deep pan with a cup of water and the olive oil, cover, and cook over a low flame until done.

This recipe is an ancestor of artichokes *alla romana*.

ARTICHOKES WITH HERB SAUCE
(APICIUS 114)

Aliter carduos elixos: Piper, cuminum, liquamen et oleum.

Another recipe for boiled cardoons: Pepper, cumin, *garum*, and oil.

Prepare the artichokes for cooking as in Apicius 112, above, then boil them in salted water (add a bit of lemon juice to maintain their color). Arrange them on a platter and serve with a sauce made from the ingredients listed in the recipe. Measure the *garum* to taste, but not less than 1 tablespoon per ½ cup of olive oil.

CELERY PUREE
(APICIUS 104)

Olus molle: Apium coques ex aqua nitrata, exprimes et concides minutatim. In mortario teres piper, ligusticum, origanum, cepam, vinum, liquamen et oleum. Coques in pultario, et sic apio commisces.

Vegetable puree: Cook celery in water with natron, squeeze out the excess liquid, and finely chop. In a mortar grind pepper, lovage, oregano, onion, wine, *garum*, and oil. Cook in a porridge pot, and mix with the celery.

Serves 4
2 large bunches celery
pinch of baking soda
2 red onions
pinch of pepper
½ Tbs. total, lovage and oregano
1 cup white wine
1 Tbs. *garum*
1 Tbs. olive oil

Boil the celery in water with the baking soda. Drain thoroughly and chop it into a pulp or pass it through a vegetable grinder.

Mince the onions and mix together with the pepper and herbs. Put this in a pot and add the wine, *garum*, and olive oil. Boil. When the onions are cooked, add the celery, mix to blend the flavors, and serve.

The addition of a pinch of natron (a naturally occurring combination of baking soda and other salts) to the cooking water kept the vegetable from discoloring, a factor the Romans considered very important.

LETTUCE PUREE WITH ONIONS
(Apicius 105)

Aliter olus molle ex foliis lactucarum cum cepis: Coques ex aqua nitrata, expressa concides minutatim. In mortario teres piper, ligusticum, apii semen, mentam siccam, cepam, liquamen, oleum et vinum.

Another vegetable puree of lettuce leaves with onions: Cook in water with natron, squeeze, and chop finely. In a mortar grind pepper, lovage, celery seeds, dried mint, onion, *garum*, oil, and wine.

Serves 4
4–5 large bunches or heads of lettuce
1 tsp. baking soda
pinch of pepper
1 Tbs. lovage, celery seeds, and mint
2 sweet red onions (or 4 baby onions), minced
1 Tbs. *garum*
½ cup olive oil
1 Tbs. white wine

Boil the lettuce in water with a teaspoon of baking soda. Drain thoroughly, gently squeezing out the excess moisture, and chop finely.

Combine the pepper, herbs, and minced onion (be sure to choose sweet onions or use baby onions or shallots, since they are to be eaten raw), and mix with the *garum*, olive oil, and wine. Put the lettuce puree in a salad bowl, pour the sauce over, and serve.

CONCICLA WITH FAVA BEANS
(Apicius 195)

Concicla cum faba: Coques. Teres piper, ligusticum, cuminum, coriandrum viridem, suffundis liquamen, vino et liquamine temperabis, mittis in caccabum, adicies oleum. Lento igni ferveat et inferes.

Concicla with fava beans: Cook. Grind pepper, lovage, cumin, fresh coriander; moisten with *garum*, mix with wine and *garum*. Put into a pot, add oil. Cook over a low fire and serve.

Serves 4
4½ lb. (2 kg.) fresh unshelled fava beans
½ cup wine
1 Tbs. *garum*
1 Tbs. olive oil
1 Tbs. total, lovage, cumin, and coriander
pinch of pepper

I have interpreted this *concicla* as a puree. It requires fresh fava beans, which may be difficult to find. Shell the beans, boil them, drain them, and pass them through a vegetable grinder. Prepare the sauce from the remaining ingredients. Put the puree in a pan, season with the sauce, and cook until any excess liquid has evaporated.

SQUASH PUREE
(APICIUS 79)

Cucurbitas frictas tritas: Piper, ligusticum, cuminum, origanum, cepam, vinum, liquamen et oleum. Amulo obligabis in patina et inferes.

Fried chopped squash: Pepper, lovage, cumin, oregano, onion, wine, *garum,* and oil. Thicken with starch in the pan and serve.

Serves 4
2 lb. (1 kg.) squash
pepper to taste
1 Tbs. total, lovage, cumin, and oregano
1 onion, minced
½ cup wine
½ cup *garum*
1 Tbs. olive oil
1 Tbs. semolina (if needed to thicken)

Peel the squash, cut it into pieces, and "fry" it. In Apicius frying does not necessarily mean cooking in oil; it can also mean simply cooking without liquid. In this case the best method is to bake it in the oven until it is quite soft. Then pass it through a vegetable grinder and season it with a sauce made by mixing together the remaining ingredients.

PEA OR FAVA BEAN PUREE A LA VITELLIUS
(APICIUS 190)

Pisam Vitellianam sive fabam: Pisam coques, lias. Teres piper, ligusticum, gingiber et super condimenta mittis vitella ovorum quae dura coxeris, mellis unc. III, liquamen, vinum et acetum. Haec omnia mittis in caccabum et condimenta quae trivisti, adiecto oleo ponis ut ferveat. Condies pisam, lias si aspera fuerit, melle mittis et inferes.

Peas or fava beans à la Vitellius: Cook the peas and press them smooth. Grind pepper, lovage, and ginger, and over these condiments put the yolks of hard-boiled eggs, 3 *unciae* of honey, *garum*, wine, and vinegar. Put all this in a pot together with the ground condiments, add oil, and bring to a boil. Season the peas, smooth out any lumps, add honey, and serve.

Serves 4
3 lb. (1½ kg.) fresh unshelled peas (or 4½ lb. [2 kg.] fresh
  unshelled fava beans)
pepper to taste
1 tsp. each, lovage and ginger
3 hard-boiled egg yolks
1 Tbs. *garum*
1 cup wine
1 tsp. honey (optional)
1 Tbs. vinegar (optional)

Shell the fresh peas or fava beans, boil them, then drain and pass through a vegetable grinder. For the sauce: Mix the pepper, lovage, and ginger with the egg yolks, *garum*, and wine. Heat in a casserole, then add the puree and heat further until the flavors blend. You can also add the honey and vinegar if you desire; the Romans believed these served to make vegetables more digestible.

Both this recipe and the next carry the name of the emperor Vitellius (reigned A.D. 69), another noted gourmand who liked to create new dishes. These two could have been either created by or dedicated to him.

PEAS OR FAVA BEANS À LA VITELLIUS
(Apicius 194)

Pisam sive fabam Vitellianam: Pisam sive fabam coques. Cum despumaverit, mittis porrum, coriandrum et flores malvarum. Dum coquitur, teres piper, ligusticum, origanum, feniculi semen, suffundis liquamen et vinum, [mittis] in caccabum, adicies oleum. Cum ferbuerit, agitas. Oleum viridem insuper mittis et inferes.

Peas or fava beans à la Vitellius: Cook the peas or beans. When they produce a froth, add leeks, coriander, and mallow flowers. While this cooks, grind pepper, lovage, oregano, and fennel seeds; moisten with *garum* and wine. [Put] in a pot, and add oil. When it boils, stir. Pour green oil over and serve.

Serves 4
3 lb. (1½ kg.) fresh unshelled peas (or 4½ lb. [2 kg.] fresh
  unshelled fava beans)
2 leeks
2 Tbs. total, coriander, mallow flowers, lovage, oregano, and
  fennel seeds
pepper to taste
1 Tbs. *garum*
1 cup wine
olive oil to taste

In contrast to the preceding recipe, here the beans or peas are not ground into a puree, but rather seasoned with a sauce after they have been boiled.

Shell the fresh peas or fava beans and boil in salted water. When they start to produce a froth, drain them and place them in a clean pot.

Chop the leeks, then add the various herbs and pepper and moisten with the *garum* and wine. Pour this sauce over the beans, and add a bit of the olive oil. Bring to a boil, then pour into a serving bowl, add another touch of olive oil, and serve.

Interestingly enough, in Rome fava beans were tabu for the chief priest of Jove (*flamen Dialis*), and among the Greeks these beans were similarly forbidden to the disciples of Pythagoras.

FRIED SQUASH
(Apicius 77)

Cucurbitas frictas: Oenogaro simplici et pipere.

Fried squash: [Season with] plain *oenogarum* and pepper.

Peel 2 lb. (1 kg.) of squash (serves 4) and cut into thin slices. Fry in olive oil at a high heat so that the squash does not soak up too much of the oil. Place on a serving dish and season with *oenogarum* and pepper.

This recipe is similar to the following, which also mixes sweet and salty flavors:

Regional Italian Recipe
(Sicily)
Sicilian Fried Squash

Prepare the squash and fry them as in the recipe above. Remove the squash from the pan, pour out all but a small amount of the oil, replace the squash, and set over a low heat. Sprinkle with a tablespoon of vinegar, then add salt, a tablespoon of sugar, and a bit of minced fresh mint. Steep and serve.

SQUASH ALEXANDRIAN STYLE
(Apicius 75)

Cucurbitas more Alexandrino: Elixatas cucurbitas exprimis, sale asparges, in patina compones. Teres piper, cuminum, coriandri semen, mentam viridem, laseris radicem, suffundes acetum. Adicies cariotam, nucleum, teres, melle, aceto, liquamine, defrito et oleo temperabis, et cucurbitas perfundes. Cum ferbuerint, piper asparges et inferes.

Squash Alexandrian style: Squeeze the excess water from boiled squash, sprinkle with salt, and place in a pan. Grind pepper, cumin, coriander seeds, fresh mint, and silphium root. Moisten with vinegar. Add dates and pine nuts; grind. Mix with honey, vinegar, *garum*, *defrutum*, and oil, and pour over the squash. When they are boiled, sprinkle with pepper and serve.

Serves 4
2 lb. (1 kg.) squash
salt and pepper to taste
6–7 pitted dates, coarsely chopped
1 handful of pine nuts
1 Tbs. total, cumin, mint, and coriander seeds
2 garlic cloves, pressed for their juice
1 tsp. honey
1 Tbs. vinegar
½ cup *garum*
½ cup olive oil

Cut the squash into large pieces and boil in water; or, better still, bake it in the oven so that it does not become too soggy. Put the cooked squash in a pan and sprinkle with salt. Prepare the sauce by grinding together the remaining ingredients (the garlic juice replaces the silphium); mix with the squash and heat. When it reaches a boil, remove from the heat, sprinkle with pepper, and serve.

If you make your own *garum* and include must as an ingredient, the *defrutum* (reduced must) can be omitted, as it has been here. Also, the quantity of the *garum*-olive oil mixture can be reduced according to taste.

BROCCOLI WITH HERB SAUCE
(APICIUS 87)

Cimas: Cuminum, salem, vinum vetus et oleum. Si voles, addes piper et ligusticum, mentam, rutam, coriandrum, folia coliclorum, liquamen, vinum, oleum.

Cabbage sprouts: Cumin, salt, aged wine, and oil. If you wish, add pepper and lovage, mint, rue, coriander, cabbage leaves, *garum*, wine, and oil.

Serves 4
2 lb. (1 kg.) broccoli (or broccoli rab)
For the basic sauce:
  1 Tbs. cumin
  salt to taste (omit if adding *garum*)
  ½ cup strong red wine
  ½ cup olive oil
For the second sauce, add:
  2–3 leaves head cabbage or savoy cabbage
  1 Tbs. total, lovage, mint, rue, and coriander
  1 Tbs. *garum*
  pepper to taste

Boil the broccoli (a member of the cabbage family) in salted water and drain when cooked. Place in a serving dish and add the sauce of your choice. For the basic sauce, simply mix together the cumin, salt, wine, and olive oil; for the second sauce, finely chop the cabbage leaves, mix with the remaining ingredients listed, and add to the original mixture. Be sure to omit the salt if you prepare this latter version because of the presence of *garum*.

BROCCOLI WITH SEMOLINA OR COUSCOUS
(APICIUS 92)

Aliter: Coliculis conditis ut supra superfundes alicam elixam cum nucleis et uva passa; piper asparges.

Another recipe: Over the young cabbage, seasoned as above, pour boiled spelt with pine nuts and raisins; sprinkle with pepper.

The "as above" in this recipe refers to Apicius 89, wherein the sauce consists of *garum*, olive oil, wine, and cumin, with a garnish of pepper, chopped leeks, cumin, and fresh coriander. Use the quantities in Apicius 87, above, as a guide.

You can use 1 cup of either semolina or couscous to prepare this recipe. The semolina should be boiled in sufficient water so that it is not too thick; add a handful of pine nuts and one of raisins that have been plumped in a bit of wine. Pour this cooked mixture over 2 pounds (1 kilo) of the boiled and seasoned broccoli. Mix and sprinkle with pepper.

Couscous, on the other hand, should be first soaked in water and then boiled with the pine nuts and plumped raisins. Pour it over the seasoned broccoli, mix well so that the flavors blend, and sprinkle with pepper.

BOILED LEEK SALAD
(APICIUS 93)

Porros maturos fieri: Pugnum salis, aquam et oleum mixtum facies et ibi coques et eximes. Cum oleo, liquamine, mero et inferes.

For large leeks: Mix a handful of salt with water and oil, and in this cook [the leeks] and remove them. [Season] with oil, *garum*, and pure wine, and serve.

This is a simple but flavorful recipe. Boil the leeks, slice them into rounds, and cover with a sauce made of olive oil, *garum*, and wine. The quantities of the ingredients may vary according to taste; if you like the strong, salty flavor of *garum*, feel free to use it generously. I find red wine is more successful here than white.

LEEKS WITH FAVA BEANS
(APICIUS 96)

Aliter porros: [Si] in aquam elixati erunt, fabae nondum conditae plurimum admisce conditurae in qua eos manducaturus es.

Another recipe for leeks: [If] they have been boiled in water, add a large quantity of unseasoned fava beans to the condiment in which you will eat them.

Boil the leeks in water, drain, and place in a serving bowl. Season them with the sauce described in the previous recipe, and add cooked or raw fava beans. You can also add fresh minced aromatic herbs if you wish.

PEAS IN HERB SAUCE
(APICIUS 186)

Pisa: Pisam coques. Cum despumaverit, porrum, coriandrum et cuminum supra mittis. Teres piper, ligusticum, careum, anetum, ocimum viridem, suffundis liquamen, vino et liquamine temperabis, facies ut ferveat. Cum ferbuerit, agitabis. Si quid defuerit, mittis et inferes.

Peas: Cook the peas. When they produce a froth, put in leek, coriander, and cumin. Grind pepper, lovage, caraway, dill, and fresh basil. Moisten with *garum*, mix with wine and *garum*, and bring to a boil. When it boils, stir. If anything should be lacking, add it, and serve.

Serves 4
3 lb. (1½ kg.) fresh peas in the shell
1 leek
1 Tbs. total, cumin and coriander
1 Tbs. olive oil
For the sauce:
pepper to taste
1 Tbs. total, lovage, caraway, dill, and basil
1 tsp. *garum*
1 Tbs. wine

Shell the fresh peas and boil them, leaving them slightly undercooked. Drain and set aside. Meanwhile, prepare the sauce by mixing together the ingredients listed above. Then finely chop the leek and sauté it in the olive oil with the cumin and coriander. Pour the peas over this and cover with the sauce. Mix over the heat (be careful not to overcook the peas) and serve.

This is the only recipe in all of *De re coquinaria* that uses basil, perhaps the most common aromatic herb in modern-day Italian cuisine.

STRING BEANS AND CHICK PEAS
(Apicius 208)

Faseoli virides et cicer ex sale, cumino, oleo et mero modico inferuntur.

Green beans and chick peas are served with salt, cumin, oil, and a bit of pure wine.

Serves 4
10 oz. (300 g.) string beans
7 oz. (200 g.) dried chick peas
1 tsp. cumin
2 Tbs. olive oil
1 Tbs. strong red wine
salt and pepper to taste

This recipe does not clearly state if the sauce is for beans and chick peas served together or if it should be used for them separately. In any case, the two are quite compatible, so you can try it this way:

Soak the chick peas overnight, then boil them. The string beans take little time to cook and can be boiled afterward. Then place both legumes in a salad bowl and dress them with the wine, oil, and cumin. Salt and pepper to taste.

The *faseoli virides* were similar to our string beans. Romans often ate young and tender beans and peas boiled in the pod, just as we do with string beans. The *faseoli* could also be left to mature for their beans, but these were not the same as the ones we eat today, which largely come from species of American origin.

LENTILS WITH ARTICHOKE BOTTOMS
(Apicius 183)

Lenticula ex sfondilis sive fondilis: Accipies caccabum mundum. Adicies in mortarium piper, cuminum, semen coriandri, mentam, rutam, puleium, fricabis, suffundis acetum, adicies mel, liquamen et defritum, aceto temperabis, reexinanies in caccabo. Sfondilos elixatos teres et mittis ut ferveat. Cum bene ferbuerit, obligas, adicies in boletari oleum viridem.

Lentils with cardoon bottoms: Take a clean pot. Put pepper, cumin, coriander seeds, mint, rue, and pennyroyal in a mortar; grind, moisten with vinegar, add honey, *garum*, and *defrutum*, mix with vinegar, and pour into the pot. Grind boiled cardoon bottoms and bring to a boil. When it has boiled well, thicken; add green oil to the serving dish.

Serves 4
10 oz. (300 g.) lentils
8 large artichoke bottoms, fresh or frozen
2 tsp. olive oil
For the sauce:
pepper to taste
1 Tbs. total, cumin, coriander seeds, mint, rue, and pennyroyal
1 Tbs. vinegar
1 tsp. honey
1 tsp. *garum*
1 Tbs. *defrutum*

Boil and drain the lentils, and set aside. Boil the artichoke bottoms. Place them whole in a pot   I find that the result is better than grinding them, as is indicated in Apicius. Prepare the sauce by mixing together the ingredients listed (a representative sampling of the herbs is sufficient), and use this to season the lentils. Add the lentils to the artichokes and heat to blend the flavors. Add a touch of olive oil and serve.

All the lentil-based recipes in Apicius mention them in the title but neglect them completely thereafter. We may nonetheless assume that the lentils are already soaked, drained, and boiled, as is perhaps hinted in the curious opening instruction to use a clean pot. The recipe then goes on to describe the preparation of the remaining ingredients—in this case the artichokes and sauce, in the next recipe the chestnuts and sauce.

The Romans actually had wild artichokes (or cardoons) and not the refined vegetable we eat today, which is the result of selective breeding begun in the fifteenth century.

The *boletarium* in this recipe and the next was a plate used primarily for serving mushrooms. Though perhaps less noble, these recipes are very good just the same.

LENTILS WITH CHESTNUTS
(Apicius 184)

Lenticulam de castaneis: Accipies caccabum novum, et castaneas purgatas diligenter mittis. Adicies aquam et nitrum modice, facies ut coquatur. Cum coquitur, mittis in mortario piper, cuminum, semen coriandri, mentam, rutam, laseris radicem, puleium, fricabis, suffundis acetum, mel, liquamen, aceto temperabis et super castaneas coctas refundis. Adicies oleum, facies ut ferveat. Cum bene ferbuerit, tutunclabis (ut in mortario teres). Gustas. Si quid deest, addes. Cum in boletar miseris, addes oleum viridem.

Lentils with chestnuts: Take a clean pot, and put in carefully shelled chestnuts. Add water and a bit of natron; cook. While this cooks, put pepper, cumin, coriander seeds, mint, rue, silphium root, and pennyroyal in a mortar; grind. Moisten with vinegar, honey, and *garum*. Mix with vinegar and pour over the cooked chestnuts. Add oil and bring to a boil. When it has boiled well, grind as if in a mortar. Taste. If anything is lacking, add it. When you have put it into a serving dish, add green oil.

Serves 4
14 oz. (400 g.) lentils
14 oz. (400 g.) shelled chestnuts
1 tsp. baking soda
For the sauce:
  pepper to taste
  1 Tbs. total, cumin, coriander seeds, mint, rue, and pennyroyal
  1 garlic clove, pressed for its juice
  1 Tbs. vinegar
  1 tsp. honey
  1 Tbs. *garum*

This is probably a chestnut puree to add to boiled lentils. Boil the chestnuts in water with the baking soda. Meanwhile, prepare the sauce by mixing together the ingredients listed. Pass the chestnuts through a vegetable grinder and mix with the sauce. Then pour this over the lentils and mix. Heat to blend the flavors and serve.

›X‹

DESSERTS

MENSA SECUNDA

The pastry cook
His hand prepares you thousands of sweet forms;
the frugal honeybee toils for him alone.

(Martial 14, 222)

Fine flour
You can list neither all the virtues of fine flour, nor all its
uses,
how often it serves the baker and the cook.

(Martial 13, 10)

Pomegranates and azaroles
The azaroles and pomegranates that we give you do not
come from Libyan branches;
they come from the trees of Nomentum.

(Martial 13, 42)

The Roman banquet ended with a rich course of sweets, fresh or dried
fruit, salted focaccias, and sometimes sausages or cheese. Those dessert
recipes surviving from the ancient Romans come from Cato and Apicius,
and the contrast in epoch and intended readership is great. Cato's recipes
are simple, economical desserts formulated for a farmer and his family.
Their three principal ingredients—flour, cheese, and honey—are used in
various imaginative combinations, which we can occasionally enrich with
the addition of eggs. The delicate desserts proposed by Apicius, on the
other hand, were created to satisfy the demanding palates of more sophisticated diners. In *De re coquinaria* we find many appealing recipes for such
things as puddings and sweet egg-based dishes.

With regard to cheeses, we can only guess what the various types were like. Nonetheless, if you offer goat or sheep cheese, such as small pear-shaped *scamorzine,* either grilled or roasted, or smoked *scamorze,* you will certainly come reasonably close to the original flavors.

In chapter 11 you will also find suggestions for stuffing dates and figs and for seasoning olives. They may be further inspiration as you prepare this final course for your meal.

MUSTACEI
(CATO 121)

Mustaceos sic facito: Farinae siligineae modium unum musto conspargito. Anesum, cuminum, adipis. P.II, casei libram, et de virga lauri deradito, eadem addito, et ubi definxeris, lauri folia subtus addito, coques.

Prepare *mustacei* thus: Moisten a *modius* of fine flour with must. Add anise, cumin, 2 *librae* of fat, 1 *libra* of cheese, and grated bay twig. When you have shaped them, place bay leaves beneath; cook.

For each ¾ cup flour:
1 Tbs. lard
½ Tbs. ricotta
1 tsp. total, anise and cumin
1 small piece of bay bark, grated
ca. 1 Tbs. must (to make a soft dough similar to that for a pie crust)
bay leaves

Cut the flour with the lard and ricotta; add the anise and cumin, and, if you can find it, the bay bark. Add enough must to form a ball (remember that flour doesn't always absorb the same amount of liquid). Form small flat focaccias from this dough; or roll out the dough to ¼ inch thickness and cut into shapes. Place 1 or 2 bay leaves beneath each one, and cook on a griddle over a low flame, turning them so they cook evenly on both sides.

The name of this dessert survives in cookies that are still made in various regions of Italy: *mustazzît* in Lombardy, *mostaccioli* in Calabria, *mustazzola di Missina* in Sicily, and *mustazzueli* in Apulia. But curiously, the must has disappeared from all of them over the centuries.

SWEET BUNS WITH MUST
(APICIUS 297)

Aliter dulcia: Musteos Afros optimos rades et in lacte infundis. Cum biberint, in furnum mittis, ne arescant, modice. Eximes eos calidos, melle perfundis, compungis ut bibant. Piper aspergis et inferes.

Another sweet dish: Remove the crust from the finest African must cakes and soak them in milk. When they have absorbed it, put them in the oven, not too long, so they do not dry out. Remove them when they are hot, pour honey over them, and puncture them so they absorb it. Sprinkle with pepper and serve.

This is nearly identical to the French recipe for *petits pains perdus*, but without the egg. Bread from Alexandria was famous throughout the ancient world for its fine quality: apparently the Egyptians were the first to discover leavening and to make soft breads with it. Though we no longer have these special breads, we can successfully substitute soft rolls made with milk. To tinge them with the delicate flavor of must, I suggest you melt 1 tablespoon of honey in a cup of must over a moderate heat before pouring it over the bread. This quantity should be sufficient to cover 8 small rolls.

FRIED BREAD
(APICIUS 298)

Aliter dulcia: Siligineos rasos frangis et buccellas maiores facies. In lacte infundis, frigis in oleo, mel superfundis et inferes.

Another sweet dish: Remove the crust from fine wheat bread and break up into large pieces. Soak them in milk, fry in oil, pour honey over them, and serve.

This is an equally delicate variation of the previous recipe. Do not soak the bread too long in the milk, or it will absorb too much oil when frying. Fry the pieces in very hot oil and pour the honey over them immediately after they are removed.

FRIED CREAMED WHEAT

(APICIUS 301)

*Aliter dulcia: Accipies similam, coques in aqua calida ita
ut durissimam pultem facias, deinde in patellam expandis.
Cum refrixerit, concidis quasi dulcia et frigis in oleo optimo. Levas, perfundis mel, piper aspergis et inferes. Melius feceris, si lac pro aqua miseris.*

Another sweet dish: Take flour, cook in hot water so that
it becomes a very firm polenta, then spread it on a plate.
When it has cooled, cut it as for sweet cakes and fry in oil
of the finest quality. Remove, pour honey over, sprinkle
with pepper, and serve. You will do even better if you use
milk instead of water.

This recipe is similar to the fried creamed wheat cakes and fried pastry
cream, two of the most appetizing elements in the Italian *fritto misto*.
Sweetened, fried creamed wheat cakes are part of the Piedmontese version
(*fricia*), while fried pastry creams (a firmer version of *crème pâtissière*) can
be found in that of Emilia.

The following is a delicious recipe from Pellegrino Artusi (*La scienza in
cucina e l'arte di mangiar bene,* 1891) for comparison:

REGIONAL ITALIAN RECIPE
(Piedmont)
Fried Creamed Wheat Cakes

½ cup fine wheat semolina
1¼ cups milk
1 pat butter
3 Tbs. sugar
1 small piece of lemon peel
pinch of salt
2 eggs
bread crumbs
powdered sugar (optional)

Heat the milk with the butter, sugar, and lemon peel; when it begins to
boil, gradually pour in the semolina, stirring constantly. Add the salt and
break in one egg; mix. When the egg has blended in, take out the lemon
peel, remove the pan from the heat, and spread the mixture to the thickness of a finger over a buttered plate or floured surface. Cut into almond

shapes. Dip them in beaten egg, then in bread crumbs, and fry in oil. Sprinkle with powdered sugar if you prefer it sweeter. Serve alone or as an accompaniment to mixed fried meats.

EGG PUDDING
(Apicius 300)

Aliter dulcia: Piper, nucleos, mel, rutam et passum teres, cum lacte et tracta coques. Coagulum coque cum modicis ovis. Perfusum melle, [pipere] aspersum inferes.

Another sweet dish: Grind pepper, pine nuts, honey, rue, and *passum;* cook with milk and *tracta.* Cook to thicken with a few eggs. Pour honey over, sprinkle [with pepper], and serve.

Serves 4
3 eggs
3 Tbs. flour
1¾ cups milk
pepper to taste
2½ oz. (70–80 g.) pine nuts
1–2 Tbs. *passum*
4 tsp. honey

This is probably a hot egg pudding. I have prepared it as a kind of *crème pâtissière* (omitting the rue prescribed in Apicius) and found it delicious.

Beat the eggs in a bowl with the flour and milk. Add pepper and heat in a pan. Meanwhile, grind the pine nuts with the *passum* in a mortar. As soon as the egg mixture begins to boil, remove from the heat. Add the honey and the pine nut mixture. Resume cooking for approximately 15 minutes more over a low heat, stirring so that no lumps form. Pour into 1 large or 4 small individual bowls; add a teaspoon of honey and a pinch of pepper to each and serve.

A TASTE OF ANCIENT ROME

HONEY CUSTARD
(Apicius 302)

Tiropatinam: Accipies lac, adversus quod patinam aesti-mabis, temperabis lac cum melle quasi ad lactantia, ova quinque ad sextarium mittis, si ad eminam, ova tria. In lacte dissolvis ita ut unum corpus facias, in cumana colas et igni lento coques. Cum duxerit ad se, piper aspargis et inferes.

Cheese patina: Take milk, pour into a pan of appropriate size, mix the milk with honey as for a milk cream, and add 5 eggs for a *sextarius*, 3 eggs for a *hemina*. Mix into the milk so that it becomes homogeneous, filter into an earthenware pot, and cook over a low fire. When it has set, sprinkle with pepper and serve.

This is one of the few recipes in Apicius where the quantities of the ingredients are carefully specified: 5 eggs to 1 pint (½ liter) of milk, or 3 eggs to 1 cup (¼ liter). The result reminds one of the French *crème au bain-marie* or *oeufs au lait*. Many older cookbooks with similar recipes maintain the instruction to filter the mixture, often specifying that it be done through a piece of gauze.

SWEET *PATINAE*
(Apicius 129 and 143)

Patina versatilis: Nucleos, nuces fractas, torres eas et teres cum melle, pipere, liquamine, lacte et ovis. Olei modicum.

Patina versatilis vice dulci: Nucleos pineos, nuces fractas et purgatas, attorebis eas, teres cum melle, pipere, liquamine, lacte, ovis, modico mero et oleo.

An inverted patina: Roast pine nuts and chopped walnuts and grind with honey, pepper, and *garum;* [add] milk and eggs, and a bit of oil.

An inverted *patina* as a dessert: Roast pine nuts and shelled and chopped walnuts; grind with honey, pepper, and *garum;* [add] milk, eggs, and a bit of pure wine and oil.

Serves 4
4 eggs
7 oz. (200 g.) roasted walnuts and pine nuts, ground
1¾ cups milk
2 Tbs. wine (red or white as you prefer)
2 Tbs. olive oil
pinch of pepper
1½ Tbs. honey

These two *patinae* are almost identical: the only difference is in the addition of wine in the second recipe. I prefer to omit the *garum*. Mix the ingredients, pour into a nonstick pan without any additional oil, and fry on both sides before placing in a serving dish.

HONEY FRITTATA
(APICIUS 303)

Ova sfongia ex lacte: Ova quattuor, lactis eminam, olei unciam in se dissolvis ita ut unum corpus facias. In patellam subtilem adicies olei modicum, facies ut bulliat et adicies inpensam quam comparasti. Una parte cum fuerit coctum, in disco vertes, melle perfundis, piper aspargis et inferes.

Egg sponge with milk: Blend 4 eggs, a *hemina* of milk, and an *uncia* of oil to make a homogeneous mixture. Put a bit of oil in a shallow pan, heat to a boil, and add your prepared mixture. When it is cooked on one side, turn onto a dish, pour honey over, sprinkle with pepper, and serve.

Serves 4
4 eggs
1 cup milk
2 Tbs. olive oil
3 Tbs. honey
pepper (or poppy seeds) to taste

This is a kind of sweet frittata. However, do not fry this one on both sides: as soon as it begins to pull away from the pan, turn it onto a plate, drizzle the honey over its surface, and sprinkle with pepper.

It would not be a serious infraction of the recipe to use poppy seeds instead of pepper; in fact, the Romans commonly used these seeds in cooking (see the following recipe).

SAVILLUM
(CATO 84)

Savillum hoc modo facito: Farinae selibram, casei P. II S una commisceto quasi libum, addito mellis P.≡et ovum unum. Catinum fictile oleo unguito. Ubi omnia bene commiscueris, in catinum indito, catinum testo operito. Videto ut bene percocas medio, ubi altissimum est. Ubi coctum erit, catinum eximito, melle unguito, papaver infriato, sub testum subde paulisper, postea eximito. Ita pone cum catillo et lingula.

Make a *savillum* thus: Mix ½ *libra* of flour and 2½ *librae* of cheese, as is done for *libum*. Add ¼ *libra* of honey and 1 egg. Grease an earthenware bowl with oil. When you have mixed the ingredients well, pour into the bowl and cover the bowl with an earthenware *testo*. See that you cook it well in the middle, where it is highest. When it is cooked, remove the bowl, spread with honey, sprinkle with poppy, put it back beneath the *testo* for a moment, and then remove. Serve it thus with a plate and spoon.

Serves 4
1⅔ lb. (750 g.) ricotta or other soft cheese
1 cup flour
6 Tbs. honey
1 egg
2 Tbs. poppy seeds

This is in effect a cheesecake. Blend the cheese with the flour, 4 tablespoons of honey, and egg. Grease a baking pan with oil, pour in the mixture, and bake in a hot oven (400°F.) for 20–30 minutes. Cover with aluminum foil for the first 10–15 minutes so that the surface does not burn.

Remove from the oven. Drizzle the remaining honey over the surface and sprinkle with poppy seeds. Replace in the oven for 5 minutes, then remove and serve.

For an illustration and explanation of the *testo*, see chapter 5, page 72; for *libum*, see Cato 75, page 169, below.

GLOBI
(CATO 79)

Globos sic facito. Caseum cum alica ad eundem modum misceto. Inde quantos voles facere facito. In ahenum caldum unguen indito. Singulos aut binos coquito versatoque crebro duabus rudibus, coctos eximito, eos melle unguito, papaver infriato, ita ponito.

Make globes thus: Mix together equal amounts of cheese and *alica*. Then shape [the globes] as large as you like. Drop them in hot fat in a copper pan. Cook one or two at a time, turning them often with two paddles. When they are cooked, remove, cover them with honey, sprinkle with poppy, and serve thus.

This is a recipe for sweet fritters. Make them with flour and ricotta and fry them in lard, as is the traditional method.

PUNIC PORRIDGE
(CATO 85)

Pultem punicam sic coquito. Libram alicae in aquam indito, facito uti bene madeat. Id infundito in alveum purum, eo addito casei recentis P. III, mellis P.S., ovum unum, omnia permisceto bene. Ita insipito in aulam novam.

Cook Punic porridge thus: Put a *libra* of *alica* in water and soak well. Then pour it into a clean bowl and add 3 *librae* of fresh cheese, ½ *libra* of honey, and 1 egg; mix everything well. Put this in a new pot.

Serves 4
2 cups flour (or couscous)
3½ cups water (or milk)
2 lb. (900 g.) ricotta or other soft cheese
3 oz. (100 g.) honey
1 or 2 eggs

Dissolve the flour in the water or milk. Add the cheese, honey, and eggs. Bake this mixture in a very hot oven (475°F.) for around 30 minutes.

If you use couscous instead of flour, soak it first in tepid water. Add the remaining ingredients, mixing well, and bake as above. The result will be less moist.

If you plan to use the *puls punica* as an appetizer, omit the honey and add some variety of aromatic herbs and pepper.

This is perhaps the most famous of Cato's recipes, wherein we discover with some relief that even the inflexible Censor had his weaknesses. *Carthago delenda est* (Carthage must be destroyed), but apparently not its *puls punica*.

The term *alica* as used by Cato is difficult to interpret. Since the writer dates from the third century B.C., he was probably referring to coarsely ground spelt; that particular grain, in fact, could not be ground into as fine a flour as we have today. However, common wheat (*triticum*) was also widely available at that time, thus *alica* could have been a type of wheat flour similar to our modern grind. For this particular recipe you can choose either interpretation.

TORTA WITH CHEESE AND HONEY (*PLACENTA*)
(CATO 76)

Placentam sic facito: Farinae siligineae L. II, unde solum facias, in tracta farinae L. IIII et alicae primae L. II. Alicam in aquam infundito. Ubi bene mollis erit, in mortarium purum indito siccatoque bene. Deinde manibus depsito. Ubi bene subactum erit, farinae L. IIII paulatim addito. Id utrumque tracta facito. In qualo ubi arescant componito. Ubi arebunt componito puriter. Cum facies singula tracta, ubi depsueris, panno oleo uncto tangito et circumtergeto unguitoque. Ubi tracta erunt, focum ibi coquas calefacito bene et testum. Postea farinae L. II conspargito condepsitoque. Inde facito solum tenue. Casei ovilli P. XIIII, ne acidum siet et bene recens, in aquam indito. Ibi macerato, aquam ter mutato. Inde eximito siccatoque bene paulatim manibus, siccum bene in mortarium imponito. Ubi omne caseum bene siccaveris, in mortarium purum manibus condepsito comminuitoque quam maxime. Deinde cribrum farinarium purum sumito, caseumque per cribrum facito transeat in mortarium. Postea indito mellis boni P. IIII S, id una bene commisceto cum caseo. Postea in tabula pura quae pateat P. I ibi balteum ponito, folia laurea uncta supponito, placentam fingito.

Tracta singula in totum solum primum ponito, deinde de mortario tracta linito, tracta addito singulatim, item linito usque adeo donec omne caseum cum melle abusus eris. In summum tracta singula indito, postea solum contrahito ornatoque focum . . . de ve primo temperatoque, tunc placentam imponito, testo caldo operito, pruna insuper, et circum operito. Videto ut bene et otiose percoquas. Aperito, dum inspicias, bis aut ter. Ubi cocta erit eximito et melle unguito. Haec erit placenta semodialis.

Make a *placenta* [cake] thus: 2 *librae* of fine flour for the crust, 4 *librae* of flour and 2 *librae* of *alica prima* for the *tracta* [sheets of dough]. Put the *alica* in water. When it has become very soft, put it in a clean mortar and drain well. Then knead with the hands. When it is well kneaded, add 4 *librae* of flour bit by bit. With this form the *tracta*. Put them in a basket where they can dry. When they are dry, place them in an orderly stack. As you make each of the *tracta,* after it has been well kneaded, press it out and wipe it all around with a cloth soaked in oil. When the *tracta* are ready, heat well the hearth where you will cook them, and also the *testo*. Then moisten the 2 *librae* of [fine] flour and knead. Make from this a thin crust. Put 14 *librae* of very fresh, sweet pecorino cheese in water. Soak it, and change the water three times. Then remove it, squeeze it well, little by little, with the hands, and when it is well dried put it in a mortar. When you have drained all the cheese well, knead it and break it up as much as you can by hand in a clean mortar. Then take a clean flour sifter and pass all the cheese through the sifter into the mortar. Then add 4½ *librae* of good honey; mix it well with the cheese. Next place the crust on a clean board that is one foot wide; put oiled bay leaves beneath the crust, and form the *placenta*. Arrange one of the *tracta* over the bottom crust, then cover with the ingredients in the mortar; continue to add *tracta* one by one and to cover them until you have used up all the cheese with honey. Place one of the *tracta* on top, then draw the crust up and arrange . . . adjust the hearth down from its first intensity of heat, then put the *placenta* on and cover it with the hot *testo;* put embers on top and around it. See that it cooks slowly and well. Open to inspect two or three times. When it is cooked, remove and spread with honey. This will be the *placenta semodialis*.

Serves 4–6
4½ cups flour
½ cup couscous
1¾ lb. (800 g.) ricotta
6 Tbs. honey
10 bay leaves
sufficient olive oil
2 eggs (optional)
2 Tbs. lard (optional)

This recipe is quite complicated, requiring two types of dough and a spread of cheese and honey. Obviously, this is an ancestor of the many Italian *torta* recipes using cheese. In my interpretation of this recipe I have chosen to make small balls instead of the sheets of dough (*tracta*) prescribed in the original.

If you prefer a softer dough, add one egg to the dough for the crust and one egg with two tablespoons of lard to the dough for the balls. Because Cato's recipe was probably intended primarily to feed slaves, it is not as rich as it could otherwise be; thus I feel fairly safe in suggesting such a variation.

The undercrust is prepared with 1½ cups of flour and sufficient water. The pastry for the balls is prepared with the remaining flour and ½ cup of soaked and cooked couscous (yielding 2 cups); this is then divided into small batches that are formed into balls. Finally, mix the ricotta and honey together for the spread.

Now you can begin to assemble the dessert. Coat the bay leaves with olive oil and place on a flat round baking pan 8 in. (20 cm.) in diameter. Roll out the crust so that it is considerably wider than the pan. Then place it on the pan over the bay leaves, allowing it to drape over the edge. Arrange half of the balls over the crust, covering this layer with a generous amount of the cheese and honey mixture; repeat with the remaining half. Bring up the edges of the crust to close around the sides. Bake in a moderately hot oven (350°–400°F.) for around 1 hour.

SCRIBLITA

(CATO 78)

Scriblitam sic facito. In balteo tractis caseo ad eundem modum facito, uti placentam, sine melle.

Make a *scriblita* thus: Make it with a crust, *tracta*, and cheese, like the *placenta,* but without the honey.

This unsweetened version of the *placenta* can also be served as an appetizer, together with warm sausages and black and green olives.

SPIRA

(Cato 77)

Spiram sic facito. Quantum voles pro ratione, ita uti placenta fit, eadem omnia facito, nisi alio modo fingito. In solo tracta cum melle oblinito bene, inde tamquam restim tractes facito, ita imponito in solo, simplicibus completo bene arte. Cetera omnia, quasi placentam facias, facito coquitoque.

Make a *spira* thus: Adjust the quantities according to the size you desire. Proceed as for the *placenta,* but form it differently. On the crust place *tracta* and spread well with honey. Then make *tracta* into rope-like shapes and arrange them skillfully over the crust. Do the rest as for the *placenta,* and cook in the same way.

Follow the general instructions for Cato 76, but shape some of the second dough into small ropes and arrange in spirals. They will take on an attractive golden color from the honey when baked.

These recipes are similar to two regional Italian desserts, *frustingolo* from the Marches and *sebada* (or *seada*) from Sardinia. The following is a recipe for *sebada,* a specialty from the province of Nuoro, for comparison:

REGIONAL ITALIAN RECIPE
(Sardinia)
Sebada

3 cups white flour
2 oz. (50 g.) lard
10 oz. (300 g.) soft cheese (e.g., ricotta)
3 Tbs. semolina
½ tsp. grated lemon peel
honey and extra soft cheese to taste
powdered sugar and honey (for fried *sebadas*)

Prepare a thin rectangular sheet of dough with the flour, lard, and sufficient water. Then prepare a mixture of soft cheese, semolina, water, and lemon peel, which should be cooked until completely blended. Cool and form many small balls, then flatten each of them to become circles 3–4 in. (8–10 cm.) in diameter.

Arrange these circles, with some space between them, in layers over one half of the sheet of pastry, spreading each layer with a bit of honey and extra cheese mixed together. Then fold the other half of the pastry over the top to enclose them. This can be placed on a baking sheet and baked in the oven; or you can cut individual circles with a cookie cutter of a diameter slightly larger than that of the fillings within and fry them in hot oil. These fried *sebadas* are then drizzled with honey and sprinkled with powdered sugar.

LIBUM
(Cato 75)

Libum hoc modo facito. Casei P. II bene disterat in mortario. Ubi bene destriverit, farinae siligineae libram, aut, si voles tenerius esse, semilibram semilaginis eodem indito, permiscetoque cum caseo bene. Ovum unum addito et una permisceto bene. Inde panem facito, folia laurea subdito: in foco caldo sub testu coquito leniter.

Make a *libum* thus: Thoroughly grind 2 *librae* of cheese in a mortar. When it is well ground, add 1 *libra* of fine flour or, if you want [the loaf to be] softer still, ½ *libra* of finest flour; mix well with the cheese. Add 1 egg and mix well. Then form a loaf, placing bay leaves beneath. Cook slowly under a *testo* on a hot hearth.

1½ lb. (700 g.) ricotta or other soft cheese
2 cups flour
2 eggs
2–3 bay leaves per loaf

Mix the ingredients as prescribed in the recipe and form small loaves, placing bay leaves beneath each one. Bake in a medium oven (350°F.) for around 30 minutes. (See p. 72 for an explanation of the *testo*.)

This bread is called *libum* (related to *libare*, to make an offering) because it was also used as a sacrificial offering. The farmer, for whom Cato wrote these recipes, was expected to make ritual sacrifices to the *Lares*, the guardian gods of home and property, "for the feast of the *Compitalia*, either at the crossroads or at the hearth" (Cato 5). We may thus assume that what was once good enough for the gods should certainly be appealing to us as well.

APOTERMUM
(APICIUS 58)

Apotermum sic facies: Alicam elixa cum nucleis et amigdalis depilatis et in aqua infusis et lotis ex creta argentaria ut ad candorem pariter perducantur. Cui ammiscebis uvam passam, carenum vel passum. Desuper [piper] confractum asparges et in boletari inferes.

Prepare an *apotermum* thus: Boil spelt with pine nuts and almonds that have been shelled and soaked in water and washed with clay used to clean silver, so that they all become equally white. Mix with raisins and *caroenum* or *passum*. Sprinkle with ground [pepper] and serve in a serving dish.

Serves 4
1 cup semolina
4 cups water (or milk)
2 oz. (50 g.) raisins
2 oz. (50 g.) pine nuts
2 oz. (50 g.) blanched almonds
2 Tbs. *passum* (or *caroenum*)
1–2 eggs (optional)

This is a delicate molded semolina pudding sweetened with *caroenum* or *passum*. I find it is better to cook the semolina in milk rather than water, omit the pepper, and add 1 or 2 eggs so that it can be baked in a pudding form and removed easily when done.

Heat the milk in a pan; when it reaches a boil, drizzle in the semolina and cook for around 10 minutes, stirring frequently. Add the remaining ingredients, then pour the mixture into a form and steam in the oven (350°F.) in a bain-marie.

Grain pudding recipes are still very common, among them the following Turkish recipe. Because it is prepared without eggs, like the Roman one above, it is served in dessert bowls instead of coming from a single form.

Serves 5–6
1 Tbs. each, finely chopped pine nuts and almonds
½ cup butter
1 cup coarse semolina
2 cups milk
1 cup sugar
½ tsp. cinnamon

Brown the almonds and pine nuts in butter in a pan. Add the semolina and sauté, stirring continuously with a wooden spoon and adding more butter if necessary. Meanwhile, mix the milk and sugar and heat to boiling. When the semolina turns golden in color, gradually blend in the milk mixture. Cover the pot securely and cook over a medium heat, checking and stirring at regular intervals until the milk has been completely absorbed. Add the cinnamon, mix, and serve.

PEACH *PATINA*
(Apicius 161)

Patina de persicis: Persica duriora purgabis, frustratim concides, elixas, in patina compones, olei modicum superstillabis et cum cuminato inferes.

A peach *patina:* Peel firm peaches, cut into pieces, and boil; place them in a dish, drizzle over a bit of oil, and serve with cumin sauce.

Serves 4
4–5 firm ripe peaches
water or white wine (to cook the peaches)
3 eggs, beaten
1½ cups milk
1 Tbs. olive oil
pepper to taste

This is undoubtedly a baked egg dish, as can be deduced from the term *patina* (which in Apicius almost always denotes a recipe using egg) and the presence of oil (which is necessary for it to be baked). Thus even if milk and eggs are not mentioned in the recipe, they seem to be a logical addition. Furthermore, the following recipe (*patina de piris*) is quite similar to this one, and it does call for eggs. It must not be forgotten that the Apician manual often took a great deal for granted.

Peel the peaches, then pit them and cut into pieces. Poach them in a little water (not too much so that they do not become too soft) or, better still, in wine. Crush them into a pulp, mix in the eggs and milk, and pour into a casserole. Drizzle over this a bit of olive oil, sprinkle with pepper, and bake for around 20 minutes at 350°F.

The cumin sauce to accompany this could be the one described on page 44 (Apicius 31), but if so I suggest you omit the *garum*. This dish is also fine as it is, without any sauce.

PEAR *PATINA*
(Apicius 162)

Patina de piris: Pira elixa et purgata e medio teres cum pipere, cumino, melle, passo, liquamine, oleo modico. Ovis missis patinam facies, piper super aspargis et inferes.

A pear *patina*: Grind boiled and cored pears with pepper, cumin, honey, *passum*, *garum*, and a bit of oil. When the eggs have been added, make a *patina*, sprinkle pepper over, and serve.

Serves 4
4 pears
water or white wine (to cook the pears)
1 Tbs. honey
pinch each of pepper and cumin
½ cup *passum*

3 eggs
1½ cups milk (optional)
1 Tbs. olive oil

Poach the whole pears in water or white wine. When they are done, peel and core them, then crush them into a puree, mixing in the honey, pepper, cumin, and *passum*. (I recommend again here that the *garum* be omitted.)

Beat the eggs, adding the milk if desired. Then blend this into the pear mixture with the olive oil. Pour into a casserole and bake for around 20 minutes at 350°F.

QUINCE *PATINA* OR PUREE
(APICIUS 164)

Patina de cydoneis: Mala cydonia cum porris, melle, liquamine, oleo, defricto coques et inferes, vel elixata ex melle.

A quince *patina*: Cook quinces with leeks, honey, *garum*, oil, and *defrutum*, and serve; or boil with honey.

Here we have two methods for preparing quinces. Both are very good.

Serves 4
For the first method:
2 large quinces
2 leeks
1 Tbs. honey
2 Tbs. *defrutum*
2 eggs, beaten

Cut the quinces into large pieces and boil them. Meanwhile, chop the leeks and boil them in another pan (they will cook more quickly). When both are done, crush and pass through a strainer. Mix with the honey and *defrutum*, then add the eggs. (Again, I suggest you omit the *garum*.) Pour into a casserole and bake.

For the second method:
2 lb. (1 kg.) quinces
2 Tbs. honey
2 Tbs. *defrutum* (optional)

Cut the quinces into large pieces and boil them; then crush them and simmer with the honey and *defrutum*. Serve hot or cold. This delicate puree is particularly appropriate for infants.

MELCA
(APICIUS 304)

Melcas: Cum pipere et liquamine vel sale, oleo et corian-dro.

Curdled milk: With pepper and *garum;* or salt, oil, and coriander.

Serves 1
1 cup curdled milk
pinch of pepper
1 tsp. *garum*
or:
    1 cup curdled milk
    pinch of salt
    2 Tbs. olive oil
    pinch of coriander

The Romans were very fond of this efficient digestive aid, a close relative of yogurt. You can prepare the milk according to the Lebanese recipe that follows. Season it with pepper and *garum,* or with salt, olive oil, and coriander.

MODERN LEBANESE RECIPE
Curdled Milk

Heat 5 quarts (liters) of goat's or sheep's milk in a pan. When it boils, remove from the heat and cool. Then add 1 lb. (500 g.) of yogurt and mix well. Cover with a thick piece of wool and let rest. After around 2 hours it will become fermented milk; after 12 hours, it will become yogurt.

This simple procedure is similar to the recipe in the *Geoponica:* "Add curdled milk to fresh milk to cause it to acidify; always retain a bit of curdled milk to make more when it has been finished" (18, 21).

Another, more complicated system recorded by Columella (12, 8) was to add a bouquet of aromatic herbs and some onion to sheep's milk, then to cover the container and let its contents ferment for five days. Then the whey was drained through a hole in the bottom of the container; this procedure was repeated after three days, at which point the herb bouquet was removed and replaced with dried herbs and leek. After two more days, the whey was drained out a final time, and the contents were salted and mixed.

This recipe, which Columella called *oxygala* (acidified milk), produces more of a cheese than a yogurt and is very similar to an old Milanese preparation called *cagiada.*

One other recipe, the Apricot Fricassee (Apicius 170, pp. 67–68), could have been included in this chapter; but since it is not very sweet and is closely related to another apricot recipe (Apicius 178, pp. 66–67) specifically called a *gustum* (appetizer), I have placed it instead in chapter 5.

In the same chapter there are two recipes for a cheese round with herbs (*Appendix Vergiliana* and Apicius 41, pp. 54–55), which could easily be served at the end of a meal, possibly with the bread described between these recipes.

Finally, in chapter 11 there are recipes for the preparation of dried fruit (figs, stuffed dates, etc.) that could be served as dessert. You can also serve fresh figs when they are in season, together with hot bread or buns flavored with must and honey (Apicius 297, p. 158).

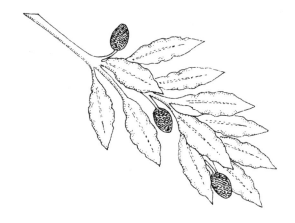

›XI‹

PRESERVES

A basket of olives
This olive, which comes to you having escaped the presses
of Picenum,
Both opens and closes banquets.

(Martial 13, 36)

Quinces
If quinces immersed in Attic honey are served to you,
you will say: "These sweet apples are delicious."

(Martial 13, 24)

Honeycombs from Sicily
When you offer Sicilian honeycombs from among the hills
of Hybla,
you can say that they are Attic.

(Martial 13, 105)

When unexpected guests arrive, every host should be able to fall back upon
a well-stocked pantry containing items with a good shelf life. Today we
have the conveniences of refrigerators, freezers, and all sorts of vacuum-
packed products; but the Romans, of course, had none of these at their
disposal as they developed methods to preserve their foods. The market
could only offer dried fish, various qualities of *garum,* and dried fruit from
the Middle East and northern Africa. Roman households would also store
dried legumes (chick peas, fava beans, lentils, etc.), grains, oil, wine, and
honey.

Many varieties of produce from garden and orchard could be preserved,
providing an extremely useful source of food for the dinner table. Further,
certain purchased items may not necessarily have been particularly fine or
fresh, in which case they were doctored rather than discarded. Most Ro-

mans did not waste their resources as frivolously as we do.

Instructions for preserves can be found in numerous manuals, whether for the experienced farmer or the accomplished cook, even in medical manuals. There are recipes to preserve turnips, figs, and truffles, procedures for improving poor honey or correcting an excessively salty *garum*, as well as hints on how to prevent fried fish or uncooked meat from developing unpleasant odors. Brine, salt, spices, oil, vinegar, honey, and mustard were the basic preservative agents, and it was important that these elements be of the best quality available.

Several interesting recipes and tips follow—some are curiosity pieces, others remain both valid and appealing for us today.

SEASONED SALTS
(Apicius 29)

Sales conditos ad multa: Sales conditos ad digestionem, ad ventrem movendum, et omnes morbos et pestilentiam et omnia frigora prohibent generari, sunt autem et suavissimi ultra quam speras. Sales communes frictos lib. I, sales ammonicos frictos lib. II, piperis albi uncias III, gingiber unc. II, ammeos unc. I semis, timi unc. I semis, apii seminis unc. I semis (si apii semen mittere nolueris, petroselini mittis unc. III), origani unc. III, erucae semen unc. I semis, piperis nigri unc. III, croci unc. I, ysopi Cretici unc. II, folium unc. II, petroselinum unc. II, aneti unc. II.

Seasoned salts for many uses: Seasoned salts are for the digestion, to move the bowels; they prevent the onset of all illnesses and pestilence and all colds. Moreover, they are more pleasant than would be expected. One *libra* of common salt, fried, 2 *librae* of sal ammoniac, fried, 3 *unciae* of white pepper, 2 *unciae* of ginger, 1½ *unciae* of ammi, 1½ *unciae* of thyme, 1½ *unciae* of celery seeds (if you do not want to use celery seeds, use 3 *unciae* of parsley seeds), 3 *unciae* of oregano, 1½ *unciae* of arugola seeds, 3 *unciae* of black pepper, 1 *uncia* of saffron, 2 *unciae* of Crete hyssop, 2 *unciae* of aromatic leaf, 2 *unciae* of parsley, and 2 *unciae* of dill.

Fried salt was prepared by putting it in an earthenware jar that was sealed and covered with a mixture of mud and straw, then placed among embers to cook until it no longer crackled in the heat.

Sal ammoniac, literally "salt of Hammon," came from the eponymous oasis (today called Sivah) in Libya.

Ammi (*Trachyspermum copticum*) is an herb of Egyptian origin, belonging to the same botanical family as cumin.

Seasoned salts were reputed to have many digestive and laxative uses, to the point that they were considered, as they are here, a kind of panacea.

DIGESTIVE AID
(Apicius 37)

Oxyporum. Cumini unc. II, zingiberis unc. I, rutae viridis unc. I, nitri scripulos VI, dactilorum pinguium scripulos XII, piperis unc. I, mellis unc. IX. Cuminum vel Ethiopicum aut Siriacum aut Libicum aceto infundes, sicca et sic tundes. Postea melle comprehendis. Cum necesse fuerit, oxygaro uteris.

Oxyporum: Two *unciae* of cumin, 1 *uncia* of ginger, 1 *uncia* of fresh rue, 6 scruples of natron, 12 scruples of plump dates, 1 *uncia* of pepper, 9 *unciae* of honey. Pour vinegar over cumin from Ethiopia, Syria, or Libya, dry it, and grind it. Then combine it with honey. Use with *oxygarum*, as needed.

This type of concoction, with a basis of herbs and spices, fruit, honey, and vinegar, was considered a very effective digestive aid. The term *oxyporum* means "that which stimulates the digestion" in Greek, implying medicinal applications. It was used after overeating, and for an upset stomach, kidney disorders and stones, and colic. The emperor Nero, who was wont to indulge in gluttony (he reputedly began his dinner at sunset and finished the following dawn), had his favorite *oxyporum*, prepared from quinces, pomegranates, and sorb apples cooked in must with Sicilian sumac (*Rhus coriaria*) and saffron.

I have not had the courage to try this recipe, but if you are more adventurous you can consult the Table of Weights and Measures for the proper conversions.

There are two more approachable recipes in Apicius under the title of *Oxygarum digestibile* (*oxygarum* as a digestive aid). The first of these (Apicius 39) includes pepper, seseli from Gaul, cardamom, cumin, aromatic leaf (bay), and dried mint, all ground, filtered through a fine sieve or gauze, and then mixed with honey, vinegar, and *garum*. The second (Apicius 40) uses pepper, parsley, caraway, and lovage, again ground and mixed with honey, vinegar, and *garum*. These recipes can be realized easily and they are actually quite effective digestive remedies. Certainly they are no less appealing than many herbal liqueurs, and could be an interesting finale for your meal.

PREPARATION OF MUSTARD
(COLUMELLA 12, 57)

Sinapim quemadmodum facias: Semen sinapis diligenter purgato et cribrato: deinde aqua frigida eluito et cum fuerit bene lotum, duabus horis in aqua sinito: postea tollito, et manibus expressum in mortarium novum aut bene emundatum conicito et pistillis conterito: cum contritum fuerit, totam intritam ad medium mortarium contrahito et comprimito manu plana: deinde cum compresseris, scarificato et impositis paucis carbonibus vivis aquam nitratam suffundito, ut omnem amaritudinem eius et pallorem exsaniet: deinde statim mortarium erigito, ut omnis humor eliquetur: post hoc album acre acetum adicito et pistillo permisceto colatoque. Hoc ius ad rapa condienda optime facit.

Caeterum si velis ad usum conviviorum praeparare, cum exsaniaveris, sinapi nucleos pineos quam recentissimos et amygdalam adicito, diligenterque conterito infuso aceto. Caetera, ut supra dixi, facito. Hoc sinapi ad embammata non solum idoneo, sed etiam specioso uteris nam est candoris eximii, si sit curiose factum.

How to prepare mustard: Carefully clean mustard seed and put it through a sieve. Then wash it with cold water and, when it is thoroughly clean, soak it for two hours in water. Afterward remove it, squeeze it by hand, put it in a mortar that is new or very clean, and grind it with a pestle. When it is ground, gather all of it in the middle of the mortar and flatten it out with an open hand. When you have flattened it, score the surface, put in a few glowing coals, and pour water with natron over, so that all the bitterness and pallid color are remedied. Lift up the mortar immediately to pour off all the liquid; after this add strong white vinegar, mix with the pestle, and strain. This sauce is very good for seasoning turnips.

If instead you want to prepare it for use in banquets,

after you have remedied it, add to the mustard very fresh pine nuts and almonds, grind together thoroughly, and pour vinegar over. Do the rest as I have stated above. This mustard is not only good for sauces, but if it is made well, it also makes a beautiful impression with its excellent white color.

Here Columella provides instructions for two versions of mustard: an ordinary one, and a more refined variation with ground almonds and pine nuts to make it white.

HOW TO BLANCH RED WINE
(Apicius 7)

Vinum ex atro candidum facies: Lomentum ex faba factum vel ovorum trium alborem in lagonam mittis et diutissime agitas: alia die erit candidum. Et cineres vitis albae idem faciunt.

To make white wine from red: Put flour made from fava beans, or the whites of three eggs, into the bottle and stir at length. The next day it will be white. The ashes of white grape vine have the same effect.

This curious recipe gives three of the most common methods both the Greeks and Romans used for clarifying red wine. Bean flour and egg white were well known as clarifying agents, and wood charcoal as an effective whitener.

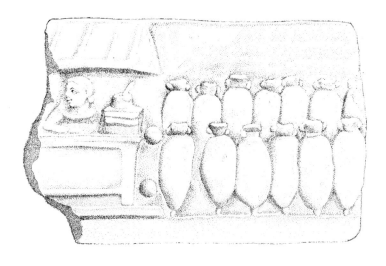

A TASTE OF ANCIENT ROME

HOW TO CORRECT GARUM
(APICIUS 8)

De liquamine emendando: Liquamen si odorem malum fecerit, vas inane inversum fumiga lauro et cupresso, et in hoc liquamen infunde ante ventilatum. Si salsum fuerit, mellis sextarium mittis et moves picas, et emendasti; sed et mustum recens idem praestat.

To correct *garum:* If the *garum* develops a bad odor, invert an empty container, smoke it with burning bay and cypress wood, then pour in it the *garum* that has previously been exposed to the air. If it is too salty, add a *sextarius* of honey and stir, and it will be adjusted. But fresh must also provides the same result.

Whether homemade or purchased, *garum* could sometimes turn out to be unsatisfactory. This recipe was an effective means of correcting unpleasant odor or excessive saltiness.

HOW TO PRESERVE MEAT WITHOUT SALT
(APICIUS 9)

Ut carnes sine sale quovis tempore recentes sint: Carnes recentes quales volueris melle tegantur, sed vas pendeat et, quando volueris, utere. Hoc hieme melius fit, aestate paucis diebus durabit. Et in carne cocta itidem facies.

To have meat always fresh without salting it: Cover the fresh meat of your choice with honey, but suspend the container and use whenever desired. It keeps better in winter; in summer it lasts only a few days. Do the same with cooked meat.

The keeping of meat was a serious problem. Preservation in salt or spices was a common method, as was smoking; but the meat could become too salty and consequently inedible. This recipe in Apicius is presented as an alternative, albeit an expensive one. The containers of preserved foods were often suspended so that the air could circulate freely around them (Columella 12, 42).

HOW TO SWEETEN SALTED MEAT
(Apicius 11)

Ut carnem salsam dulcem facias: Carnem salsam dulcem facies, si prius in lacte coquas et postea in aquam.

To make salted meat sweet: Make salted meat sweet by cooking it first in milk and then in water.

HOW TO PRESERVE FRIED FISH
(Apicius 12)

Ut pisces fricti diu durent: Eodem momento quo friguntur et levantur, ab aceto calido perfunduntur.

To preserve fried fish: The very moment they are fried and removed, they are sprinkled with hot vinegar.

The following sausage recipes provide an interesting picture of how they were made. Predictably, all three contain the seemingly ubiquitous *garum*.

LUCANIAN SAUSAGES
(Apicius 61)

Lucanicae: . . . Teritur piper, cuminum, satureia, ruta, petroselinum, condimentum, bacae lauri, liquamen, et admiscetur pulpa bene tunsa ita ut denuo bene cum ipso subtrito fricetur. Cum liquamine admixto, pipere integro et abundanti pinguedine et nucleis inicies in intestinum perquam tenuatim perductum, et sic ad fumum suspenditur.

Lucanian sausages: . . . Pepper is ground with cumin, savory, rue, parsley, condiments, bay berries, and *garum*. Finely ground meat is mixed in, then ground again together with the other ground ingredients. Mix with *garum*, peppercorns, and plenty of fat, and pine nuts; fill a casing stretched extremely thin, and thus it is hung in smoke.

See page 13 for a brief discussion of these sausages.

SAUSAGES

(APICIUS 62 AND 63)

Farcimina: Ova et cerebella teres, nucleos pineos, piper, liquamen, laser modicum, et his intestinum implebis. Elixas, postea assas et inferes.

Aliter: Coctam alicam et tritam cum pulpa concisa et trita una cum pipere et liquamine et nucleis. Farcies intestinum et elixabis, deinde cum sale assabis et cum senapi inferes, vel sic concisum in disco.

Sausage: Grind eggs and brains, pine nuts, pepper, *garum*, and a bit of silphium, and fill a casing with this. Boil, then roast and serve.

Another recipe: [Mix] cooked and ground spelt with chopped meat that has been ground together with pepper and *garum* and pine nuts. Stuff a casing and boil, then roast with salt, and serve with mustard or sliced thus on a dish.

HOW TO PRESERVE TURNIPS AND RUTABAGAS

(COLUMELLA 12, 56)

Rapas et napos quomodo condias. Rapa quam rotundissima sumito eaque, si sunt lutosa, detergito et summam cutem novacula decerpito: deinde (sicut consueverunt salgamarii) decussatim ferramento lunato incidito: sed caveto, ne usque ad imum praecidas rapa. Tum salem inter incisuras raporum, non nimium minutum aspergito et rapa in alveo aut seria componito et sale plusculo aspersa triduo sinito, dum exudent: post tertiam diem mediam fibram rapi gustato, si receperit salem: deinde cum videbitur satis recepisse, exemptis omnibus, singula suo sibi iure eluito: vel si non multum liquoris fuerit, muriam duram adicito, et ita eluito: et postea in quadratam cistam vimineam, quae neque spisse, solide tamen et crassis viminibus contexta sit, rapa componito: deinde sic aptatam tabulam superponito, ut usque ad fundum, si res exigat, intra cistam deprimi possit. Cum autem eam tabulam sic aptaveris, gravia pondera superponito, et sinito nocte tota et uno die siccari: tum in dolio picato fictili, vel in vitreo componito et sic infundito sinapi et aceto, ut a iure contegantur.

Napi quoque, sed integri, si minuti sunt, maiores autem insecti, eodem iure, quo rapa, condiri possunt: sed curandum est ut haec utraque antequam caulem agant et cymam faciant, dum sunt tenera, componantur.

Napos minutos integros, aut rursus amplos in tres aut quattuor partes divisos, in vas conicito, et aceto infundito, salis quoque cocti unum sextarium in congium aceti adicito: post trigesimum diem uti poteris.

How to preserve turnips and rutabagas. Take nice round turnips, clean them if they are dirty, and remove the outer peel with a knife; then (as the manufacturers of preserves usually have done) make crosswise incisions with a curved iron knife. But be careful not to cut the turnips completely through. Then sprinkle salt that has not been ground too finely into the incisions, arrange the turnips in a pot or jar, and, after sprinkling them with a good deal of salt, leave them for three days so that they sweat. After the third day, taste the center fiber of a turnip to see if it has absorbed the salt. Then when it seems to have absorbed enough, remove them all, and rinse each one in the liquid they have left; or if there is not much liquid, add strong brine and wash them with that. Afterward put the turnips in a square wicker basket woven not too tightly, but solidly and of thick wicker. Then place a plank over them, fitted so that it can be pressed down into the basket all the way to the bottom if necessary. After fitting the plank in this way, put heavy weights on it and leave [the turnips] to dry for an entire night and a day. Then arrange them in a pitched jar or a glass jar, and pour mustard and vinegar over them so that they are covered with liquid.

Rutabagas, whole if they are small, cut up if they are large, can also be preserved in the same liquid as for turnips; but take care that both of these are collected while they are still tender, before they form a stalk and shoots.

Put the rutabagas, whole if they are small, cut into three or four pieces if they are large, in a jar, pour vinegar over them, and add one *sextarius* of roasted salt to a *congius* of vinegar. You can use them after the thirtieth day.

The following two recipes for turnip preserves in Apicius are, in contrast to that by Columella, mercifully brief.

HOW TO PRESERVE TURNIPS
(APICIUS 25 AND 26)

Rapae ut diu serventur: Ante accuratas et compositas asperges mirtae bacis cum melle et aceto.

Aliter: Senapi tempera melle, aceto, sale et super compositas rapas infundes.

How turnips are preserved: First clean them and arrange them [in a container]; pour myrtle berries over them with honey and vinegar.

Another recipe: Mix mustard with honey, vinegar, and salt, and pour over turnips that have been arranged [in a container].

HOW TO PRESERVE TRUFFLES
(APICIUS 27)

Tubera ut diu serventur: Tubera quae aquae non vexaverint componis in vas alternis, alternis scobem siccam mittis et gipsas et loco frigido pones.

How truffles are preserved: Arrange truffles that have not been damaged by water in a jar, alternating in layers with dry sawdust; seal [the lid] with gypsum plaster and keep in a cool place.

Certainly this recipe is convincing evidence that truffles were once not so prohibitively expensive, if in fact one could preserve layers of them in jars. For us, unfortunately, there is no choice but to read such instructions with envy.

HOW TO PRESERVE GREEN OLIVES
(CATO 117)

Olae albae quo modo condiantur: Antequam nigrae fiant, contundantur et in aquam deiciantur. Crebro aquam mutet. Deinde, ubi satis maceratae erunt, exprimat et in acetum coiciat et oleum addat, salis selibram in modium olearum. Feniculum et lentiscum seorsum condat in acetum. . . . Manibus siccis cum voles sumito.

How green olives may be seasoned: Before they turn black, they are crushed and placed in water. Change the water frequently. Then, when they have soaked enough, squeeze them and put them in vinegar and add oil and ½ *libra* of salt for each *modius* of olives. Place fennel and lentiscus separately in the vinegar. . . . When you desire some, take them out with dry hands.

ANOTHER WAY TO PREPARE GREEN OLIVES
(Cato 118)

Oleam albam, quam secundum vindemmiam uti voles, sic condito. Musti tantundem addito, quantum aceti. Cetera item condito ita uti supra scriptum est.

Season thus green olives that you want to use following their harvest. Add must and vinegar in equal quantities. For the rest, season them as is written above.

Columella wrote that most people "mix crushed olives with minced leeks, rue, young celery, and mint; they then add a small amount of vinegar seasoned with pepper and a bit of honey or *mulsum,* pour on a generous amount of green olive oil, and then cover them with a bouquet of fresh celery" (12, 49). We too can follow this procedure, buying green olives, pounding them slightly with a meat pounder (or making one or two small incisions in each one) and then marinating them in oil, vinegar, and aromatic herbs in an airtight container.

REGIONAL ITALIAN RECIPE
(Calabria)

In Calabria olives are prepared similarly, but with the addition of a bit of minced hot pepper to the oil. After around 10 days the olives thus become very flavorful. Of course, the hot pepper, which came from America, is an ingredient that dates centuries after the ancient Romans.

HOW TO PRESERVE GRAPES
(Apicius 18)

Uvae ut diu serventur: Accipies uvas de vite inlaesas, et aquam pluvialem ad tertias decoques, et mittis in vas in quo et uvas mittis. Vas picari et gipsari facies, et in locum

*frigidum ubi soli accessum non habet reponi facies et,
quando volueris, uvas virides invenies. Et ipsam aquam
pro idromelli aegris dabis. Et si in ordeo obruas, inlaesas
invenies.*

To preserve grapes: Take unblemished bunches of grapes;
reduce rainwater to one third, and put it in a jar in which
you also put the grapes. Coat the jar with pitch and seal
[the lid] with gypsum plaster, and store it in a cool place
where the sun cannot enter; when you want them, you will
find fresh grapes. Give the water to the sick instead of
honey water. If you keep them in barley, you will find them
unblemished.

This same recipe can be found in ancient Greek texts on agriculture; evidently it was a fairly common procedure. Barley was also used to preserve
citrons and quinces. As late as the end of the nineteenth century, grapes
were still stored in barrels and mixed with millet seeds or other grains so
that they would be available during the winter.

HOW TO PRESERVE MULBERRIES
(Apicius 23)

*Mora ut diu durent: Ex moris sucum facito et cum sapa
misce et in vitrio vase cum mora mitte: custodies multo
tempore.*

To preserve mulberries: Make a juice from mulberries and
mix it with *sapa* and put it in a glass jar with mulberries.
You can keep them for a long time.

Note that this recipe calls for mulberries, not blackberries. Make a syrup
by cooking 1 pound (500 grams) of them for around 20 minutes. Pass
them through a strainer, add 4–5 tablespoons of *sapa,* and pour this mixture over whole mulberries in marmalade jars, covering them completely.
They can be used for cakes, puddings, or ice cream.

HOW TO PRESERVE APPLES AND POMEGRANATES
(Apicius 19)

Ut mala et mala granata diu durent: In calidam ferventem merge, et statim leva et suspende.

To preserve apples and pomegranates: Immerse them in boiling water, remove immediately, and suspend.

This recipe seems incomplete; in fact, other ancient sources (for example, Columella 12, 46) say to immerse them in sea water or brine, dry them in the sun, and then suspend them, which is more convincing.

HOW TO PRESERVE QUINCES
(Apicius 20)

Ut mala cidonia diu serventur: Eligis mala sine vitio cum ramulis et foliis et condes in vas et suffundes mel et defritum et diu servabis.

To preserve quinces: Select unblemished quinces with stems and leaves; put them in a jar and pour honey and *defrutum* over them, and you will keep them a long time.

Columella (12, 47) suggested instead that quinces be preserved in honey alone. He warned that they must be fully ripe, otherwise they cannot be cut when needed; also, they must not press against each other in the container. The honey (a fine pourable variety) would form a liquid called *melomeli* as it sat in storage with the fruit.

HOW TO PRESERVE CITRONS
(Apicius 22)

Citria ut diu durent: In vas citrium mitte, gipsa, suspende.

To preserve citrons: Put [each] citron in a jar, seal [the lid] with gypsum plaster, and suspend.

Citrons were also preserved in barley or, more often, they were individually enclosed in clay. The clay would then dry in the sun and form a container around the citron; every time a citron was desired, the clay was cracked open to obtain the fruit inside.

HOW TO PRESERVE
VARIOUS TYPES OF FRUIT
(Apicius 21)

Ficum recentem, mala, pruna, pira, cerasia ut diu serves:
Omnia cum peciolis diligenter legito et in melle ponito ne
se contingant.

To preserve fresh figs, apples, plums, pears, and cherries:
Carefully pick everything with their stems and put them in
honey so that they do not touch each other.

HOW TO PRESERVE WHOLE DRIED FIGS
(Cato 99)

Fici aridae si voles uti integrae sint, in vas fictile condito.
Id amurca decocta unguito.

If you want dried figs to remain whole, keep them in an
earthenware jar. Grease it with boiled dregs of olive oil.

Regional Italian Recipe
(Apulia)

In Apulia it is customary to dry figs in the sun, then preserve them in layers,
separated by bay leaves, in earthenware containers. This gives the figs an
extraordinary fragrance.

STUFFED DATES
(Apicius 296)

Dulcia domestica: Palmulas vel dactilos excepto semine,
nuce vel nucleis vel pipere trito infercies. Sale foris contin-
gis, frigis in melle cocto et inferes.

A homemade sweet: Remove the pits from palmyra fruits
or dates, and stuff them with walnuts or pine nuts or
ground pepper. Roll them in salt, fry in cooked honey, and
serve.

The ancient Romans stuffed figs and dates with walnuts, hazelnuts, or pine nuts. If they are simply stuffed, dried dates can be used; but if they are to be cooked, it is better to use fresh ones.

Pit the dates and stuff some with chopped walnuts, others with chopped pine nuts. (I omit the salt prescribed in Apicius.) Cook in a bit of liquid honey that has been heated in a pan. Use 5–6 dates for each serving. This recipe produces a delicate warm dessert.

›XII‹

BEVERAGES

Fundanum
This wine of Fundi is the product of a prosperous autumn
harvest under Opimius.
The consul himself pressed the grapes and drank the
must.

(Martial 13, 113)

Mulsum
Attic honey only spoils the nectar of Falernus.
This fine wine should be mixed by Ganymede.

(Martial 13, 108)

Falernum
These Massic wines come from the presses of Sinuessa.
Do you ask who was consul when the wine was bottled?
There were not yet consuls.

(Martial 13, 111)

The ancient Romans had a limited range of hot and cold beverages available to them, quite unlike the variety we have today. Only water, milk, wine, beer, and a few herbal teas were available.

Milk (*lac*) was not an important element in the urban adult diet: it was fed to children and used in the preparation of an occasional dish such as pudding or porridge. But in the country both children and adults drank milk. The most commonly consumed varieties were obtained from goats and sheep because these animals were (and still are) more plentiful than cattle in the Mediterranean region. Cows were left to nourish their young and were not routinely milked. Camel milk was also consumed, though almost exclusively in the provinces of Asia and Africa where these animals flourished. It was considered the sweetest and most nutritious but was not easy to procure. Milk from horses and donkeys, which was occasionally mentioned by ancient authors, was used predominantly for cosmetic or medicinal purposes.

Beer (*cervisia*) had been produced in large quantities already from the epoch of the ancient Egyptians, to whom its invention is attributed. Romans made beer from wheat and barley; the lack of hops, which give beer a longer shelf life, required that it be consumed much sooner. Hops are also the source of the mildly bitter flavor and more aromatic character of modern beer.

But even though beer was widely produced and consumed in Egypt, Spain, and the provinces north of the Alps, Romans for the most part considered it a therapeutic beverage for the ill. Only common soldiers in the outlying garrisons drank it on a regular basis, and certainly no host would have offered it to his guests. The following epigram, attributed to the emperor Julian the Apostate (360–363), reflects this more sophisticated opinion:

> Wine from the vine has a fragrance like nectar;
> wine from barley stinks like a goat.
> Wine from the vine comes from Bacchus,
> son of the goddess Semele;
> wine from barley comes from bread.

Thus wine was considered divine, beer vulgar. In fact, wine was the most respected and consumed beverage in the ancient world: no dinner, great or small, would have been complete without it. The more famous zones of production were Campania, which provided the celebrated Falernian and Massic wines; Gaul, which provided aromatic wines and smoked wines (like that from Marseilles); Spain; and naturally, Greece, the source of the most sought-after wines (such as those from Knossos, Chios, Kos, and Rhodes). Wine was produced north of the Alps even before the region was conquered by the Romans; but afterward production was greatly expanded and improved, particularly in the Moselle and Rhineland regions. Wine grapes were even cultivated in England under the Roman Empire.

The methods for the cultivation of grapes and the production of wine were an established part of ancient Italian heritage (the original name of a large zone of southern Italy was Enotria, or "land of wine"). We have precise descriptions of these procedures in the agricultural writings of Cato and Columella. While the systems of cultivation are remarkably similar to those used in Italy as recently as seventy or eighty years ago, the production and preservation of wine involved methods that were much more primitive. The quantity of wine produced was enormous, but each winery had to find a way to preserve it. Wine would easily turn to vinegar, particularly during transport by sea (as is still the case today); therefore, after the grapes were pressed and the juice was filtered through large reed baskets, all types of stabilizers and preservatives were added. In Greece, sea water was the most frequent additive, while Cato and Columella suggested resin, tar, iris and gladiolus roots, even calcium and lead salts. These may actually have served their purpose to some extent, but there were many other suggestions based upon pure superstition: for example, if an animal were to fall into a vat of fermenting must and drown, Columella (12, 31) wrote that the wine would be saved by retrieving the animal's body, burning it, and then mixing the cooled ashes back into the vat.

The must was placed in large earthenware jars, or in wooden casks that were coated with pitch and washed with sea water. When it turned to wine, it was poured into amphoras that were often marked with the place of production, the year, and the volume of the container (more prestigious wines even had identification tags, called *pittacia,* made of leather, fabric, or parchment, that were attached to the necks of the amphoras), and thus it traveled far and wide. Wine amphoras have been discovered hundreds, sometimes thousands, of kilometers from their place of origin. One archaeological excavation in Israel unearthed twelve Roman amphoras among the ruins of the royal palaces of Herod. They had come to Palestine by sea and were expressly marked: "I am for Herod, king of Judea."

Because wine was generally very strong, it was diluted in the proportion of three parts water to one part wine when served. This adjustment was the responsibility of the wine steward of the epoch, the *cellarius.* He used an *authepsa,* a kind of samovar that sat over a small stove of embers (when heated wine was desired during the winter) or a bowl of snow (in the summer), and that was equipped with a filter at the top to collect any sediment from the wine as it was decanted. Sometimes the *cellarius* would place fennel seeds or other fragrant seeds in the filter to give the wine a particular "character."

It was one thing to dilute wine to make it more palatable; but quite another to "stretch" it with inordinate amounts of water, as did for instance a certain dishonest merchant named Coranus, in order to sell greater quantities:

> The proceeds of the grape harvest have not been ruined
>   everywhere, Ovidius:
> the great rain itself has borne fruit.
> Coranus has been able to fill a hundred amphoras
> by means of this water.
>
>   (Martial 9, 98)

It was also common to cut bad wine with good:

What pleasure does it give you, Tucca,
to mix the must of inferior Vatican casks with an aged
          Falernian wine?
What great good have the bad wines done you,
or what harm the fine ones?
To us it is clear: it is a crime to murder the Falernian,
to administer terrible toxins to that Campanian wine.
Perhaps your guests deserved to die;
but that precious amphora did not.

(Martial 1, 18)

. . . and it must be said that little has changed over these many years.

There was a cheap wine for slaves made from the residue of grapes after they had been pressed. The following interesting recipe for this "wine" was contributed by the miserly Cato:

> To make wine for the slaves to drink during winter, pour 10 *quadrantalia* of must in a vat, add 2 *quandrantalia* of strong vinegar, 2 *quadrantalia* of *sapa*, and 50 *quadrantalia* of fresh water. Stir these ingredients with a large pole 3 times a day for 5 consecutive days. Add 64 *sextarii* of old sea water, put a cover on the vat, and after 10 days seal it with a layer of gypsum plaster. This wine will last until the solstice.

(Cato 104)

The quantities in modern measurements are: 258 quarts of must, 51½ quarts of *sapa,* 1,290 quarts of fresh water, and 34½ quarts of stagnant sea water! Cato then added a pointed and undoubtedly accurate observation: "If a bit is left over after the solstice, it will be a strong, excellent vinegar."

This beverage was actually closer to *posca,* a drink of vinegar or acidified wine and water that is often mentioned in the ancient sources. It was used for the military troops and considered to be refreshing and invigorating. With this in mind, one may find it interesting to recall a portion of the Passion according to St. John: "After this, Jesus, knowing that all things were now accomplished, that the Scripture might be fulfilled, said, I thirst. Now there was set a vessel full of vinegar: and they filled a sponge with vinegar, and put it upon hyssop, and put it to his mouth" (John 19: 28–29). This seemingly heartless action was therefore simply a gesture of compassion for a dying man.

But let us return to the various forms of wine, principal drink at dinners and in taverns, and the main ingredient of many recipes. One of these variations was *passum,* a raisin wine made from grapes that were left to dry on the vine and then harvested and pressed. This wine was stronger and sweeter than normal wine and was served with dessert.

Wine was also reduced to become *caroenum*. Its name comes directly from the Greek *karoinon* (*oinos* = wine; *kariunon* = in the form of a walnut) cited by Galen (*De victu attenante* 12, 99), possibly derived from the custom of keeping it in containers in the form of a walnut shell. Other authors used the term to refer to reduced must.

Wine could be seasoned (*vinum conditum*) with spices (most commonly pepper), herbs (absinthium, cumin), floral essences (violets, roses), roots (irises, gladioli), and various seeds (fennel, cumin). More discriminating Romans were so fond of these variations that they kept a package of their favorite mixture with them when they traveled so that it was always ready to be added to the wine they were served in taverns along the way.

When absinthium (wormwood) was used, the resulting wine was called *vinum absinthiatum*, which the Germans translated literally as *Wermut-Wein* (*Wermut* = wormwood). This name (eventually becoming more common than the Latin-derived *absinthe*) was gradually corrupted into *vermouth*, a popular aperitif and digestive drink made of wine and herbs, among which wormwood gives it its slightly bitter flavor.

The first recipe in Apicius is for one of these seasoned wines:

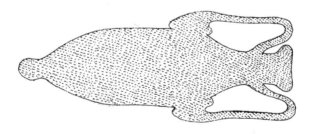

CONDITUM PARADOXUM
(APICIUS 1)

Conditi paradoxi compositio: Mellis p. XV in aeneum vas mittuntur, praemissis vini sextariis duobus, ut in coctura mellis vinum decoquas. Quod igni lento et aridis lignis ca-lefactum, commotum ferula dum coquitur, si effervere coe-perit, vini rore conpescitur, praeter quod subtracto igni in se redit. Cum perfrixerit, rursus accenditur. Hoc secundo ac tertio fiet, ac tum demum remotum a foco postridie des-

pumatur. Tum [mittis] piperis uncias quattuor iam triti, masticis scripulos III, folii et croci dragmae singulae, dactilorum ossibus torridis quinque, isdemque dactilis vino mollitis, intercedente prius suffusione vini de suo modo ac numero, ut tritura lenis habeatur. His omnibus paratis supermittis vini lenis sextaria XVIII. Carbones perfecto aderunt.

To prepare a marvelous seasoned wine: 15 *librae* of honey are placed in a bronze pot, in which you have previously placed 2 *sextarii* of wine, in order to reduce the wine in the cooking honey. It is heated over a low fire of dry wood, and stirred with a stick while it is cooked. If it begins to boil, it is stopped by adding wine or removing it from the flame. When it has cooled, it is heated again. This is done a second and a third time, and finally it is removed from the fire and skimmed the day after. Then [add] 4 *unciae* of ground pepper, 3 scruples of mastic, 1 drachma each of aromatic leaf and saffron, 5 roasted date pits, the dates themselves soaked in wine, having been steeped beforehand in wine of sufficient quality and quantity so that a sweet mash is produced. When you have prepared all this, pour over it 18 *sextarii* of sweet wine. The resulting mixture is treated with charcoal.

Charcoal was often used as a purifying and deodorizing agent; see Columella 12, 57 (pp. 179–80) for a similar prescription in the preparation of mustard.

ROMAN ABSINTHE
(APICIUS 3)

Absintium romanum sic facies: . . . absinti Pontici purgati terendique unciam, Thebaicam dabis, masticis, folii [scripulos] III, costi scripulos senos, croci scripulos III, vini eius modi sectarios XVIII. Carbones amaritudo non exigit.

Make Roman absinthe thus: . . . use an *uncia* of clean ground absinthium from Pontus, one date from Thebes, 3 [*scruples*] of mastic and of aromatic leaf, 6 scruples of costusroot, 3 scruples of saffron, 18 *sextarii* of appropriate wine. It is unnecessary to use charcoal to remove its bitterness.

Could this possibly be the secret recipe of a certain famous Turinese distillery for the vermouth it has produced since the late eighteenth century? It would be an intriguing thought indeed.

MULSUM

1 bottle aromatic dry white wine
3 Tbs. liquid honey

Dissolve the honey in a bit of the wine. Funnel this into the remaining wine in the bottle and place it in the refrigerator for at least 2 hours. If any of the honey has settled on the bottom, mix well before serving. You can decant it into an earthenware pitcher as a more historically appropriate serving vessel if you prefer.

The Romans added honey to wine or must to obtain *mulsum,* the drink that was served with appetizers. Columella (12, 41) described it as must that was mixed with honey and then left to ferment for a month; he suggested 10 *librae* of honey for an *urna* (about 13 quarts or liters) of must, thus a proportion of about 2 pounds (1 kilo) of honey for every 4 quarts or liters) of must. This recipe is both too time-consuming and certainly too sweet for our tastes. In the *Geoponica* (8, 25) the proportions are instead one part honey to four parts wine.

Pliny (*Naturalis historia* 22, 113–14) suggested using dry wine, claiming that the honey would mix perfectly with it. He went on to record that Augustus once asked a certain centenarian named Pollio Romilius how he was able to keep himself so healthy and youthful. The old man responded that he used *mulsum* on the inside and oil on the outside.

The Romans also consumed wines made from fermented fruit, such as pears, quinces, pomegranates, and even dates. And they enjoyed a refreshing drink called *hydromeli* or *aqua mulsa,* prepared with one part honey to two parts water (Pliny, *Naturalis historia* 14, 113). If it was served as soon as it was made it was called *aqua mulsa subita;* if aged it was called *aqua mulsa inveterata.* This latter version, according to Pliny, "took on the flavor of wine"—in other words, it underwent fermentation. But the proportion of honey to water must have been adjusted, or the concentration of sugar would have been too great for fermentation to take place.

Finally, there was reduced must, called *sapa, defrutum,* or *defritum.* Because it was not used as a beverage but rather as an ingredient in the preparation of sauces, sweets, and other dishes, its description is included in chapter 4.

›XIII‹

MENUS

The pantry steward
Tell me the number of guests, and at what price you wish
      to dine.
Don't add another word: dinner is ready for you.
                    (Martial 14, 218)

Punishment
I seem cruel and too gluttonous to you, Rusticus,
when for a poor dinner I strike the cook.
If this appears to you an insufficient motive for the
      lashing,
for what reason then would you strike the cook?
                    (Martial 8, 23)

The typical menu for a Roman *cena* consisted of three parts. The first, corresponding to a course of appetizers, was called *gustum* (or *gustatio* or *promulsis*) and included a selection from among such elements as dishes based on eggs, raw or cooked vegetables (such as asparagus, squash, or cucumbers), salads, mushrooms, salt-cured fish, oysters, mixed shellfish, and the ever-popular dormice (see page 75). The beverage served with this course was *mulsum* (see page 197).

The second part was called the *mensa prima* or *caput cenae*. Dishes varied in number from two to seven (proportionate to the host's ambition and ability to impress his guests) and were based on domestic meat, game, and fish. They were accompanied with wine.

Finally, the *mensa secunda* consisted generally of sweets and fruit, although sometimes salted dishes, sausages, cheese, and even mollusks were served.

This evening meal was considered the high point of the day, the focal point of business and social relationships, whether between a *dominus* and his *clientes* (that is, between the rich man and his entourage of admirers and profiteers), or in the imperial court, in various intellectual circles, or in the entire well-to-do class of *equites*.

Each host was judged according to his personal ability to graciously entertain his guests, the luxuriance of his *triclinium* and table setting, and naturally the food he offered. The excesses of the nouveaux riches, who strove to overwhelm at any cost, were ridiculed by Petronius in the *Cena Trimalchionis* (which we will touch upon later in this chapter); but the penurious host was also ridiculed:

> Yesterday you invited sixty of us to dinner, Mancinus, yet there was nothing more than a boar placed before us; not preserved ripe grapes that clung late upon the vine, nor apples as sweet as honeycomb; not pears dangling from a long genista branch, nor pomegranates the color of fleeting roses; not conic cheeses from rustic Sassina, nor olives from Picenian jars. Just a miserable boar, and so small that it could have been killed by an unarmed dwarf. And none of it was given us; we all simply gazed upon it. We are used to having a boar presented to us in this manner at the arena. After such a gesture, may no boar be served to you, but rather you yourself be served to the boar before which [the thief] Charidemus was served.
>
> (Martial 1, 43)

A remorseless critic as a guest, Martial also played host to his friends upon occasion. Let us see if his own menu is more appealing:

> With me you will eat well, Julius Cerialis; do come if you haven't a better invitation. You can keep the eighth hour. We will bathe together; you know how close the baths of Stephanus are to my home. First you will be given lettuce that is useful for moving the bowels, and sliced stalks of leeks; then full-grown tuna that is larger than the slender mackerel, garnished with eggs on leaves of rue; other eggs cooked in embers will not be lacking, and cheese set on a Velabrian hearth, and olives that have felt the Picenian cold. This will suffice as appetizer. Do you wish to know what follows? I will lie so that you will come: fish, mollusks, sow's paps, fattened birds from courtyard and marsh, that not even Stella, save on rare occasion, is wont to serve at dinner. Still more I promise you: I will recite nothing for you, while you will be free to read once more your Giants or your Georgics, worthy of the immortal Virgil.
>
> (Martial 11, 52)

Obviously the poet exaggerates in this waggish lure to his friend, but the list of food is nonetheless fairly typical for a dinner devised without regard for expense. Martial's rich variety of dishes is an admirable proposition for a summer dinner, a genuine buffet. We can dress the salad with one of the vinaigrettes or the cheese sauce in Apicius (see chapter 4).

Martial addressed this poem of invitation to several of his close friends for an informal, pleasant luncheon among men:

> Acolytes announce the eighth hour to the Pharian heifer [Isis], and the javelin-armed temple guard changes. At this hour the baths are temperate; while in the previous hour they emit too much steam, and in the sixth hour the baths of Nero are excessively hot. Stella, Nepos, Canius, Cerialis, Flaccus, will you come? The *sigma* [*triclinium*] holds seven; we are six, so we can add Lupus. The countrywoman has brought me mallows that liberate the stomach, and various treasures of the garden: digestive lettuce and cut leeks; mint that stimulates belching and aphrodisiac arugola. Slices of egg will crown mackerel in rue, and there will be sow's paps swimming in tuna sauce. This as appetizer. The luncheon proper will consist of a single course: a kid snatched from the jaws of a cruel wolf, cutlets that do not require the knife of a carver, fava beans, the food of laborers, and young cabbages. A chicken will be added to this meal, and a ham remaining from three dinners before. When you have had your fill, I will offer ripe fruit, and wine without sediment from a Nomentan bottle, aged three years at the time of the second consulate of Frontinus. There will be games free of malice, and no liberties taken that would cause regret the following day, nor words spoken and later desired unsaid. My guests may discuss the green and blue teams [in the circus races]; and one cup too many will make no man guilty.
>
> (Martial 10, 48)

From feast to friendly debate, this savory meal is one we too can enjoy. Only the sow's paps need be replaced with cold veal roast sliced and then covered with the tuna sauce, thus becoming a kind of *vitello tonnato*. And of course we would do well to avoid serving leftovers to our guests . . .

Yet another tempting invitation is the one Martial wrote to his friend Toranius:

> If you dread a solitary dinner at home, Toranius, you can come suffer your hunger with me. If appetizers are your

habit, there will be common Cappadocian lettuces and strong-smelling leeks, and tuna hidden beneath slices of egg. A green cabbage, fresh from the cool garden and hot enough to burn your fingers, will be served on a black plate, as well as a sausage settled over snow-white porridge, and pale fava beans with rosy bacon. If you desire the luxury of another course, you will be given raisins, and pears fine enough to have come from Syria, and chestnuts, creation of the learned Naples, roasted over a slow fire. You will bring worth to my wine by drinking it. If after all this Bacchus excites further hunger, as is often the case, you will be relieved by excellent olives freshly harvested from Picenian branches, with hot chick peas and tepid lupines. The dinner is humble—who can deny it?—but you will have no need to invent falsehoods, nor to hear them, and you can repose just as you are. . . . This is the dinner. You will be placed behind Claudia. Which woman would you desire before me?

(Martial 5, 78)

This time it is a frugal proposal that could serve perhaps as a picnic or an informal gathering on a summer terrace.

Another good example is the menu proposed by Juvenal (*Satires* 11, 64–76): an appetizer of eggs and asparagus, *caput cenae* of kid and chicken, and a dessert of fruit. We can choose how to cook the meats and how to prepare the eggs and asparagus—for example, a *patina de asparagis,* (Apicius 133, pages 52–53) or the eggs with a pine nut sauce (Apicius 329, page 47) and the asparagus with a vinaigrette sauce (such as Apicius 84, pages 45–46).

The most famous Roman menu is undoubtedly that in Petronius's *Cena Trimalchionis. Gustum* consisted of green and black olives, roasted dormice in a sauce of honey and poppy seeds, sausages, and figpeckers in shells made of pastry. The *mensa prima* offered first a rich choice of chicken, hare, sow's paps, and fish in a spicy sauce; then there was a roasted pig stuffed with sausages and blood sausages, and, to conclude the course, an entire boiled calf. The *mensa secunda* brought the meal to a close with fruit and various cakes. But this dry synopsis cannot compare with a translation of the lively, entertaining text itself:

GUSTUM

In the middle of the appetizer tray stood a donkey made of Corinthian bronze with two panniers, one containing green olives and the other black. Two dishes flanked the donkey, around the edges of which Trimalchio's name and the weight of the silver were engraved. Small iron bridges held dormice dipped in honey and sprinkled with poppy seeds. There were also sausages "roasting" on a silver grill, and beneath were dark Syrian plums and pomegranate kernels [to simulate a crackling fire]. . . .

While we were still eating the appetizers, a tray was brought in. Upon it was a basket in which a wooden hen, with wings outstretched, sat as if it were hatching eggs. . . . Trimalchio turned and said: "Friends, I ordered peahen eggs to be placed beneath that hen and, by Hercules, I'm afraid they have already hatched. But let us see if we can still suck them." We were handed spoons weighing at least a half *libra* each and cracked open the eggs, which were made of rich pastry. . . . I found inside a plump figpecker in egg sauce, well seasoned with pepper.

(*Cena Trimalchionis*, Petronius chapters 31 and 33)

MENSA PRIMA

A circular tray was brought in that had the twelve signs of the zodiac around it, and over each of these the chef had placed an appropriate food. Over Aries were ram's-head chick peas; over Taurus a slice of beef; over Gemini a pair of testicles and kidneys; over Cancer a wreath; over Leo an African fig; over Virgo a barren sow's womb; over Libra a pair of scales with a *scriblita* in one pan and a *placenta* in the other; over Scorpio a small seafish; over Sagittarius a hare; over Capricorn a lobster; over Aquarius a goose; and over Pisces two mullet. In the middle lay a clod of turf with grass, topped by a honeycomb. An Egyptian boy served bread around in a silver portable oven. . . .

(chapter 35)

But this was only the cover for another tray; four slaves lifted it to reveal the actual course to be eaten:

Beneath it we saw fattened fowl and sow's wombs, and a hare in the middle with wings attached to resemble Pegasus. We also noted at the corners of the tray four small vessels resembling [the satyr] Marsyas, with spicy *garum* dripping from their bellies over fish that looked as if they were swimming about in a canal.

(chapter 36)

Then three beasts were brought in, the first of which was only for show: an enormous sow stuffed with live thrushes, who flew forth once the sow was cut open and were caught by waiting slaves. Nestled around the sow were pastry piglets that seemed to be suckling their mother. The second beast was a large roasted hog:

> Trimalchio, who had been closely scrutinizing the pig, suddenly exclaimed: "What? What's this? Has this pig not been gutted? By Hercules, it has not! Have the cook come in at once!" The cook appeared with an expression of dismay and admitted that he had forgotten to gut it. "What? You forgot?" Trimalchio exclaimed. "You would think it no worse than omitting the pepper and cumin! . . . Well, since your memory is so poor, gut the pig here before us all!" . . . The cook took up a knife, and with a trembling hand he slashed here and there at the pig's belly. Immediately sausages and blood sausages poured out of the gashes, which widened from the pressure inside.
>
> (chapter 49)

The last dish of the *mensa prima* was an entire boiled calf:

> While the slaves scurried about, a boiled calf wearing a helmet was presented on a platter weighing two hundred [librae]. [A servant dressed as] Ajax followed with drawn sword and, as if he were mad, he cut it, slashing back and forth; then with the point he skewered the pieces of calf and passed them around to the astonished spectators.
>
> (chapter 59)

MENSA SECUNDA

> In the middle of a tray garnished with *placentae* was a pastry figure of Priapus, his generous belly full of every variety of fruit and grape. . . .
>
> (chapter 60)

It must be remembered, however, that this is a parody of a banquet—and further, that banquets were not daily affairs. Even at court a certain moderation was demanded by several emperors. For example, in the *Historia Augusta, Pertinax* 12, we read: "He was such a miser that, before he became emperor, he provided his guests only cardoons and half portions of lettuce. When he invited friends, unless he had received some gift of food he always offered (regardless of the number of people at table) nine *librae* of meat in three courses. If anything remained thereafter, he kept it for the next day because he always had many guests. Even after he became emperor, his habits did not change, at least when he dined alone. When he wished to send his friends a part of his meal, it always consisted of a few bites of meat or a piece of tripe or sometimes chicken thighs; but never pheasant, because this item never appeared on his table."

The usual family dinner certainly consisted of items similar to those we still consume, with perhaps hot soup in the winter, some cheese, eggs, fruit, and a bit of meat on the tables of those who could afford it.

The following menus are only a few of many possible suggestions, based on a more contemporary approach to putting meals together. Naturally, your imagination may lead you to many other combinations of your own.

WINTER MENUS

Menu 1

Gustum
Lettuce *Patina* (page 53)
Hard-Boiled Eggs with *Garum* Sauce
(pages 46–47)

Mensa prima
Roasted Boar with Cooked Sauce
(pages 116–17)

Mensa secunda
Stuffed Dates (pages 189–90)

Menu 2

Gustum
Lentils with Artichoke Bottoms
(pages 153–54)
Fresh Cheese

Mensa prima
Ham in Pastry (pages 96–97)

Mensa secunda
Honey Custard (page 161)

Menu 3

Gustum
Medium-Boiled Eggs in Pine Nut
Sauce (page 47)
Fried Squash (page 145)

Mensa prima
Duck in Prune Sauce (pages 109–10)

Mensa secunda
Sweet Buns with Must (page 158)

Menu 4

Gustum
Artichokes with Egg (page 46)
Sweet-and-Sour Turnips (pages
61–62)

Mensa prima
Stuffed Chicken (pages 103–4)

Mensa secunda
Sweet *Patina* (pages 161–62)

SUMMER MENUS

Menu 1

Gustum
Beets with Mustard (page 140)
Mixed Shellfish Salad with Cumin
Sauce (pages 171–72)

Mensa prima
Pork Stew with Apples (pages 93–94)

Mensa secunda
Fruit in Season

Menu 2

Gustum
Cheese Round with Herbs (pages
54–55)

Mensa prima
Seasoned Mussels (page 130)

Mensa secunda
Fried Creamed Wheat (page 159)

Menu 3

Gustum
Seasoned Melon (page 63)

Mensa prima
Grilled Lobster (pages 128–29)

Mensa secunda
Melca (page 174)
Mustacei (page 157)

Menu 4

Gustum
Fried Anchovy *Patina* (pages 63–64)
Herbal Bread and Cheese (page 58)

Mensa prima
Stuffed Pigeons (pages 112–13)

Mensa secunda
Figs

EVERYDAY MENUS

Menu 1

Gustum
Green and Black Olives
Sausages (page 182)

Mensa prima
Chicken à la Fronto (page 105)

Mensa secunda
Quince *Patina* (page 173)

Menu 2

Gustum
Olive Paste on Toast (pages 59–60)
Fresh Cheese

Mensa prima
Scaloppine in Date Sauce (page 34)

Mensa secunda
Fruit in Season

Menu 3

Gustum
Beets with Mustard (page 140)
Cheese Round with Herbs (pages
54–55)

Mensa prima
Baked Fish with Coriander Seeds
(pages 122–23)

Mensa secunda
Pear *Patina* (pages 172–73)

Menu 4

Gustum
Green and Black Olives
Smoked *Scamorzine*

Mensa prima
Stuffed Meat Patties (pages 89–90)

Mensa secunda
Fruit in Season

ELEGANT MENUS

Menu 1

Gustum
Seafood Patties (pages 132–33)
Lettuce with Cheese Sauce (pages 47–48)
Seasoned Green and Black Olives

Mensa prima
Parthian Lamb (pages 99–100)

Mensa secunda
Stuffed Dates (pages 189–90)
Fried Bread (page 158)

Menu 2

Gustum
Olive Paste with Toast (pages 59–60)
Asparagus and Figpecker *Patina* (pages 51–52)

Mensa prima
Roasted Sea Bream (page 126)

Mensa secunda
Egg Pudding (page 160)

Menu 3

Gustum
Mushroom Caps (page 65)
Medium-Boiled Eggs in Pine Nut Sauce (page 44)

Mensa prima
Duck with Turnips (pages 110–11)

Mensa secunda
Peach *Patina* (pages 171–72)

Menu 4

Gustum
Truffle Salad (page 65)
Onion Appetizer (pages 68–69)

Mensa prima
Guinea Hen with Sweet-and-Sour Sauce (pages 107–8)

Mensa secunda
Fried Creamed Wheat (page 159)
Pomegranates

›XIV‹

AT THE TAVERN

... and these idlers pass
the entire day closed up in a tavern.

(Seneca, *De providentia* 4)

Nero had hospices raised at intervals along the banks of
the Tiber and on the coast of the gulf of Baiae, and every
time he traveled to Ostia or took a boat excursion in the
gulf, splendid receptions were organized in these hospices,
and matrons dressed as hostesses were sent to them beforehand to welcome the emperor when he arrived.

(Suetonius, *De vita Caesarum, Nero,* 28)

From sunrise to sunset, Roman urbanites passed the entire day outside
their homes—at the Forum, in government offices, at the tribunals and the
Senate, among the various shops, concluding with a visit to the thermal
baths. It was a life of continuous activity.

Inevitably, many of them would grab a bite to eat in the city center. This
custom brought about the appearance of restorative establishments that
came to flourish in the Forum and around the thermal baths: from simple
taverns (*popinae* or *thermopolia*), which offered hot or cold wine according to the season, cakes made with chick peas, focaccias, and other ready-
to-eat items; to inns (*cauponae*), which had beds available for visitors who
needed a place to sleep.

These public gathering places (of which traces abound in the streets of
Pompeii, Herculaneum, and Ostia) looked approximately like this: a
brickwork serving bar facing the street, containing large amphoras for
wine, water, and oil; shelves for mugs and glasses; and against the back
wall, stoves for preparing a few hot foods or for a quick reheating. Further
within there was usually at least one room sparsely furnished with tables

and benches for those customers with the time and desire to eat seated, as was the custom among the lower strata of society. Those taverns with more decorous intentions also had a few *triclinia* for their sophisticated clientele.

The staff in these places is always described in the ancient sources as an assorted collection of lowlife: the proprietor was on the same social scale as a thief, and the servants commonly provided less than reputable services to their customers upon request. Gambling often went on in the back rooms; although it was condemned by the building authorities, the proprietor was not held responsible for activities that took place in his business concern. However, he was not permitted to protest any damage to his property resulting from the numerous fights that broke out therein. These taverns did not have fixed hours, remaining open well into the night and frequently disturbing the population with their bacchanalia. Thieves, idlers, gamblers, sailors and escaped slaves were an omnipresent component of the tavern's trade.

But the more self-respecting among the population had no need to mix with this beastly breed of habitué: one could purchase his hot spiced wine, fresh focaccia, plate of warm *puls* (porridge), or fruit directly from a street

A TASTE OF ANCIENT ROME

vendor. The more ambitious of these vendors (and along with them the *salarii*, vendors of salamis and cooked meats) did not hesitate to send waiters into the Forum, around the central thoroughfares, and into the thermal baths to offer sausages and similar snacks. For every type of food they had a particular call to attract the attention of passersby, just as Italian street hawkers would sell their merchandise long after. Now extinct or disappearing, they include the Florentines with their tripe or hot chestnuts, the Milanese with hot crayfish from the Lambro river or poached pears, and the Neapolitans with *u'musu* (boiled heads of calf and pig). Among the ancient Romans the most popular items were cakes of chick peas; their vendors were assured a lucrative business.

The thermal baths opened at noon or, from the reign of Hadrian, at two o'clock in the afternoon. Many *popinae* were conveniently located immediately inside the baths and in the porticoes around the outside. The lengthy alternating hot and cold baths, races, gymnastics, and massages must have left participants exhausted and hungry, so that a snack between one endeavor and another was certainly welcome. One entertaining source of information on the practice of eating inside the baths is found in Martial, who satirized the habits of a certain Aemilius with these verses:

> At the baths Aemilius eats lettuce, eggs, and mackerel,
>   and then refuses to eat at home.
> (Martial 12, 19)

Medical treatises also recommended several specific foods and medicines to consume *a balneo*, upon leaving the bath. Apicius 55 is a curious recipe for "starched meat patties after leaving the bath"; perhaps it was originally part of some diet prescribed in a medical treatise and later made its way into the cooking manual.

Naturally, only men ate in the *popinae*. Even in the epoch when women attended the baths (in special reserved sections), no woman of decent reputation would have entered one of these eateries; rather, she would send a slave to purchase something for her.

The *cauponae*, which offered sleeping accommodations as well as hot meals, were generally frequented by such travelers as merchants and military ambassadors. They would order a hot dinner from the owner or, if they were accompanied by slaves, they would send their attendants into the kitchen to prepare their meals.

We have an engaging description of a tavern and its *copa* (hostess) contained in a brief elegiac poem entitled *Copa* and inserted in the *Appendix Vergiliana*. The setting is summer, the street is dusty and sunny, the cicadas are deafening. In the doorway of her tavern, a young Syrian hostess sings and dances and invites the weary traveler to come into her establishment, full of refreshments and amusements:

> . . . there is also young wine, just poured from the pitched jar, and the hoarse murmur of a warbling stream; there are small wreaths of crocus flowers with violet petals, and garlands of red roses intertwined with yellow flowers and lilies gathered on the banks of the virgin brook by the maiden Acheloias, who brought them in woven baskets. Here is delicate cheese, placed in reed baskets to dry, and the blond plums of autumn; and chestnuts and pleasantly rosy apples. The innocent Ceres, Amor, and Bromius reign here. And still more, there are blood-red mulberries and grapes in tender clusters, and the deep green cucumber hangs from the vine. . . .
>
> (Copa, vv. 11–22)

A rough-hewn bas-relief from Aesernia (modern-day Isernia) portrays a hostess and a traveler engaged in the following dialogue, which is inscribed beneath the scene. With this final vibrant image, our own brief excursion now comes to a close.

—Hostess, let us settle the bill.
—You have a *sextarius* of wine. For the bread, 1 *as;* for
        that which went with the bread, 2 *asses.*
—Agreed.
—For the girl, 8 *asses.*
—Agreed on that as well.
—The hay for your mule, 2 *asses.*

TABLE OF WEIGHTS AND MEASURES

These are the most common weights and measures used by the ancient Romans, along with modern conversions of the principal units.

Liquid Measures

Amphora (standard of measure): 25.8 liters (ca. 27¼ quarts.)

Urna = ½ *amphora*

Modius = ⅓ *amphora*

Congius = ⅛ *amphora*

Sextarius = ¹⁄₄₈ *amphora* (⅙ *congius*): .54 liter (ca. 18 oz. or 2¼ cups)

Hemina = ½ *sextarius*

Quartarius = ¼ *sextarius*

Acetabulum = ⅛ *sextarius*

Ciatus (cyathus) = ¹⁄₁₂ *sextarius*

Cochlear = perhaps ¼ *ciatus* (ca. 2 tsp.)

Calix: ca. 1 cup

Dry Measures

Libra (standard of measure): 327.45 grams (ca. 11.5 oz.)

Selibra = ½ *libra*

Quadrans = ¼ *libra*

Uncia = ¹⁄₁₂ *libra:* 27.3 grams (almost exactly 1 oz.)

Semuncia = ½ *uncia*

Drachma (dragma) = ca. ⅙ *uncia*

Scripulus (scriptulus) = ¹⁄₂₄ *uncia*

GLOSSARY

ACETABULUM: container for vinegar or sauce; unit of measure for liquids; see the Table of Weights and Measures.

ALICA: semolina or coarsely ground spelt; see p. 165.

ALLEC (or ALLEX): residue from the production of *garum;* see p. 28.

AMPHORA: container used for both liquids and grains; see the Table of Weights and Measures.

AMULUM: starch, derived from rice or other grains such as rye or wheat; see p. 30.

AQUA MULSA: hydromel, a mixture of honey and water; see p. 197.

CALIX: cup; measure for liquids. See the Table of Weights and Measures.

CARENUM (or CAROENUM): reduced wine.

CIATUS (or CYATHUS): ladle used for serving wine and as a liquid measure; see the Table of Weights and Measures.

CIPERUS (or CIPERIS): cyperus (*Cyperus rotundus*); a sedge-like plant, of which the aromatic roots or tubers were used.

CONCICLA (or CONCHICULA): from the Greek κόγχη (shell), originally referring to the pods of legumes, it came to signify a dish of cooked fava beans or peas.

CONDITUM (VINUM CONDITUM): spiced wine; see p. 195.

CONGIUS: unit of liquid measure; see the Table of Weights and Measures.

COSTUM: costusroot; the fragrant root of the *Saussurea lappa,* imported from India.

DRACHMA (or DRAGMA): unit of dry measure; see the Table of Weights and Measures.

DEFRUTUM (or DEFRITUM): reduced must, or *sapa;* see pp. 29–30.

EMBRACTUM: a sauce or stew.

EMINA (or HEMINA): unit of liquid measure; see the Table of Weights and Measures.

EPITYRUM: olive paste; see pp. 59–60.

ESICIUM: see *isicium.*

FAR (or SPELTA): spelt; a type of hard wheat (*Triticum spelta*), which was crushed for use prior to the introduction of soft wheat for flour.

FOLIUM: any aromatic plant leaf, such as laurel or bay leaf, nard, or malabathrum.

GARUM: fermented fish sauce; see pp. 27–29.

GARUM CASTIMONIALE: *garum* prepared for the Jews; see p. 28.

GARUM SOCIORUM: the most expensive *garum,* made exclusively from mackerel; see p. 28.

GUSTUM (or GUSTATIO): the appetizer course of a Roman banquet.

HEMINA: see *emina.*

HYDROGARUM: *garum* diluted with water; see p. 28.

IENTACULUM: breakfast, the first meal of the day.

ISICIUM (or ESICIUM): a patty made from ground meat or ground fish.

LASER (or LASERPICIUM): Latin name for silphium, a plant of the genus *Ferula,* now extinct; see pp. 30–31.

LIQUAMEN: another name for *garum.*

LIBRA: unit of dry measure; see the Table of Weights and Measures.

MENSA PRIMA: the main course of a Roman banquet, following the *gustum.*

MENSA SECUNDA: dessert, the final course of a Roman banquet.

MINUTAL: a stew or fricassee, usually including pieces of meat and patties of meat or of fish.

MODIUS: unit of liquid and dry measure; see the Table of Weights and Measures.

MULSUM: wine mixed with honey; see p. 197.

MURIA: another name for *garum.*

OENOGARUM: *garum* diluted with wine; see p. 28.

OFELLA; a small piece of meat cut for use in stew or for roasting on a skewer; may also refer to a cutlet.

OXYGARUM: *garum* diluted with vinegar; see p. 28.

PASSUM: raisin wine, see pp. 194–95.

PATINA (or PATELLA): a shallow metal or earthenware pan especially useful for cooking egg-based dishes; over time these particular dishes took on the name of the vessel itself.

POSCA: beverage of water and vinegar; see p. 194.

PULS: a thick soup or porridge.

PYRETHRUM: pyrethrum, a plant of African origin (*Anacyclus pyrethrum*) resembling chamomile, providing a pungent, bitter-tasting root that is no longer used in cooking.

QUADRANS: unit of dry measure; see the Table of Weights and Measures.

QUARTARIUS: unit of liquid measure; see the Table of Weights and Measures.

SAPA: reduced must, or *defrutum;* see pp. 29–30.

SCRIPULUS (or SCRIPTULUS): scruple, unit of dry measure; see the Table of Weights and Measures.

SELIBRA: ½ *libra,* unit of dry measure; see the Table of Weights and Measures.

SEMUNCIA: ½ *uncia,* unit of dry measure; see the Table of Weights and Measures.

SEXTARIUS: unit of liquid measure; see the Table of Weights and Measures.

SILIGO (or POLLEN): fine wheat flour; see p. 16.

SILPHIUM: silphium, the Greek name for *laser* or *laserpicium;* see *laser.*

SIMILAGO (or SIMILA): wheat flour sifted to a degree between that of fine and whole wheat flour; see p. 16.

SPELTA: see *far.*

SPICA INDICA (or SPICA NARDI): east Indian spikenard (*Nardostachys jatamansi*).

TRACTA (also TRACTUM): a sheet of dough made from flour and water, often dried and broken into pieces for use as a thickening agent in sauces; see p. 30.

TRITICUM: soft wheat.

UNCIA: unit of dry measure; see the Table of Weights and Measures.

VINUM CONDITUM: see *conditum.*

SELECT BIBLIOGRAPHY

ANCIENT SOURCES

Apicius, M. Gavius

Apicius. *L'art culinaire*. Translated (French) by Jacques André. Paris: Les belles lettres, 1974.

———. *The Roman Cookery Book*. Translated by Barbara Flower and Elisabeth Rosenbaum. London: George G. Harrap and Co., 1958.

———. *De re coquinaria*. Edited by C. Giarratano and Fr. Vollmer. Leipzig: Teubner, 1922.

———. *De re coquinaria*. Edited by Aldo Marsili. Pisa: Colombo Cursi, 1957.

Appendix Vergiliana

Appendix Vergiliana. Translated (Italian) by Armando Salvatore. Naples: Libreria Scientifica Editrice, 1964.

Cato, Marcus Porcius, Censorius

Cato. *Liber de agricultura*. Translated (Italian) by Rose Calzecchi Onesti. Rome: Ramo Editoriale degli Agricoltori, 1948.

———. *On Agriculture*. In Cato and Varro, *On Agriculture,* translated by William Davis Hooper, and revised by Harrison Boyd Ash. Loeb Classical Library. Cambridge: Harvard University Press; London: William Heinemann, 1935.

Columella, Lucius Junius Moderatus

Columella. *De re rustica libri XIII*. Translated (Italian) by Rosa Calzecchi Onesti. Rome: Ramo Editoriale degli Agricoltori, 1948.

———. *On Agriculture*. Translated by Harrison Boyd Ash. Loeb Classical Library. Cambridge: Harvard University Press; London: William Heinemann, 1941–55.

Geoponica

Geoponicorum sive de re rustica libri XX. Edited by Heinrich Beckh. Leipzig: Teubner, 1895.

Historia Augusta

Scriptores historiae Augustae. Edited by Ernestus Hohl. Leipzig: Teubner, 1927–55.

———. Translated by David Magie. Loeb Classical Library. New York: G. P. Putnam's Sons; London: Heinemann, 1924–32.

Juvenalis, Decimus Junius

Juvenal. *Satire.* Translated (Italian) by G. Vitali. Bologna: Zanichelli, 1965.

Martialis, Marcus Valerius

Martial. *Epigrammi.* Translated (Italian) by Guido Ceronetti. Turin: Einaudi, 1964.

———. *Epigrammi.* Translated (Italian) by G. Norico. Turin: Unione Tipografico-Editrice Torinese, 1980.

———. *The Epigrams.* Bohn's Classical Library. London: George Bell and Sons, 1888.

Gargilius Martialis, Quintus

Martialis, Gargilius. *De medicina et de virtute herbarum.* Edited by Valentin Rose. Leipzig: Teubner, 1893.

Petronius Arbiter

Petronius. *Satyricon.* Edited by Carlo Pellegrino. Rome: Edizioni dell'Ateneo, 1975.

———. *The Satyricon.* Translated by J. M. Mitchell. 2d edition. Broadway Translations. London: George Routledge and Sons; New York: E. P. Dutton, 1923.

Plinius Secundus, C.

Pliny the Elder. *Natural History.* Translated by H. Rackham et al. Loeb Classical Library. Cambridge: Harvard University Press; London: William Heinemann, 1938–63.

Seneca, Lucius Annaeus

Seneca. *Moral Essays.* Translated by J. W. Basore. Loeb Classical Library. Cambridge: Harvard University Press; London: William Heinemann, 28–35.

Tacitus, Cornelius

Tacitus. *The Annals.* Edited by Henry Furneaux. 2d edition. Oxford: Clarendon Press, 1956.

MODERN SOURCES ON THE LIFE AND CUSTOMS OF ANCIENT ROME

André, Jacques. *L'alimentation et la cuisine à Rome.* Paris: Klincksieck, 1961.

———. *Lexique des termes de botanique en latin.* Paris: Klincksieck, 1956.

Carcopino, Jerome. *Daily Life in Ancient Rome*. Translated by E. O. Lorimer. Edited by Henry T. Rowell. New Haven: Yale University Press, 1940.

Levi, Mario A. *Roma antica*. Turin: Unione Tipografico-Editrice Torinese, 1963.

Paoli, Ugo E. *Vita romana*. Florence: Le Monnier, 1975.

GENERAL REFERENCE

Daremberg, Charles Victor, and Edmund Saglio. *Dictionnaire des antiquités grecques et romaines*. Paris: Hachette, 1877–1919.

Oxford Classical Dictionary. 2d ed. 1970.

Pauly, August Friedrich von. *Real-Encyclopaedie der classischen Alterthumswissenschaft*. Stuttgart: J. B. Metzler, 1894–.

ILLUSTRATIONS

Plates 5 and 6: recipes realized by the author at the restaurant Ariotto di Terruggia, Monferrato.

Photo credits: Pl. 1: IGDA, Novara. Pls. 2, 3, 4, 11, 13: Pedicini, Naples. Pls. 7, 8, 9, 10, 12, 14, 15, used with permission of Credito Italiano.

Some line drawings have been taken from Daremberg and Saglio, *Dictionnaire des antiquités grecques et romaines* (Paris, 1877–1919), and Guhl and Koner, *La vita dei Greci e dei Romani* (Turin, 1875).

The original pen and ink drawings for this English edition were done by Patricia Smith.

Index

Boldface page numbers indicate recipes.

bread, 2, 14, 16; Alexandrian, 58; as thickener, 27, 30; whole-wheat, 57–58
   fried, **158**
breakfast, 2
brine, 177
broccoli
   with couscous, **150**
   with herb sauce, **149–50**
Bromius, 210
Brummel, Beau, 9
buccelli, 30
buns, sweet, with must, **158**
butter, 12, 26

Cabbage, 13, 200, 201
Caecilius, 139
cagiada, 174
Calabria, 157
Calabrian olives, **186**
calf: boiled, 201, 203; heads, boiled, 209
calix, 21
camel heels, 26
Campania, 9, 122, 192
canard aux navets, 111
capon, 2
caput cenae. See mensa prima
caraway, 15, 16
cardamom, 27
cardoons, 13, **46, 141–42, 153–54,** 203
carduos, 141–42
careota, 36–37
caroenum (or *sapa*), 29, 195; preparation of, 30.
   See also defrutum; must
carrots, 13
   with cumin sauce, **141**
   fried, **140**
   marinade for, **45**
Carthage, 6, 108, 165
caryota, dates, 36–37
cassoeula, 70
catillus, 21
catinus, 21
Cato, vii, 5–7, 17, 192–93; as source of recipes, 59, 77, 97, 156, 157, 163–69, 185, 189, 194
caul fat, 90
cauponae, 207, 209–10
celery: family; ix; leaves, 31; seed, 16, 27
   puree, **143**
cellarius, 22, 193
Celsus, 11, 16
cena (or *coena*), 3
Cena Trimalchionis (Petronius) 7, 9, 21, 22, 24–

25, 75, 98, 199; quoted, 202–3. *See also* Petronius
cepes. *See* mushrooms
Ceres, 210
cervisia, 16–17, 28, 192
Cetarii, 94
charcoal, 20, 180, 196
Charidemus, 199
charta emporetica, 126
cheese, 2, 3, 13–14, 49, 156–57, 198, 199, 204, 210; Parmesan, 57; pecorino, 53, 57, 78, 91, 166; ricotta, 54–56, 58, 64–65, 68, 69, 157, 167; Roquefort, 48; *scamorze,* 157; *scamorzine,* 157; Vestine, 58
   chicken liver and, pâté, **55–56**
   chicken, sweetbreads, and, pâté, **57–58**
   herbal bread and, 58
   round with herbs, **54–55,** 175
   sauce, **47–48,** 60
cherries, 14
chervil, 27
chestnuts, 201, 209, 210
   with lentils, **154–55**
chick peas, 13, 76, 202; cakes, 207, 209
   and string beans, **152**
chicken, 12, 60, 90, 200, 201, 204
   breasts, **52, 57–58**
   Circassian, **33**
   à la Elagabalus, **106–7**
   à la Fronto, **105**
   livers, **55–56**
   with prunes: **109;** Moroccan, **110**
   with squash, **102–3**
   sweetbread and cheese pâté, **57–58**
   stuffed, **103–4**
chicory, 13, 60
Chinese potato, 92
Chios, 192
ciatus, 21
cibarium, 16
Cicero, 86
Cincinnatus, vii
circuses, 200
citrons, 187
   pork stew with, **95–96**
   preserved, **188**
clams, Venus, **129**
classical cooking, compared with medieval, ix
Claudius, emperor, 121
Clazomenae, 27
cliens, clientes, 3, 10, 22
cloves, 27
coci, 21
Coci (book of recipes), 94

garlic, 14, 31

garum, ix, 20, 26, **27–29**, 31–32, **181**, 202; *cas-timoniale,* 28; *sociorum,* 26, 28
    sauce for boiled eggs, **46–47**

Gaul, 13, 16, 178, 192

Geoponica, 16, 29, 124, 197

Georgics, 199

gilthead, 12, 121
    sauce for, **42**

ginger, 27

gladioli, 195

glirarii, 75

globi, **164**

goat, 12, 13, 86–87. *See also* kid

goose, 12, 86, 108, 202; liver, 49
    boiled, à la Apicius, **108–9**

grains, 14–16, 18. *See also specific grains*

granturco, 11

grape juice, 29

grape must. *See* must

grapes, 14, 29–30, 49, 199, 210; cultivation of, 192–93; Nuragus, 29
    preserved, **186–87**

Greece, 12, 20, 65, 192

gudgeon, 121

guinea hen, 108
    with sweet-and-sour sauce, **107–8**

gustum (or gustatio). *See* appetizers

gypsum, used in preserving, 186–87, 194

Hadrian, emperor, 10, 209

hake, 123

halibut, 12

ham, 13, 200
    in pastry, **96–97,** 98

Hannibal, 108

hard-boiled egg sauce, **33–34**

hare, 12, 87; "winged," 202. *See also* rabbit
    roasted with herb sauce, **114–15**
    stuffed, **113–14**

hazelnuts, 14

hen, 85

herbal bread and cheese, **58**

herb sauce for fish, **42–43**

herbs, substituting, 31

Herculaneum, 19, 207

Herod, 193

Historia (Herodotus), 24–25

Historia Augusta, 8, 37, 79, 87, 120, 203

honey, ix, 2, 16–17, 32, 33, 177, 197; as preservative, 181, 185, 186, 188. *See also mulsum*

custard, **161**

frittata, **162**

hops, in modern beer, 192

Horace, 19–20

hydrogarum, 28

hydromel, 16–17, 197

hyssop, 177, 194

Iecur *ficatum,* 13, 101

ientaculum, 2

India, 16

instrumentum vocale (slave), 113

irises, 195

Isauricus, 121

Isernia, bas-relief from, 210

isicia, 8

Isis, 200

Islam, expansion of, viii

Israel, 193

Jellyfish, 129–30

Jericho, 37

Jerusalem artichokes, 92

Jesus, 194

Jews, *garum* made for, 28

John, St., 194

Jove, Capitoline, 77

Jove, priests of, dietary restrictions, 147

Judea, 193

Julian the Apostate, emperor, 22, 79, 192

Julian of Pannonia, 79

Julius Caesar, 2, 86, 94, 121

juniper berries, 27, 40

Juvenal, 5, 10, 201

Kaiseraugst, Switzerland, 22

kale soup, **83–84**

karoenum. See caroenum

kibbé, **135–36**

kid, 200. *See also* goat, lamb
    Parthian, **99–100**
    roasted, **98–99**

kidneys, 202

knives, use of, 2–3

Knossos, 192

Kos, 192

Lac. *See* milk.

laganum, viii